D0477284

THE GOLD COINS OF ENGLAND.

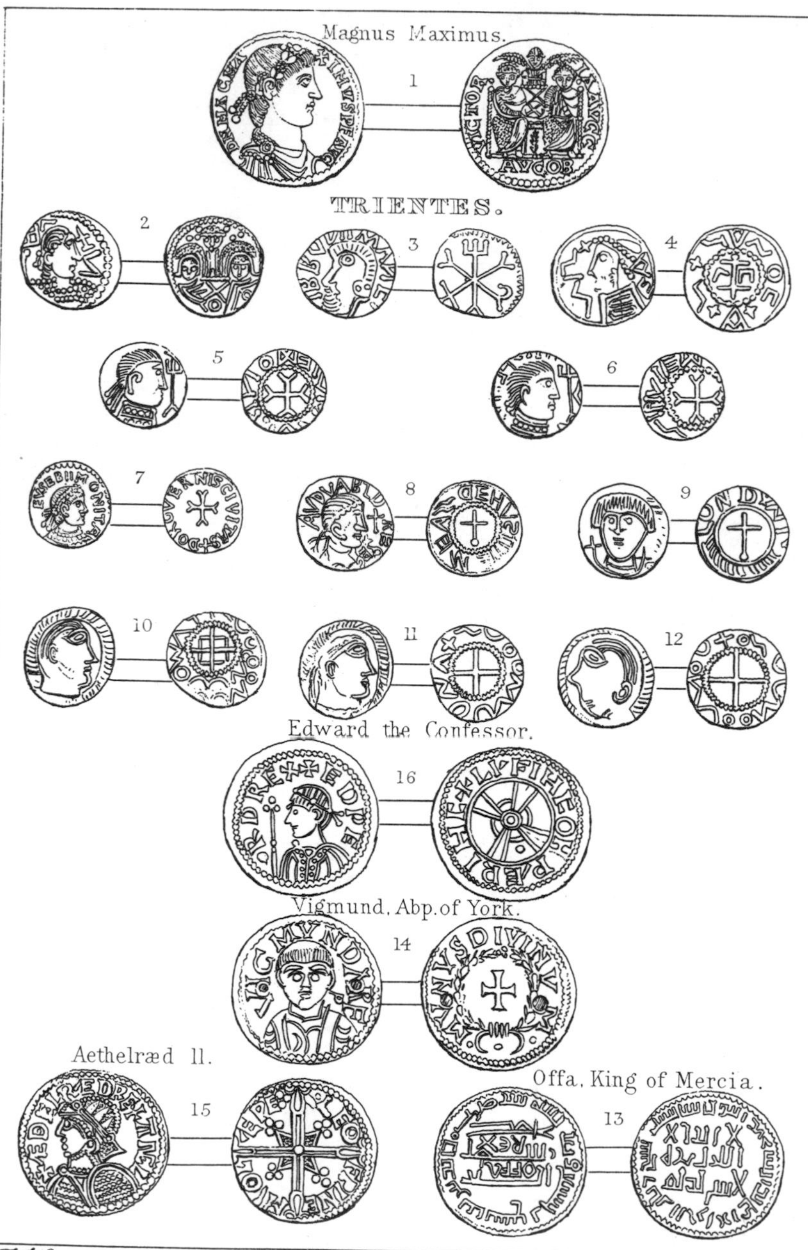
Magnus Maximus.
1
TRIENTES.
2
3
4
5
6
7
8
9
10
11
12
Edward the Confessor.
16
Vigmund, Abp. of York.
14
Aethelræd II.
15
Offa, King of Mercia.
13
F. J. Lees.

KENYON'S GOLD COINS OF ENGLAND

ROBERT LLOYD KENYON

Including an addendum by
NORRIS D. McWHIRTER, M.A. (OXON.)
Listing gold coins issued up to 1969

FIRECREST PUBLISHING LIMITED
BATH

First published 1884 by Bernard Quaritch

This edition reprinted by
arrangement with the
copyright holder

Standard Book Number 85119 000 6

Reproduced and Printed in Great Britain by
Redwood Press Limited
Trowbridge & London

PREFACE TO 1969 EDITION

Kenyon's *Gold Coins of England* was the classic source for our information on gold coinage at a time when the sovereign and half sovereign were the everyday medium of exchange.

The Imperial Gold coinage continued for another 30 years to reach both its zenith and its extinction in the same year of 1914. Thus, Robert Lloyd Kenyon was writing about a subject which had little mystery to his readers and which had few students.

Now that paper and base metal coinage has, in accordance with Gresham's Law, invaded each and every one of the world's 145 sovereign countries, gold coinage is a lingering memory of the elderly and a fascinating curiosity to the newer generations.

Since 1917, the United Kingdom has not issued any Imperial gold coins for general circulation although no fewer than 24 varieties have been struck as proofs, patterns or for controlled circulation.

It has thus been felt that since our gold coinage is a continuing story of which Mr. Kenyon could only be a partial chronicler, some up-dating would render a reprint of his work more useful to collectors and numismatists.

It would seem that Elizabeth II sovereigns will continue to be issued in small numbers if only as a deterrent to counterfeiters of previous issues, i.e. mainly those of her grandfather (King George V) and great grandfather (King Edward VII). The legal tender status of sovereigns cannot be described by Italian or Lebanese courts as a legal fiction if the series is continued, albeit in small mintages.

It seems highly unlikely that in the 15 generations left to the human race, now set on overbreeding itself into extinction, gold coins will ever again circulate as everyday coinage. Their continued tenuous existence seems however to enhance rather than diminish their perennial fascination.

NORRIS McWHIRTER

THE

GOLD COINS OF ENGLAND.

As gold coins are now the sole standard measure of value in this kingdom, so their prototypes of the same metal are believed to have been the earliest coins struck in Britain. About 150 years before Christ the ancient Britons are thought to have made their first coins, taking for their model the coins then current in Gaul, which were themselves copied from those of Philip of Macedon, which have the laureate head of Apollo, or as some think, of Mars, on the one side, and a two-horsed chariot on the other. This head, therefore, and this chariot, more or less unsuccessfully imitated, form the types of our earliest known coins. The metal used was gold. Silver and copper coins of similar types were soon afterwards introduced, and the original designs were gradually more and more departed from as time went on, and as successive artists took for their models the imitations made by their predecessors, instead of earlier copies, or the original Macedonian prototype. After the landing of Julius Cæsar the influence of Roman art becomes very apparent on these British coins, and about the reign of Claudius they were altogether discontinued, and gave way to the regular Roman coins, which were thenceforward for more than 300 years the sole currency of the island. The last Emperor who is believed to have struck coins here is Magnus Maximus, who assumed the purple in this country in A.D. 383, and was defeated and put to death by Theodosius at Aquileia in A.D. 388.

The gold coins of Philip of Macedon weigh about 133 grains. The British gold coins vary in weight from about

120 to 84 grains, becoming, like most other series of coins, gradually lighter as time went on. The Aureus of the early Roman Empire was in like manner from time to time diminished in weight, and Diocletian in A.D. 296 abolished all other gold coins and fixed the weight of his Aureus at 72 grains. Constantine introduced a new coinage, which lasted as long as the empire of Rome, consisting of a double Solidus, a Solidus weighing the same as the former Aureus, 72 grains, and a Triens which weighed 24 grains. A Solidus of Magnus Maximus, in the British Museum, is engraved in the frontispiece to this volume, fig. 1. The letters AVG in the exergue are interpreted to mean Augusta, by which name Ammianus Marcellinus, a contemporary historian, informs us that the ancient city of Lundinium was then called. See *Num. Chron.* N. S. vii. 61, 329. The letters OB which follow it stand for 72, and indicate that 72 of these solidi were coined out of a pound of gold.

We do not, however, propose to enter upon a description of the British and Roman coins in this volume. They form two series, very distinct from each other, and very distinct also from the coins afterwards struck in England. The British are fully described by Mr. Evans in his "Ancient British Coins," and a short account of them, including the gold and copper as well as the silver, is given at the beginning of Hawkins' "Silver Coins of England," 2nd edition. Such of the Roman coins as were known in 1844 are included in Akerman's "Coins of the Romans relating to Britain."

At the beginning of the 5th century, about twenty years after the death of Maximus, the Emperor Honorius "committed to the Britons the care of their own safety," and the Romans finally retired from the island. From this time till the 8th century the history of the coinage is involved in great obscurity. During the 5th century Roman coins would no doubt continue to form the bulk of the currency, and coins would be imported in some numbers from the continent by the bands of Saxon invaders, who were continually arriving here during the latter part of the 4th, and the whole of the 5th century; and at the end of the 6th century the landing of Augustine established a new link between Britain and the other countries of Europe. The fact, therefore, that early barbaric coins have from time to time been found in England, goes but a short way to establish a presumption that they were struck here, especially as they have nearly always been found in the southern counties, between which and the continent the intercourse would be the greatest. Nevertheless, we believe that it is certain that between the 5th century, when the Saxons got possession of the island, and the 8th century when the coinage of pennies was introduced, some coins were struck here both of gold and silver. It is probable, *à priori*, that some of the numerous princes or ecclesiastical foundations would try to imitate on their own account the Roman or other foreign money circulating in their neighbourhood, and the inscriptions on some of the coins which have been found here show that they actually did so. The silver coins of this period, which were called sceattæ, from the Saxon word sceat, "a portion," are described in Hawkins' "Silver Coins of England," 2nd ed., pp. 23 to 30, but none of those to which dates can with any confidence be assigned were struck before the middle of the 7th century. The laws of Ethelbert, King of Kent, at the beginning of that century, mention Solidi and Sceattæ, but although coins must have been then circulating under those names, this does not prove that they were struck in England. Such gold coins as seem to have the best claim to have been struck in this country, we will now proceed to describe.

2. Obv. bust in profile to right, in armour, a cross and perhaps a letter in front of the face, A behind the head. Rev. three small heads with other ornaments, but without inscription. *Frontispiece*, fig. 2. There are four specimens of this coin in the British Museum, which also contains a

silver sceatta of the same type, engraved in Hawkins' "Silver Coins" (554). They are evidently imitations of the coins of Magnus Maximus, fig. 1. This type was a common one upon Roman coins, and was by no means confined to the London mint; but a remarkable penny of Ceolwlf II, A.D. 874, Hawkins' "Silver Coins" (580), on which the same type is reproduced, affords a curious proof that it was long well known in England, and may justify us in claiming these coins as being not improbably struck in this country, though it does not appear where they were found, nor can an exact date be at present with any confidence assigned to them. The A behind the head connects them with several of the coins afterwards described. The gold pieces are of the weight of a French triens, about 20 grains, a denomination of coin commonly used in France under the Merovingian dynasty. In the time of Archbishop Ælfric, at the end of the 10th century, a triens was equivalent to 10 pennies.

3. Obv. very rude head to left, legend, probably, ABBONI MANET, but the first and last letters are imperfect. Rev. an uninterpreted device, possibly imitated from the Christian symbol, or labarum, common on Roman Christian coins. No legend. *Frontispiece*, fig. 3. *Unique*. The hoard of coins of which this and several of those afterwards described form part, was found at Crondale, in Hampshire, in 1828, by C. E. Lefroy, Esq., of Itchell Manor, Winchfield, to whose son and successor, C. J. Maxwell-Lefroy, Esq., it now belongs. It has been twice described in *The Numismatic Chronicle*, vol. vi, p. 171, and New Series, vol. x, p. 164, with engravings of nearly every variety of coin contained in it; and the whole has been most kindly placed in the hands of the author for examination. It is to this hoard that we owe the greater part of our knowledge of the earliest Anglo-Saxon coins.

The Crondale hoard consists of exactly 100 pieces, together with two small gold chains, each having a hook at one end, and at the other a triangular ornament set with rubies, having a cross in the centre, and evidently intended to symbolize the Trinity. The workmanship is pronounced by Mr. Akerman to be doubtless anterior to the 8th century. Three of the coins are blanks, which seems to prove that the whole belonged to a moneyer. Nine are imitations of coins of Licinius, and one of Leo, Emperors of the East, 308 to 324, and 451 to 474, respectively. Five bear the names of French cities, Mettis, Marsallo, Parisius. Thirty-nine are of the seven types described in these pages. The remaining forty-three are of twenty-two different types, and all are in weight and general appearance similar to Merovingian trientes. The average weight is 19·9 grains, and very few individual coins differ much from this.

With respect to Abbo, whose name appears on this coin, the Vicomte de Ponton d'Amécourt, who has paid great attention to the Merovingian series, has shown in the "Annuaire de la Société Francaise de Numismatique" for 1873, that Abbo was a moneyer at Châlon-sur-Saône, probably under Gontran, King of Burgundy, A.D. 561 to 593; that to Abbo, a moneyer at Limoges, probably the same person, was intrusted the education of St. Eligius, about A.D. 604; and that this coin found at Crondale bears a considerable resemblance, especially in the form of the letters of the legend, to those struck by Abbo at Châlons and Limoges. Assuming as an indisputable fact that the greater part of the coins found at Crondale were struck in England, he concludes that Abbo was one of the Franks who accompanied St. Augustine to England in 596 or 597, that he established a mint in this country, and that after staying here some years, he returned to France and settled at Limoges in or before A.D. 604. If this be so,—and the ascertained facts certainly seem to make it probable,—then this coin, rude as it is, becomes of extreme interest, as being struck under the immediate influence of St. Augustine himself, and forming the connecting link between the coinage of this country and that of France.

4. Obv. bust to left, two or three letters in front, EA behind. Rev. a device like an anchor, between letters, perhaps V and C, within a beaded circle. The letters outside this do not seem to form a legend. The letter A is at the top and bottom of the coin, and others seem to be repeated merely to fill up the space. *Frontispiece,* fig. 4. *Found at Crondale. Unique.*

This coin, quite worthy of Abbo in point of design, is included in the English series on account of the letter A, which is peculiarly and carefully formed, and seems to be intended as a distinguishing mark on the coin. The shape of the letter is not uncommon in the legends of other coins, and occurs on some of those struck by Abbo at Châlons. The same letter, however, formed in the same manner, and used in the same prominent way, occurs on fig. 6 of the frontispiece, and on some of the early English silver coins with Runic legends described in Hawkins' "Silver Coins of England," 2nd ed., pp. 25-27; as well as on other coins not yet attributed (see Ruding's Plates of Sceattæ, I. 1, ii. 22). It is true that it is also used as a symbol, perhaps of the town of Aristalium or Herstal, on coins of Pépin-le-bref; but the coins with Runic legends on which it appears are almost certainly English, and the type and place of finding of this coin make it probable that it ought not to be separated from them. The letter A probably denotes the town or kingdom where the coïn was struck, just as on the Merovingian series the town is often denoted by the first one or two letters of its name, and as this same letter was used in the 9th century as the symbol of East Anglia on the pennies of that kingdom. This coin is probably of nearly the same date with that of Abbo, in company with which it was found.

5. Obv. bust in profile to right, in armour, an object like a trident in front of the face, three ornaments pendent from the back of the head. No legend. Rev. a cross moline within a beaded circle, round which is a legend

wholly or partly in Runic characters, which has not yet been interpreted. *Frontispiece*, fig. 5. This figure is taken from an electrotype in the British Museum of a coin found near Canterbury, and published in *Num. Chron.*, N. S., v. 166. Mr. Akerman considered it to be an Anglo-Saxon prelatical coin, probably of Canterbury, and this attribution is confirmed by the fact that no less than twenty-one coins of this type, though differing from each other in some details, were included in the Crondale hoard described on page 5; and still more by their resemblance to our figure 7, which has the inscription Dorovernis Civitas. The bust is evidently copied from a Roman coin. The trident is similar to that on the reverse of Abbo's coin, figure 3, but has an addition to the central prong, which is probably not accidental.

6. Similar to the last, but having a legend, much clipped, behind the head, a letter apparently in front of the trident, and A at the foot of it. *Frontispiece*, fig. 6. Of the twenty-one coins of this type found at Crondale, only two had any trace of this legend, and from one of them our engraving is taken. On the other specimen, of which there is a woodcut in *The Numismatic Chronicle*, N. S., vol. x, p. 172, much less of the legend is visible, but the A is very distinct, and a lower row of five or six beads is shown on the collar. The A, which is of the same shape with that on figure 4, connects these coins with it, and with the silver coins with Runic legends mentioned on p. 6.

7. Obv. bust in profile to right, filleted, in armour. Around it is the legend EVSEBII MONITA. Rev. Cross moline, legend + DOROVERNIS CIVITAS. *Frontispiece*, fig. 7. The engraving is from an electrotype, in the British Museum, of a coin in the French national collection. This coin was the first triens ever attributed to the Anglo-Saxons, and was so attributed by M. de Longpérier in *The Numismatic Journal*, vol. ii, p. 232. The bust is copied from Roman coins of the 6th century, and the reverse is similar to that of the coins just described, figures 5 and 6.

Of Eusebius, who was probably, from his name, an ecclesiastic, we know nothing; but Dorovernis is the name given to Canterbury by Bede, and in the charters of the 7th and 8th centuries, and we know of no other town which can be signified by that name. The weight of this coin is given in *The Numismatic Chronicle*, vol. ii, p. 204, as 25 grains, which is heavier than other English or French trientes of the 6th and 7th centuries.

8. Obv. bust to right, filleted, a cross in front of face, a smaller one below it. Legend AVDVARLD REGE. Rev. cross resting on a small globe, within a beaded circle. Legend MEALLDENVS. *Frontispiece*, fig. 8. From the Crondale hoard. *Unique*. These legends were read by Mr. Haigh, "Audvarid Reges," and "Meassgenus." The author, however, believes the above readings to be more correct, and if so the coin may be safely attributed to Mealdunesberg, or Malmesbury. The name on the obverse of the coin has no resemblance to that of any known king of the West Saxons, in which kingdom Malmesbury was situated; but it may perhaps be meant for Eadbald, King of Kent, A.D. 616 to 640, whose father Ethelbert held a supremacy over the West Saxons for a considerable time. Eadbald lost this supremacy, but he may have retained it sufficiently long to allow of coins being struck at Malmesbury in his name. The first extant charter to the monastery of Malmesbury is dated 675, but it existed in a humbler manner for a considerable time previously. Eadbald at the beginning of his reign rejected Christianity, to which he soon afterwards returned. But even if this coin were struck while the king was Pagan, the Bishop or Abbot striking it is not unlikely to have placed on it the crosses which were the emblems of his own religion. The Vicomte de Ponton d'Amécourt possesses a coin of this type, which is said to read pretty distinctly on the reverse AMBALLONDENVS; but it seems not improbable that it is intended for the same legend as on our coin.—*Num. Chron.* N. S., xii. 72.

9. Obv. head, full-faced, tonsured, a small cross rising from each shoulder, no legend. Rev. cross resting on a small globe, the same as on the last coin, within a plain circle, legend LONDVNIV. *Frontispiece*, fig. 9. Seven specimens of this were found at Crondale, and are the only ones known. The legend is quite distinct, and there can be no doubt that the coins were struck at London, and that the portrait is that of an ecclesiastic, perhaps Mellitus, first Bishop of London, 604 to 617. The cross above each shoulder is probably meant for the termination of the stole. Mellitus was expelled in 617, when the East Saxon kingdom (which included London) returned to Paganism, and the next Bishop of London was Cedd, who was consecrated about 656, and died 664. These coins are closely connected with that last described by the type of the reverses, and are more likely to have been struck in the time of Mellitus than in that of Cedd.

10. Obv. head to right, surrounded by a rude ornament. No legend. Rev. cross crosslet within a beaded circle. The legend is double struck, but is apparently the same as that of the coin next described. *Frontispiece*, fig. 10. Found at Crondale. Mr. Evans has a similar but not identical coin found near Dover and engraved in *Smith's Collectanea Antiqua*, Vol. I., Pl. xxii. 9; and a gold-plated coin of nearly the same type was found in Ayrshire. *Arch. and Hist. Coll. of Ayr and Wigton*, 1882, p. 46.

11. Obv. as the last, though not from the same die. Rev. plain cross within a beaded circle, legend + LUOON MONA. *Frontispiece*, fig. 11. Six of these coins were found at Crondale, but they are from several different dies. The one engraved has perhaps the clearest legend. The others seem to read LUOONUS MVÁL. The first letter on all of them is like a Z, and may be intended for N. The placing a moneyer's name on the coins, and omitting that of the king, is very common on Merovingian coins, and very inconvenient to the modern numismatist.

12. Obv. head to left. Otherwise as the last. The legend

appears to be composed of the same letters as the last, but arranged almost at haphazard. The coin is perhaps copied from the last by a moneyer who did not understand the legend. *Frontispiece,* fig. 12. Found at Crondale. *Unique.*

These coins, figures 10, 11 and 12, cannot be attributed to any individual, but the fact of their having been all found in Britain raises a presumption that they were struck here; and moreover they resemble the London coins too much in workmanship and general appearance to be removed far from them either in locality or in date.

We have now come to the end of the trientes at present attributable to England. The coins enumerated above are of unquestioned authenticity, and were all found in England, excepting perhaps Nos. 2 and 7, whose place of finding is not known. This of itself raises some presumption that they are English coins. Moreover, an English gold coinage of this sort in the 7th century is, *à priori,* highly probable, as we know that a similar one prevailed at that time in France, with which country after the landing of Augustine there was considerable intercourse, so that we should naturally expect to find coins struck in England of the same general appearance, type, and weight, as those current in France, an expectation to which the coins before us exactly answer. The names Dorovernis, Londuni and Mealldenus, can only mean Canterbury, London and Malmesbury; and the other coins described are too closely associated both by type and by place of finding with those bearing these names to be assigned to a different country. We have, therefore, no hesitation in claiming them as English, and it is probable that some of the other coins found at Crondale may also belong to this country, but it would be premature to claim them until some further progress has been made in deciphering their legends.

With respect to date, the evidence is not conclusive, as none of the coins in the Crondale hoard can be assigned with certainty to a known individual. Figure 2 may possibly be of the 6th century, though if the cross on it be intended, as it probably is, for the Christian symbol, it can hardly be earlier than the 7th. As to the coin by Abbo, fig. 3, a considerable probability has been shown that it is of the time of St. Augustine. We see no reason to think that the others are very much later, and in our opinion all the evidence at present obtainable points to the whole of these trientes belonging to the first half of the 7th century. Gold would be likely to be used as the first material for a native currency, on account of its dignity, and silver coins to have been struck afterwards, as was the case with the ancient British coinage; and the earliest date to which any silver sceatta has with any confidence been attributed is the reign of Peada, King of Mercia, A.D. 656. How long a gold coinage continued to exist in England later discoveries may show, but probably the metal was not sufficiently plentiful to keep it up very long. The pieces we are about to describe are very much later in date than the trientes, and were probably rather medals or pattern pieces than current coins.

13. In the collection of the late Duc de Blacas was an Arabic Dinar, equivalent in weight and value to a mancus (30 pence), which bore the name of Offa, King of Mercia, A.D. 757 to 796. The following is a description of this curious coin. Obv. round the coin an Arabic legend, meaning, "*In the name of God was coined this dinar in the year* 157" (A.D. 774). Across the field, "*Mahommed is the Apostle of God,*" in three lines, between which, but upside down, are the words OFFA REX. Rev. round the coin, "*Mahommed is the Apostle of God, who sent him with the doctrine and true faith to prevail over every other religion.*" Across the field, "*There is no other God but the one God; He has no equal.*" *Frontispiece*, fig. 13. The figure is placed last in our plate by mistake. M. de Longpérier and Mr. Akerman were probably right in thinking that this is a copy of an Arabic coin, made in England by a workman ignorant of the Arabic language, and is a specimen of

the coins sent by Offa to the Pope in fulfilment of his promise to send him 365 gold mancuses every year. It was procured in Rome, *Num. Chr.* O. S., iv. 232. There is reason to believe that gold coins both of the Greek Empire and of Arabic princes had some circulation in England during Saxon times, as they are occasionally found in this country; and if this coin was really struck for the purpose of paying Offa's tribute to the Pope, it would be pretty conclusive evidence that there was no native gold currency in which that tribute could be paid. The coin is unique, and it is very unlikely that any great number of such pieces were ever struck. When the tribute was paid at all, it was probably paid in foreign gold, and a few pieces of this sort may have been struck to make up a deficiency in such gold procurable in some one year.

14. A gold piece in the British Museum, of the size and weight of a mancus, has on the obverse a full-faced bust of an ecclesiastic, with the legend VIGMVND AREP. Rev. a small cross within a wreath; MVNVS DIVINVM. Weight, 68 grs. *Frontispiece*, fig. 14. Vigmund was Archbishop of York, A.D. 831 to 854. The place of finding this piece is not known, and its authenticity has been questioned. It has a hole drilled on each side of the neck, as if for suspension; and it is curious that a coin in the British Museum of Louis le Debonnaire, of the same denomination and with the same type and inscription on the reverse, found in Scotland, has exactly similar holes. Vigmund's piece, which is unique, must be considered rather as a medal than a coin, and was perhaps intended to be suspended as an ornament or amulet round the neck.

15. Obv. ÆTHELRÆD REX ANGL. King's bust to left, helmeted and with a radiated crown, oval shield on left shoulder, within beaded circle. Rev. LEOFWINE MIO LÆWE. A long cross voided, with pellet in the centre, each limb terminating in three crescents and dividing the legend, over a lozenge-shaped compartment with concave

sides and three pellets at each corner. Weight, 51½ grs. *Frontispiece*, fig. 15. This coin was found at Hellingly, in Sussex, about the year 1808, and was immediately bought by Mr. Martin, in the possession of whose daughter, Mrs. Holroyd, it now is. The type is exactly the same as that of some silver pennies of the same king, Hawkins (203), and the place where it was found is only thirteen miles from Lewes, its place of mintage. See *Num. Chron.* N. S., xix. 62. We are indebted to the courtesy of the Rev. J. Carter, Mrs. Holroyd's son-in-law, for the cast from which our engraving is taken. The coin has either been worn, or is struck from worn dies.

16. Obv. EDWERD REX. King's bust to left, filleted; sceptre in front. Rev. LVFINC ON WÆRINC. Cross, limbs gradually expanding, issuing from a central circle, with four crescents in the angles, and a pellet in the third quarter. Wt. 54¼ grs. *Frontispiece*, fig. 16, which is copied from Rud. H. 44, and has accidentally been transposed in our plate with fig. 13. The type is the same as that of the silver pennies, Hawkins (219), and there is, perhaps, no sufficient reason to doubt its authenticity, though its place of finding is not known. It was in the collection of Mr. T. H. Spurrier, of Edgbaston, near Birmingham, in which town it was bought. See *Num. Journ.* ii. 54. Wærinc signifies Warwick, the place of mintage. The four last-named coins are the only known Saxon pieces, other than the trientes, struck in gold, and we have thought it desirable to bring them together and engrave them in our frontispiece. The Arabic Dinar, however, was clearly not a current coin, and tends strongly to disprove the existence of any native gold currency in Offa's time. Vigmund's piece is probably a medal; and those of Æthelred and Edward the Confessor appear to have been struck from dies intended for silver pennies, either as pattern pieces or by a mere freak of the moneyer. We do not believe that there was any regular Saxon gold coinage later than the trientes.

HENRY III, 1216 TO 1272.

From the end of the 9th century there was no gold coinage either in England or in any of the neighbouring countries till the reign of Henry III. The gold bezants of the Greek Empire, and the gold coins struck during the 9th and 10th centuries by the Arabic princes in Sicily, were probably used more or less in mercantile transactions all over Europe, and are found occasionally in this country, but they had no legal currency here and were probably accepted merely as bullion. In the middle of the 13th century, however—an age of revolutions and of new ideas all over the world—a native gold coinage was almost simultaneously adopted by the European nations. The first gold "Florin" was issued by the republic of Florence in 1252. Louis IX introduced gold coins in France, and the Emperor Frederick II in his kingdom of Naples, and at about the same time the same innovation took place in England. On the 16th of August, 1257, a writ dated at Chester was issued commanding the Mayor of London to proclaim in that city that "the Gold Money which the king had caused to be made should be immediately current there and elsewhere within the realm of England, in all transactions of buying and selling, at the rate of 20 pennies of sterlings (*i.e.*, 20 silver pennies) for every gold penny." The times, however, were by no means favourable to the issue of pieces of a denomination so much higher than had been previously known. The kingdom was in a very disturbed state; the "mad parliament," by which the king was practically deposed, was to meet the next year, and so great distress prevailed throughout the country that a quarter of wheat, the average price of which was about 7*s*, is said to have sold this year for as much as 24*s*. Accordingly, on the 4th of November in the same year, the City of London petitioned against these coins, and the king had to issue another proclamation that no one was obliged to take them, and that whoever did might bring them to his Exchange, and receive there the value at which they had been made current, deducting only a halfpenny for each piece. The coins nevertheless continued to be current, and are mentioned in several records down to the year 1270; and in 1265, the year of Montfort's Parliament, their value was raised by proclamation from 20 to 24 pence; probably equivalent in purchasing power to £2. 10*s* at the present day. It is not likely that any great number of these coins was ever struck, and being unpopular and, from their high value, inconvenient, they would soon be melted down, a process which would be greatly facilitated by the fact that they were of pure gold, without alloy of any kind; and this will account for their being at present of extreme rarity, only three or four specimens being known. The type is, obv. the king crowned, in royal robes, seated on his throne, holding a sceptre in his right hand, an orb in his left; the legend, HENRIC REX III, is interrupted both at top and bottom by the king's figure, and the cross on the orb separates the H in Henric from the E. Rev. a cross of double limbs, each botone, extending nearly to the edge of the coin, as on the silver pennies of 1248, a pellet in the centre of the cross, and a rose surrounded by three pellets in each angle; a beaded inner circle; legend, WILLEM ON LVND. *MB.* Rud. Suppl. pl. vi. 18. Or with the arms and legs of the throne formed by pellets instead of straight lines, legend WILLEM ON LVNDE. *MB. Num. Chron.* N. S., iii. 190. The weight of both these coins is 45⅕ grains. One of them was bought for £41. 10*s*. See *woodcut on title-page.* Another, reading LVNDEN, sold at Capt. Murchison's sale in 1864 for £140. Mr. J. Evans has a fourth specimen, reading LVND, and having a hole through the field, which was formerly Mr. Cuff's and Mr. Wigan's. They are the last English gold coins on which the name of a moneyer appears, and are the only ones which have been struck of pure gold. The amount of gold contained in them is about $\frac{2}{5}$ of that in a modern sovereign, but their purchasing power may be considered equal to that of £2 or £2. 10*s* of our present money.

Edward III, 1327 to 1377.

No further attempts were made, after the ill-received coinage of Henry III, to provide a gold currency for this kingdom, until the 17th year of King Edward III, 1343. Gold coins were, however, used in the countries with which our principal commerce was carried on, notably in North Italy, France, and Flanders; and in 1343, in order to increase the quantity of money in the kingdom and to facilitate the trade with Flanders, the Council resolved, after examining before Parliament certain merchants, goldsmiths, and moneyers, that one kind of gold money should be made both in England and Flanders, provided the Flemings were willing, to be current at such weight, alloy, and value, as should be appointed by the king and Council, and that all other gold money should be prohibited in both countries. Accordingly, in that year an indenture was made between the king and the masters and workers and changers of the money, according to which three monies of gold were to be made; one, which was called a florin, to be current at 6*s*, to be equal in weight to two petit florins of Florence of good weight, *i.e.*, 108 grains; and of the same fineness, namely, 23 carats 3½ grains pure gold to ½ grain alloy; and the half and quarter florin in proportion. This money was made current by a proclamation on the 27th of January, 1343 (*O. S.*), in which the new coins were described as "one coin with two leopards, each piece to be current for six shillings, another piece of one leopard, and another piece of one helm, being respectively the half and quarter of the larger coin, and of proportional value," and were ordered to be received by all persons throughout the realm. The same indenture was renewed the next year, 1344, with a new master and worker; but it was discovered that the coins were valued too high in proportion to the silver, and were consequently generally refused, and accordingly a proclamation was issued on the 9th of July to order that they should be taken in payment only with the consent of those to whom they were offered, and another on the 20th of August of the same year, 1344, declared them no longer current without the consent of the receiver, but they were to be considered as bullion and taken according to their value as such.

It is not to be wondered at that under these circumstances the florin and its parts are extremely rare. Of the florin two specimens only are known, both of which were found together in the river Tyne. They have on the obv. the king crowned and robed, seated under a canopy, holding a sceptre in his right hand, an orb in his left; two leopards, as mentioned in the proclamation, are placed one on each side the throne; fleur-de-lys are sprinkled over the field. Legend, EDWR ° D ° GRA ° REX ° ANGL ° Z ° FRANC ° DNS ° HIB. Rev. tressure of four curves, with a beaded interior foliated at each angle, containing a short cross with quatrefoiled and foliated ends, and a quatrefoil in the centre, upon a beaded cross voided; in each curve of the tressure is a crown, and outside each angle of the tressure is a lion or leopard. Legend ⁑ IHC ⁑ TRANSIENS ⁑ PE ⁑ MEDIVM ⁑ ILLORVM ⁑ IBAT ⁑ One of these pieces is in MB., pl. 1 (1); the other, which differs in having a fleur-de-lys between the king's right arm and his body, and a greater number of fleur-de-lys in the field, was sold at Mr. Forster's sale in 1868 for £113, and is now in the collection of Mr. Evans. It weighs 107 grs.

HALF-FLORIN. Obv. a leopard crowned, a banner

bearing the arms of France and England quartered is fastened to his neck and flows back on his shoulder. EDWAR ° D ° GRA ° REX ° ANGL ° Z ° FRANC ° DNS ° HIB. Rev. a tressure of four curves, with a beaded interior with a lis at each angle, containing a cross nearly the same as that on the florin ; a lion outside each angle. ⁝ DOMINE ⁝ NE ⁝ IN ⁝ FVRORE ⁝ TVO ⁝ ARGVAS ⁝ ME ⁝ *MB*. Pl. 1. (2). Rud. Suppl. part ii, plate iii, 6. Or without the ⁝ before and after the legend. *EVANS*. These are the only two specimens at present known.

QUARTER FLORIN. Obv. a lion crowned standing on a cap of maintenance surmounting a helmet, attached to which is the mantling or curtain, which was worn both for ornament and as a protection against the sun. The field is strewn with lys. EDWR ⁝ R ⁝ ANGL ⁝ Z ⁝ FRANC ⁝ D ⁝ HIB. Rev. a short cross potent upon a beaded cross voided, with foliated ends, a quatrefoil in the centre. ⁝ EXALTABITVR ⁝ IN ⁝ GLORIA ⁝ Pl. 1 (3). *MB*. Wt. 27 grs. A brilliant specimen of the quarter florin was sold at Capt. Murchison's sale in 1864 for £170. One in the Hunter Museum at Glasgow is engraved in Rud. Gold Coins, I. 1, Suppl. part ii, pl. iii, 5. Mr. Evans has one like this, but reading EXALTABITAR.

SECOND COINAGE, 1344. The issue of gold florins had been as unsuccessful as that of gold pennies ; but in the same year in which the florins were called in, a new indenture was entered into between the king and the master of the mint, by virtue of which a Tower pound of gold was to be coined into 39½ nobles, at 6*s* 8*d* each, or a proportionable number of half and quarter nobles ; and this new money was made current by a proclamation which declared that the coins were to be called Nobles, Maille Nobles, and Ferling Nobles respectively, and that no one could refuse to take them in payment of sums of 20*s* and upwards, and it was ordered that no person should carry, nor cause to be carried out of the realm gold or silver in plate or in money, *except the king's money of gold aforesaid.* It had been long unlawful to export silver plate or money, and this prohibition was extended to gold plate in 1331. The principal object of the gold coinage, however, was to facilitate the trade between England and Flanders, and the exportation of the gold coins was therefore freely allowed for the present, though it was stopped upon the representations of the Commons, a few years afterwards. The reason for preventing the exportation of uncoined gold was probably that it might be brought to the mint to be coined, and a certain profit obtained thereby for the king.

The weight of the new noble was $138\frac{6}{13}$ grs., and the fineness the same as before. The type is, obv. the king in armour, crowned, holding in his right hand a sword, in his left a shield, bearing the arms of France and England quarterly, standing in a ship, the upper part of the side of which is ornamented with three lions, behind each of which are two lis. There are three ropes from the mast to the stern of the ship, two to the prow. The French arms are not, as they subsequently became, three lis only, but *semé de lys, i.e.*, an indefinite number of lis on the shield. Legend EDWAR × D × GRA × REX × ANGL × Z × FRANC × DNS × HYB. Rev. within a compartment of double moulding of eight arches, having a trefoil in each spandril, is a short cross potent upon a beaded cross voided with foliated ends, having L (for London) in the centre, within a compartment of four arches and four angles, with a trefoil at each angle; and there is a lis opposite each end of the cross, and a lion passant guardant with a crown above it in each angle. × IHC × TRANSIENS × PER × MEDIVM × ILLORVM × IBAT × Pl. i. (4). Rud. ii. 1. *MB.* Wt. 135 grs. *Ext. rare.*

The half-noble of this coinage is not known.

The quarter noble has on the obv. a shield with the arms of France and England quarterly, within a double tressure of six arches, a trefoil in each spandril, a pellet at each angle. EDWAR REX ANGL Z FRANC D HYB. A mark like an inverted comma between each word. Rev. within a compartment of eight arches is a cross with foliated ends, having L in the centre, within a compartment of four arches and four angles, with a trefoil at each angle; there is a lis opposite each end of the cross, and a lion passant guardant in each angle. ⁑ EXALTABITVR ⁑ IN ⁑ GLORIA ⁑ Pl. i. (5). *MB.* Wt. 33½ grs. *Ext. rare.* One was sold at Mr. Cuff's sale in 1854 for £10, and another at Mr. Forster's sale in 1868 for £9. Mr. Rashleigh has a quarter noble weighing 34½ grs. which has Є instead of L in the centre of the reverse. It was bought at Mr. Whitbourn's sale in 1869.

The ship which appears upon these nobles is said to commemorate the great naval victory which the English fleet, commanded by the king in person, obtained over the French fleet off Sluys, on Midsummer Day, 1340, and also to be intended to assert Edward's claim to the sovereignty of the seas. Their name is supposed to be derived from the *noble* nature of the metal of which they are composed, and however this may be, their beauty seems to have made a great impression on the people, and a legend was long current that they were made by alchemy, and the inscription, "Jesus autem transiens per medium illorum ibat" (Luke iv. 30) was explained to mean that "as Jesus passed invisible and in most secret manner by the middest of the Pharisees, so gold was made by invisible and secret art amidst the ignorant;" and it was said that it was put upon the coins "because Ripley, the Alchymist, when he made gold in the Tower, the first time he found it spoke these words 'per medium eorum,' *i.e.*, per medium ignis et sulphuris." It appears, however, that this text was considered to be a charm against dangers in war and also against thieves; and it was perhaps its virtue in this last respect which caused the authorities to place it on so valuable a coin as the gold Noble.

THIRD COINAGE, 1346. In the King's 20th year, 1346, by indenture with Percival de Porche, master of the mint, the weight of the money, both of gold and silver, was diminished, 42 nobles instead of $39\frac{1}{2}$ being ordered to be made out of the Tower pound, so that the noble was now to weigh only $128\frac{4}{7}$ grs., and the half and quarter in proportion. In the same year also, upon the petition of the Commons, an ordinance was made that no person, of what estate or condition soever, should carry out of the realm the king's good money, including apparently the gold coins, which it had hitherto been lawful to export. The coins of this period, like all previous ones, are very rare.

NOBLE. Exactly the same as that of 1344, except that it has Є, the initial of the king's name, instead of L in the centre of the reverse. Rud. ii. 2. *MB.* Wt. 127 grs. *Very rare.* Three specimens were sold at Mr. Cuff's sale in 1854, of which Mr. Evans has one.

HALF NOBLE. Type as the noble, but three ropes from each end of the ship, and three lions each followed by a lis on the side. EDWAR. DEI. G. REX. ANGL. Z. FRANC. D Rev. DOMINE × NE × IN × FVRORE × TVO ⁑ ARGVAS × ME. Є in centre, lis before head of lion in second quarter, two dots over upper limb of cross. Pl. i. (6). *MB.* Wt. $60\frac{1}{2}$ grs., considerably clipped. *Very rare.* The object in the centre of the reverse is probably an Є, but is not very distinct. The Ns on the reverse of this coin are of the Roman shape, not, as on all previous coins, Lombardic.

QUARTER NOBLE. Type as the previous issue of 1344, but the compartment on the reverse is double, and it has Є instead of L in the centre. ⁑ EDWAR ⁑ R ⁑ ANGL ⁑ Z ⁑ FRANE ⁑ D ⁑ HYB ⁑ ⁑ EXALTABITVR ⁑ IN ⁑ GLORIA ⁑ Pl. i. (7). *MB.* Wt. 32·3 grs. Two of these were sold at Mr. Cuff's sale in 1854 for 12*s* and 13*s* respectively, and one at Mr. Duncombe's sale in June, 1869. *Very rare.*

FOURTH COINAGE, 1351. Notwithstanding the diminution made in the weight of the noble in 1346, it was still found that the English coins "had hitherto been so much better than those of any other nation, that they were exported, and base money brought into the realm, to the impoverishment of the people;" and accordingly in 1351 the weight of the coins both of gold and silver was still further reduced, and the noble, retaining the same nominal value of 6*s* 8*d*, was now to weigh only 120 grs., 45 being made out of the Tower pound, and the others in proportion. An ordinance was made at the same time forbidding all persons to carry out of the realm any gold or silver, either in plate or in money; but this would appear to be repealed by the Statute of the Staple, in 1353, which provided that "no one should carry out of the realm the old sterlings *nor any other money but the king's new money of gold and silver,*" so that an implied permission was given to export new money. This permission was revoked by a statute of 1381.

The pieces of the fourth coinage are of the same type as those of former years, but they may be divided by their legends into three periods, namely, from 1351 to 1360, when the title of King of France appears on the coins, but not that of Lord of Aquitaine; from 1360 to 1369, when, in accordance with the treaty of Bretigny in the former year, the title of King of France was omitted and that of Lord of Aquitaine substituted for it; and from 1369 to the king's death in 1377, when, the treaty of Bretigny having been broken by Charles V, both titles were used. The pieces of this coinage are by no means uncommon.

NOBLES. Type like those of 1346, having Є in the centre of the reverse, and trefoils in the spandrils.

1351 to 1360. The title King of France appears upon all of these, but never that of Duke of Aquitaine; and with the exception of the first coin described, all of them have a lis over the head of the lion in one quarter or other of the reverse, and are ornamented, either between the words or in the field of the reverse, with annulets. The letters of the legend are generally of the old English or Lombardic shape, but with one exception (No. 16), the Ns are always of the Roman shape. 1. EDWARD × DEI × GRA × REX × ANGL × Z × FRANC × D h. Three ropes from stern, one from prow; three lions, each preceded by two lis, on the side of the ship. Rev. IHE × AVTEM × TRANCIENS ⁑ P × MEDIVM × ILLORVM × YBAT. Two dots over upper limb of cross. *MB*. This coin was found with No. 12 in the cloisters of Westminster Abbey. 2. Same but D HYB, three ropes from each end of ship, three lis only in French arms on shield, IBAT, two annulets instead of dots over upper limb of cross, lis over head of lion in second quarter. *MB*. 3. EDWARD × DEI × GRA × REX × ANGL × Z × FRANC × D × HYB. Three ropes from stern, none from prow, three lis only in French arms, ornaments on ship as 1. Rev. IHC ° AVTEM ° TRANCIENS ° P ° MEDIVM ° ILLORVM ° IBAT, MM crown, lis over head of lion in second quarter. *MB*. 4. Same, but with one rope from the prow, French arms *semé de lys;* the stops are an annulet before Edward and between all the words except after Edward, Rex, D, and Illorum. Pl. ii. (8). *MB*. 5. ° E ° DWARD ° DEI ° GRA ° ANGL ° Z ° FRANC ° D ° HY ° B ° E. Ropes and ornaments as No. 1. Rev. legend as No. 3, lis in second quarter. *MB*. Mr. Evans has one like 3, but without the MM; two ropes from prow, EDVARD, no × after D; and another in bad condition but apparently like 3, without the MM, three ropes from prow, IB for Ibat. 6. As No. 1, but D HYB, IBAT, ornaments on side of ship are lion, lis, lion, lis, lion. Lis in second quarter, two annulets over upper limb of cross. Rud. ii. 3. *MB*. 7. Obv. as No. 6. Rev. IHC × AVEM (*sic*) × TRANCIENS × P × MEDIVM × ILLORVM × IBAT. One annulet to right of upper limb of cross, lis in 2nd quarter. *MB*. 8. × EDWERD × DEI × GRA × REX × ANGL × Z × FRANC D B, two ropes from stern, one from prow, three lis only in French arms, ornaments on ship as

No. 6. Rev. as No. 1, but IHC, IBAT, two annulets over upper limb of cross, lis in 2nd quarter. *MB.* 9. EDWARD ° DEI ° GRA ° REX ° ANGL ° Z ° FRANC ° D ° HYB; two ropes from stern, one from prow, ornaments on ship as No. 6. Rev. IHC × AVTEM × TRANCIENS × P × MEDIVM ILLORVM IBAT. Lis in second quarter. *EVANS.* 10. Same as last, but three ropes from prow, no annulet after D, saltire after every word on rev. *MB.* 11. Obv. legend as 9, but FR ° ANC °; three ropes from each end of ship, ornaments on ship lis, lion, lis, lion, lis, lion, lis; lettering smaller than usual. Rev. IHES ° AVTEM ° TRANCIENS ° PER ° MEDIV ° ILDORVM ° IBAT, lis in second quarter. *EVANS.* 12. Obv. legend as 9, but HYBE, no stops between the words, three ropes from each end of the ship, ornaments on ship one lis, lion, two lis, lion, two lis, lion, two lis, lettering small. Rev. as the last. *MB.* Mr. Evans has one reading EDWAD & ILLORV, and with ° between the words on rev. 13. Legends as 9, but HI for Hyb, ropes and ornaments as 12, annulet between words on both sides, lis in third quarter. *MB.* 14. Same as last, but HYB, IBA, and with lis in first quarter instead of third. Rud. i. 2. *MB.* 15. Legends as 9, three ropes from stern, four from prow, annulet between words on both sides, lis in first quarter, ornaments on ship are two lis, lion, two lis, lion, two lis, lion, two lis. *MB.* 16. Obv. legend as 9, three ropes from each end of ship, ornaments on ship one lis, lion, two lis, lion, two lis, lion, one lis. Rev. IHC ⁑ TRANSIENS ⁑ PER ⁑ MEDIVM ⁑ ILLORVM ⁑ IBAT. Lis over head of lion in first quarter. *MB.* The Ns on the reverse of this coin are of the Lombardic not the Roman form. 17. Obv. as last. Rev. IHE ° AVTEM ° TRANCIENS ° P ° MEDIVM ° ILLORVM ° IBA°, lis over head of lion in second quarter. *MB.*

1360 to 1369. These differ from the previous nobles in that, in consequence of the treaty of Bretigny, the name of France never appears on them, but that of Aquitaine generally does. Most of them are marked with annulets, but these never occur, as on former nobles, between the words of the legend. On many coins of this time annulets are substituted for trefoils at the angles of the central compartment on the reverse.

18. EDWARDVS ⁑ DEI ⁑ GRA × REX × ANGL × DENS ⁑ HYB. Three ropes from stern, two from prow; ornaments on ship as Nos. 16 and 17. Rev. IHC × AVTEM ⁑ PER ⁑ MEDIVM ⁑ ILLORVM ⁑ IBAT. Lis over head of lion in second quarter, annulet instead of trefoil at each angle of centre compartment, three pellets, for trefoil, in each spandril. Pl. ii (11) *MB*. On this coin the N in ANGL is of the Roman shape, that in DENS of the Lombardic. On all subsequent nobles the Lombardic shape only is used. 19. Obv. from the same die as the last. Rev. IHC × AVTEM ⁑ TRANSIENS ⁑ PER ⁑ MED × ILLORR ⁑ IBAT. Lis and annulets as the last. *MB*. The last two coins omit the French title but do not add that of Aquitaine; but the lis over the head of the lion in the second quarter, and the ornaments on the ship, connect them closely with the last of the coins struck before 1360, and show that they must have been struck very soon after that date. The blunders in the legends on these and the next coins seem to show that the change of title caused some confusion in the mint. 20. EDWARDVS × DEI × GRA × REX ⁑ ANGLIE ⁑ Z ⁑ AQVTA × D × E'. Three ropes from each end, ornaments on ship as Nos. 16-19. Rev. IHC × AVTEM × TRANSIEVS ⁑ P × MEDIVM ⁑ ILLORR × IBAT Lis and annulets as the two last. *MB*. 21. EDWARD × DEI × GRA × REX × ANGL × DNS × HIBN × Z × AQ. Three ropes from each end, ornaments as Nos. 16-20. Rev. IHC × AVTE × TRANSIENS ⁑ PER ⁑ MEDVM ⁑ ILLORR × IBAT. Lis and annulets as the three last. *MB*. 22. Obv. legend as last but HYB × Z × AQT, two saltires between all the other words, and before Edward; three ropes from stern, two from prow; ornaments on side of ship are a lion, two lis, a lion, two lis. Rev. IHC ⁑

AVTEM ⁑ TRANSIENS ⁑ PER ⁑ MEDIVM ⁑ ILLORV ⁑ IBAT. Trefoils at angles of centre compartment. *MB.* 23. Same as last without saltires before Edward, and reading MEDIV ⁑ ILLORVM ⁑ *MB.* 24. Same as last with annulet before Edward. *MB.*

Calais. The foregoing coins all have Є, for the name of the king, in the centre of the reverse, with the possible exception of No. 20, on which the letter may be either Є or C; but there are three coins of this period, 1360 to 1369, in the British Museum which have a C instead of Є in that place, and which also differ from the others in having a flag at the stern of the ship; and it is supposed that these coins were struck at Calais. A mint was established at Calais as early as the year 1347, immediately after its conquest by the English, but it is not till the year 1363 that there is any proof of gold being coined there. In that year the Mayor was commanded to enforce an ordinance which had been previously published forbidding the currency of any money in the town except that which was coined at the mint there; and all persons importing wool from England to Calais were ordered to bring, for every sack of wool so imported, five shillings in weight of fine gold, or other bullion of gold or silver, to the Calais mint. In 1364 Guater de Barde, master of the mint in the Tower of London, undertook to coin the king's money of gold and silver at Calais, of the same weight and alloy as the money of the Tower. It is probable that the three following coins are specimens of this money; and although, as being struck at Calais, they cannot strictly claim a place among English coins, yet we insert them here for the present because, even though struck at Calais, they no doubt had a legal currency in England; and also because it is possible that, after all, the C, on which we rest their appropriation, may have been intended for an E, and that they may therefore, like the rest, have been struck at the Tower. In any case it is probable that the dies were made at the Tower, in order to ensure their uniformity with those of the English coins. 25. Same as 22, but with no saltires before Edward, a flag at the stern of the ship, and Œ in the centre of the reverse. *MB*. 26. Same as the last, with small open quatrefoil before Edward. See Rud. i. 4. *MB*. 27. Same as the last, omitting the saltires after PER. *MB*. A Calais noble without the flag was sold at Mr. Cuff's sale in 1854 for £3. 1*s*. Mr. Evans has one exactly like 23, but reading HYB AQVT.

1369 to 1377. During this period the names both of France and Aquitaine appear upon the coins. The annulet mark is sometimes used, but never either between the words of the legend or at the angles of the central compartment on the reverse. All except the first mentioned in this class have three ropes from the stern, one from the prow of the ship, and have the side of the ship ornamented by a lis, lion, lis, lion, lis, lion, lis.

28. ° EDWARD ⁑ DEI ⁑ G ⁑ REX ⁑ ANG × Z × FRA ⁑ DNS ⁑ HYB × Z × AT. Otherwise exactly the same as No. 24. *MB*. See Rud. i. 3. 29. EDWARD × DI × GRA × REX × ANGL × Z × FRANC × DNS × HIB × Z × AQVIT. Flag at stern. Rev. IHC ⁑ AVTEM ⁑ TRANSIENS ⁑ PER ⁑ MEDIVM ⁑ ILLORVM ⁑ IBAT. Pellet after the E in the centre, two dots over the lis on the top and bottom limbs of the cross. Rud. Suppl. pl. vi. 19. *MB*. This is the only noble with a flag at the stern of the ship which has not got Œ instead of E in the centre of the reverse. 30. Like the last, but without the flag, no pellets over the limbs of the cross, saltire after Ibat. *MB*. 31. Same but reading EDWARDVS, AQT. *MB*. 32. Same, with no saltire after Ibat. *MB*. 33. Legends as 29 but AQ, small cross after the E in the centre, annulet at spring of first arch. *MB*. 34. Legends as 29 but AQ, MEDIV, ILLORV. E in centre reversed, two saltires before Gra and Aq. *MB*. A noble with Edward's name, but with R in the centre of the reverse, will be found described under Richard II's reign.

CALAIS. C in centre of reverse. Otherwise exactly like 28, but AQT, ILLORV. *EVANS.*

HALF NOBLES, 1351 to 1360. These, like the nobles of the same period, which they very closely resemble, have the titles of England and France but not of Aquitaine. The type and legends are similar to those of the earlier half nobles. Annulets occur between the words of the legends on coins of this class only. 1. EDWAR × DEI × G × REX × ANGL × Z × FRANC D (Hyb omitted). Three ropes from stern, one from prow. Ornaments on ship lis, lion, lis, lion, lis, lion, lis. Rev. DOMINE NE × IN × FVRORE × TVO × ARGVAS × ME. Two dots over upper limb of cross on rev. *MB.* Cf. noble No. 1, and half noble of 1346. 2. EDWAR ° D ° GRA ° REX ° ANGL Z FRA ° D ° HY. Three ropes from stern, four from prow. Ornaments on ship two lis, lion, one lis, lion, two lis. Rev. DOMINE NE ×× IN ×× FVRORE ×× TVO ×× ARGVAS ×× ME. Lis over head of lion in second quarter. *MB.* 3. Same but HYB, no annulet before Gra, E in centre of reverse placed diagonally, no lis in second quarter. Pl. ii (9). *MB.* Cf. nobles, Nos. 15-17.

1360 to 1369. Without the title of France, but generally with that of Aquitaine. All of these have three ropes from the stern, two from the prow. 4. EDWARDVS ×× DEI ×× G ×× REX ANGL × D × H. Ornaments on ship lis, lion, lis, lion, lis, lion. Rev. DOMINE ×× IN ×× FVRORE ×× TVO ×× ARGVAS ×× M (omitting the important word NE). Annulet at each angle of central compartment, lis over head of lion in second quarter. *MB.* Major Thorburn has one reading EDWARD and HIB with × between each word on obv.; and ME on rev. Cf. nobles, Nos. 18, 19. 5. ED × DEI ×× GRA × REX × ANGL × DNS × HIB × Z × AQ Q Rev. DOMINE ×× IN ×× FVRORE ×× TVO ×× ARGVTS ×× ME. Otherwise as the last. *MB.* 6. Obv. from same die as the last. Rev. as last, but ARGVAS instead of arguts, one saltire after each word on rev. *MB.* 7. × EDWARD ××

DEI × G × REX × ANGL × D × HYB × Z × AQT. Ornaments on ship lion, two lis, lion, two lis. Rev. DOMINE × NE × IN × FVRORE × TVO × ARGVAS × ME. Cf. noble, No. 22. *MB*. 8. Same as the last, with annulet instead of saltire before Edward. *MB*. Cf. noble, No. 24. Major Stewart Thorburn has two similar ones with no mark before Edward, one of which has a small trefoil instead of × each side of Z.

Calais.—These have C instead of E in the centre of the reverse. 9. Same as 7, but with no mark before Edward. Pl. ii. (12) *MB*. 10. Same as the last, but with a flag at the stern. Rud. i. 5. *MB*.

1369 to 1377. The nobles of this period have the titles both of France and Aquitaine, but the latter does not appear upon any half nobles. We attribute, however, to this period those half nobles which, bearing the French title, differ from the others which bear it by having a flag at the stern of the ship and three ropes from the stern and only one from the prow, like the nobles of the same period. The flag appears upon no coins before the treaty of Bretigny in 1360.

11. EDWARD × DI × GRA × REX × ANGL × Z × FRANC × D. Ornaments on ship, lis, lion, lis, lion, lis. Rev. legend as 7, with saltire after ME. Cf. noble, No. 30. (14) *MB*. 12. Same as last, omitting D. It is not clear whether this coin has E or C or even R in the centre of the reverse.

Calais. Same as No. 12, with no saltire after Franc or Me, and with C in the centre of the reverse. *MB*.

QUARTER NOBLES, 1351-1360. These have for type, obv. a shield with the arms of France and England quarterly within a double tressure of eight arches, a trefoil at the angle of each arch; the whole within an inner circle. The name of France always appears in the legend, but never that of Aquitaine. Rev. within a double tressure of eight arches is a cross having some ornament in the centre, the extremities are foliated, and there is a lis opposite each of them, and a lion passant guardant in each angle. The whole within an inner circle. The following varieties occur: 1. EDWAR × R × ANGL × Z × FRANC × D × HY. Rev. EXALTABITVR × IN × GLORIA. Doubtful object in centre, two dots over upper limb of cross. *MB.* 2. Obv. as last, but annulet instead of saltire between the words. Rev. GAhLORI for Gloria, pellet? in centre, one annulet over upper limb of cross; saltire between words. *MB.* 3. Same as 2, but GhLORIA, annulet between words on both sides and after Ghloria, none over cross, pellet in centre of cross. *MB.* 4. EDWAR ° D ° G ° REX ° ANGL ° Z ° FRANC. Rev. EXALTABITVR × IN × GhLORIA °° Є in centre of cross. Pl. ii. (10) *MB.* 5. Same as 4, but annulet after exaltabitur, no marks after the other words on rev. *MB.* 6. Obv. as 5. Rev. EXALTABITVR °° IN °° GLORIA ° A; Є in centre of cross. *MB.* 7. EDWAR ° R ° ANGL Z FRANC ° D ° HYBER. Rev. as 6. *MB.* 8. EDWAR ° D ° G ° REX ° ANGL Z FRAE ° D ° HYB. Rev. as 6, but AI instead of A, one annulet after exaltabitur and in, two after Gloria. Rud. i. 9. *MB.* 9. Obv. legend as 1, but two saltires after R, none after D. Rev. EXATABITVR (*sic*) × IN × GLORIA; Є in centre of cross. *MB.* 10. EDWR × R × ANGLIE × F × DNVS × HV. Rev. EXALTABITVR × IN × GLORIA ××××. Є in centre of cross. *MB.*

1360 to 1369. These quarter nobles are distinguished from the previous ones by the omission of the title of King of France. The title of Duke of Aquitaine, however, which was placed upon the larger coins of this period, does not appear on these, and the French title does not seem to have been reintroduced upon them in 1369, so that the quarter nobles struck during the observance of the treaty of Bretigny are not distinguishable by their legends from those struck after the breach of that treaty. Those which we are now about to describe may, however, safely be attributed to this period, on account of having annulets in the angles of the cross on the reverse, a peculiarity which appears on nobles and half nobles of this date only. In other respects they resemble the previous quarter nobles in type, except that the ornaments in the centre of the cross on the reverse are different, and that they never have annulets between the words of their legends. Neither Є nor C ever occurs in the centre of the cross.

11. EDWAR × DEI ×× GRAC × REX ×× ANGL × D. Annulet instead of trefoil at the angle of each arch, trefoil in each spandril. Rev. EXALTABITVR ×× IN ×× GLORIA ×× Pellet within annulet in centre of cross, annulet in each angle, pellet in each spandril. Pl. ii. (13) *MB*. 12. Obv. as 11, omitting D, with one saltire only between each word, and pellet instead of trefoil in each spandril. Rev. as 11, omitting the saltires after Gloria. Rud. i. 7. *MB*. 13. Obv. legend as 11, trefoil at each angle, pellet in each spandril. Rev. as the last. *MB*. Major Thorburn has one with obv. as 12, but with trefoil at each angle, ERWAR, GRA; rev. as 11, but GLRIA ××. 14. Obv. as 13, but trefoil instead of pellet in each spandril. Rev. legend as 11, pellet within compartment in centre of cross, annulet in each angle, trefoil in each spandril, no saltires after Gloria. *MB*. 15. EDWAR × DEI × GRA × REX × ANGL. Trefoil at each angle, pellet in each spandril. Rev. EXALTBITVR × IN × GLORIA × Pellet in centre of cross, in each angle, and in each spandril. *MB*. This coin much more closely resembles those that have than those that have not annulets in the angles of the cross, and is therefore placed with them, but at the end of the period. The legend is blundered, as is the case on so many of the coins struck about the time when a change of type or legend was in progress at the mint.

1369 to 1377. Legend like the quarter nobles of the last period, and type the same except that in the centre of the cross on the reverse is a compartment having a trefoil at each angle, like that on the coins previous to 1360; within the compartment is some ornament.

16. EDWARD ⁑ DEI ⁑ GRA ⁑ REX ⁑ ANGL. Trefoil at each angle, nothing in the spandrils, cross within annulet over shield. Rev. EXALTABITVR ⁑ IN ⁑ GLORIA, annulet in centre of cross, nothing in spandrils. *MB.* 17. Same as last with pellet or annulet before Edward. *MB.* 18. Obv. as 16, but cross over shield. Rev. as last, but open quatrefoil in centre of cross. (15) *MB.* 19. Legends as 16. Obv. trefoil at each angle, nothing in spandrils. Rev. quatrefoil in centre of cross, nothing in spandrils. Rud. i. 8. *MB.* 20. Obv. as last, with annulet before Edward. Rev. as last, but lis in centre of cross. *MB.* 21. Obv. as 19. Rev. as 19, but lis in centre of cross; one saltire only between each word. *MB.* On some of these last coins the trefoils at the angles on the obverse look more like rosettes.

London and Calais seem to have been the only places at which gold coins of the English type were struck during this reign, for though the king had a mint at York it does not appear to have issued gold coins, and those which were struck in Aquitaine were of an entirely different denomination and type. The ecclesiastical mints, at which the smaller silver pieces were coined, were never allowed to strike gold. In 1346 the king made a treaty with the Flemings for the purpose of making a uniform gold currency for the two countries, of having his own gold coins struck in Flanders, and of dividing between the two countries the profits which should arise from such a coinage; and he appointed William Stury and Gilbert de Wendlyngburgh to coin Pennies, Halfpennies, and Farthings (of gold) called Nobles, in Ghent, Bruges, and Ipre. It does not appear, however, that this coinage was ever actually carried out.

Mint-marks, usually so called, that is to say, peculiar marks placed at the beginning of the legend on one or both sides of the coin, for the purpose of distinguishing one coinage from another, were not regularly used until the reign of Edward IV. But Edward III and all succeeding monarchs placed marks for this purpose on some part or other of the coins in order that the pieces for which one master of the mint or one moneyer was responsible might be known from those of another; and if proper records of the proceedings of the mint could be found, we should no doubt be able to arrange the coins by means of these marks almost as accurately as if they had dates upon them.

The following is a table of the principal of these marks on the money of Edward III, the crosses showing upon what coins in the British Museum the marks in question are now found :—

TABULAR VIEW.	Flor.	½ Flor.	¼ Flor.
1ST COINAGE, 1343, *florins.*	+	+	+
	Noble.	½ Noble.	¼ Noble.
2ND COINAGE, 1344, *nobles, Wt.* $138\frac{6}{13}$ *grs.*			
L in centre of reverse . . .	+		+ Rash-leigh.
Є in centre of reverse . . .			
3RD COINAGE, 1346, *nobles, Wt.* $128\frac{4}{7}$ *grs.*			
Є in centre of reverse . . .	+		+
,, ,, lis in second quarter, two dots over upper limb of cross .		+	
4TH COINAGE, 1351, *nobles, Wt.* 120 *grs.*			
1351-1360. *Title of King of England and France.*			
Two dots over upper limb of cross on rev.	+	+	+
Lis in 2nd quarter, 2 annulets over upper limb of cross	+		
,, MM crown, annulets in rev. legend	+		
,, MM crown, annulets in legends	+		
,, annulets in legends . .	+		
,, 2 annulets over upper limb of cross, 3 lions and 2 lis on ship . .	+		
,, 1 annulet over upper limb of cross, 3 lions and 2 lis on ship	+		
Pellet in centre of rev., 1 annulet over upper limb of cross, annulets in obv. legend			+
Lis in 2nd quarter, annulets in obv. legend	+	+	

	Noble.	½ Noble.	¼ Noble.
Lis in 2nd quarter, annulets in legends, 3 lions and 4 lis on ship . .	Evans.		
,, ,, ,, rev. legend, 3 lions and 7 lis on ship . .	+		
Lis in 2nd quarter, annulets in legends, 3 lions and 7 lis on ship . .	Evans.		
Pellet in centre of rev. annulets in legends			+
Є in centre of rev., annulets in legends			+
Lis in 3rd quarter, annulets in legends	+		
,, 1st ,, ,, ,,	+		
,, ,, annulets in legends, 3 lions and 8 lis on ship . .	+		
,, ,, ,, obv. legend 3 lions and 6 lis on ship . .	+		
,, 2nd ,, ,, legends, 3 lions and 6 lis on ship . .	+		
Annulets in obv. legend . .	+		
Є in centre of rev., no annulets .			+
1360-1369, *title of King of France omitted. That of Duke of Aquitaine is generally used on the nobles and half nobles.*			
Lis in 2nd quarter, annulet at each angle of centre compartment on rev. .	+	+	
Pellet within annulet in centre of cross on rev., annulet at angle of each arch on obv. and in each angle of cross on rev.			+
Pellet within annulet in centre of cross on rev., annulet in each angle .			+
Pellet within compartment in centre of cross on rev., annulet in each angle .			+
Pellet in centre of cross on rev. and in each angle			+
No lis in field, trefoils at angles .	+	+	
Same, with annulet before Edward .	+	+	
CALAIS.—No peculiar marks . .	Evans.	+	
Flag at stern of ship .	+	+	
,, quatrefoil before Edward	+		
1369 to 1377, *titles of King of France and Duke of Aquitaine both used on nobles. Flag at stern of ship on half nobles.*			
Annulet in centre of rev., cross within annulet over shield on obv. . .			+
Same as last with annulet before Edward			+
Annulet before Edward . .	+		
Є and pellet in centre of rev., two dots over lis on top and bottom limbs of cross, flag at stern of ship . .	+		
Flag at stern of ship . . .		+	
Є and pellet in centre of rev. . .	+		
Є and cross in centre of rev., annulet at spring of first arch . . .	+		

	Noble.	½ Noble.	¼ Noble.
Ɛ reversed in centre of rev. . .	+		
Open quatrefoil in centre of rev., cross over shield on obv. . . .			+
Quatrefoil in centre of rev. . .			+
Lis ,, ,, annulet before Edward			+
Lis in centre of rev. . . .			+
CALAIS.—Flag at stern of ship . .		+	
No flag . . .	Evans.		

RICHARD II, 1377 TO 1399.

The coins of Richard II resemble in all respects the last issued by his grandfather, excepting that they have Richard's name on the obverse, and R instead of E in the centre of the reverse. The noble continued to weigh 120 grs., and was current for 6*s* 8*d*, and the others in proportion; but from several petitions presented to Parliament in this reign, and from the examination of some witnesses upon this point before the House of Lords in 1381 and 1382, it appears that the intrinsic value of the gold coins was higher than their nominal value. Great complaints were also made of the clipping of the coins, both of gold and silver, and of their exportation; and accordingly a statute was passed in 1381 forbidding their exportation except for the wages of the king's fortresses beyond the sea. The gold coins are not common. At Mr. Bergnes' sale, in 1873, two half nobles sold for £10. 10*s* and £15 respectively.

NOBLES. Type exactly like Edward III's last nobles, with, like them, three ropes from the stern, one from the prow. 1. Obv. from a die of Edward III, EDWARD × DI × GRA × REX × ANGL × Z × FRANC × DNS × HIB × Z × AQ Annulet ? before Edward. No flag. Ornaments on ship's side, lis, lion, lis, lion, lis, lion, lis. Rev. IHC ⁑ AVTEM ⁑ TRANSIENS ⁑ PER ⁑ MEDIVM ⁑ ILLORVM ⁑ IBAT ⁑ R (for Richard) in centre of cross. *MB*. 2. RICARD ⁑ D ⁑ G ⁑ REX ⁑ ANGL × Z ⁑ FRANC × D ⁑ HIB × Z × AQ Flag at stern, ornaments on ship as No. 1. Rev. from a die of Edward III, with Ɛ in the centre. Legend as the last but

ILLORV. *MB.* Mr. Evans has one with obv. as 2, rev. as 1 but ILLORV × IBAT. 3. Obv. same, but omitting A in Ricard, and having no flag at stern. Rev. as 1, but MEDIV ×× ILLORV ×× no saltires after Ibat. *MB.* This coin, and Nos. 4, 7, and 11, were found in the cloisters of Westminster Abbey. Captain Stewart Thorburn has a similar one with only one cross after Ricard and Z, and reading TRANSIES. 4. RICARD × DI ×× G ×× REX ×× ANGL × Z ×× FRANC × D ×× HIB × Z × AQ. No flag; ornaments on ship as 1. Rev. as 1, but MEDIV ××, no saltires after Ibat. *MB.* 5. RICARD × DEI ×× GRA × REX ×× ANGL × DNS × HIB × Z × AQT. Flag at stern, ornaments as 1. Rev. as the last. *MB.* See Rud. i. 10, which reads DI. 6. Same as the last, but without the flag; two saltires after Ricard. Rev. legend IHC × AVTEM ×× TRANSIENS ×× PER ×× MEDIV × ILLORV × IBAT. (16) *MB.* 7. Obv. as 5, but omitting Z and the last lis on the ship's side, and reading AQ. No flag. Rev. as last but IHC ××. *MB.* 8. RICARD × DI × GRA × REX ×× ANGL × Z × FRANC × DNS × HIB × Z × AQ. No flag; ornaments on ship as 1, lis on the rudder. Rev. as 1, but MEDIV ×; no saltires after Transiens or Ibat. *MB.* 9. RICARD × DI × GRA × REX × ANGL × Z × FRANC × DNS × HIB Z AQ. Flag at stern, ornaments on ship as 1, pellet above the shield. Rev. as 1, but only one saltire after Ihc, none after Ibat. *MB.* 10. Same, but D instead of Dns, and AQT (?); ornaments on ship lion, lis, lion, lis, lion; MEDIV ×× instead of Medium. *MB.* 11. Obv. as 9 but AQT; ornaments on ship as 10, small dot at corner of shield instead of pellet above it. Rev. as 7. *MB.* 12. Rud. ii. 4 gives an obverse like this without the dot at the corner of the shield, and with no flag, but with an escallop shell on the rudder. 13. Obv. as 11 without the dot. Rev. IHC ×× AVTEM ×× TRANSIENS ×× PER ×× MEDIV ×× ILLORVM ×× IBAT. *MB.*

HALF NOBLES. Type like the previous ones. The ornaments on the ship seem always to be three lions, with a lis between each, as on the last nobles, except No. 3, which has none. 1. RICARD × D ×× G × REX ×× ANGL × Z × FRANC ×

D × h. Flag at stern. Rev. DOMINE ×× NE ×× IN ×× FVRORE ×× TVO ×× ARGVAS ×× ME. Ɑ in centre, from a reverse die of Edward III. Cf. noble, No. 2. *MB.* Rud. ii. 5 gives an obverse similar to this but reading DI × GRA × REX × ANGL × Z FRANC × D ×× HYB. 2. Obv. as 1, but with AQ following h, a saltire in the field near the rudder, two after Rex, one between the other words. Rev. as 1, but R stamped over Ɑ in the centre. *MB.* 3. RICARD × DI × GRA × REX × ANGL × Z × FR × D ×× h ×× Z × No flag, and no lion or lis on side of ship. Rev. as No. 1, except that in the die an R seems to have been cut upside down over the Ɑ. (17) *MB.* 4. RICARD × DI × G × REX × ANGL × Z × F × DNS HIB A. No flag. Rev. as 1, but R in centre, saltire after Me. *MB.* 5. RICARD ×× D ×× G ×× REX ×× ANGL ×× Z ×× F ×× D ×× HIB ×× Z ×× AQ. No flag. Rev. as 1, but R in centre. *MB.* 6. RICARD × DEI × GRA × REX ×× ANGL × DNS × HIB Z AQ. No flag. Rev. as last. Rud. i. 11. *MB.* 7. Same, but D, AQT. *THORBURN.*

QUARTER NOBLES. Like the last ones of Edward III. 1. RICARD × DEI ×× GRA ×× REX ×× ANGL. Trefoil at each angle, nothing in spandrils. Rev. EXALTABITVR ×× IN ×× GLORIA. Lis in centre of cross, nothing in spandrils. Except the king's name, this is almost identical with the last of Edward III's quarter nobles. (18) *MB.* 2. Same, but DI ××, ANG ×× *MB.* or ANGL, dot before and two after rev. legend. *EVANS.* 3. RICARD ×× D ×× GRA ×× REX ×× ANGL ×× Z ×× F. Small cross or quatrefoil above shield on obv., a single saltire between words on rev. Otherwise as 1. *EVANS.* 4. RICARD × D × GRA × REX × ANGLIE; obv. as last. Rev. EXALTABITVR × IN × GLORIA. Pellet in centre. *MB.* 5. RICARD DI G × REX ×× ANGL Z FRAC. Trefoil at each angle, nothing in spandrils; trefoil, or three annulets united, above shield. Rev. EXALTABITVR ×× IN ×× GLORIA. Pellet in centre of rev. This is in the collection of Mr. H. Montagu, 34, Queen's Gardens. 6. As 1, but escallop over shield on obv., pellet in centre of rev., two saltires after every word. *MB.*

7. Same as 2, but pellet in centre of reverse. *MB.* 8. RICARD × DI × GRA × REX × ANGL × Z × F. Trefoil at each angle and in each spandril. Rev. as 1, but pellet in the centre. *MB.* 9. Same as 1, but legends RICARD ⁑ DI ⁑ GRA ⁑ REX ⁑ ANG × Rev. EXALTABITVR × IN ⁑ GLORIA. Two pellets in centre of reverse. *THORBURN.* 10. Same as 1, but two saltires after Ricard, R in centre. *MB.*

Richard II does not appear to have used any mint except that in the Tower.

TABULAR VIEW.

	Noble.	½ Noble.	¼ Noble.
Obverse from die of Edward III .	+		
Reverse from die of Edward III, flag at stern	+	+	
,, ,, flag at stern, saltire in field near rudder .		+	
,, ,, no flag, no lions or lis on ship . .		+	
No flag nor special marks . .	+	+	
Flag, no special marks . . .	+		
Lis in centre of cross on rev. . .			+
No flag, last lis on ship's side omitted	+		
,, lis on rudder . . .	+		
Flag, pellet above shield . .	+		
Lis in centre of rev., cross or quatrefoil above shield			Evans
Pellet in centre of rev., cross or quatrefoil above shield . . .			+
Pellet in centre of rev., trefoil above shield			Montagu
Flag, dot at corner of shield . .	+		
Pellet in centre of rev., escallop above shield			+
No flag, escallop on rudder . .	Rud.		
Pellet in centre of rev., no special marks			+
,, ,, ,, trefoils in spandrils . . , .			+
Two pellets in centre of rev. . .			Thorburn
R in centre of rev. . . .			+

HENRY IV, 1399 TO 1413.

Henry IV's coinage, until the year 1412, when the weight was reduced, was continued on the same principles as that of his predecessors, the noble remaining of the weight of 120 grs., and of the current value of 6*s* 8*d*, and the fineness being, as before, 23 carats 3½ grs. pure gold to ½ gr. alloy. The type also continued exactly the same.

NOBLES. 1399-1412. Type as before; obv., the king in armour, crowned, holding in his right hand a sword, in his left a shield bearing the arms of France and England quarterly, standing in a ship ornamented on the side with lions and lis. The number of lis in the French arms varies. Rev. within a compartment of double moulding of eight arches, having a trefoil in each spandril, is a cross potent upon a beaded cross voided, with corniced and foliated ends. In the centre of the cross is h for Henry within a compartment of four arches and four angles, with a trefoil at each angle; opposite each extremity is a lis, and in each angle is a lion passant guardant with a crown above it. The known varieties are, 1. HENRIC DI GRA REX ANGL Z FRANC DNS HI Z AQ. No flag, French arms *semé de lys,* three ropes from stern, one from prow, as on Richard II's coins, ornaments on ship, lis, lion, lis, lion, lis, lion. Rev. IHC AVTEM TRANSIENS PER MEDIV ILLORVM IBAT. Rud. Suppl. vi. 20. Wt. 119½ grs. 2. HENRIC . . . . . ANGL × Z ×× FRANC × D × HIB × Z AQE. Flag at stern, French arms *semé de lys,* three ropes from stern, one from prow, ornaments on ship, lion, lis, lion, lis, lion, lis. Rev. as 1, with saltire between each word. Rud. i. 13. The weight of this coin is given as only 105 grs., but it has evidently suffered so much from clipping that it must originally have belonged to the heavy coinage. 3. Obv. legend as 1, flag at stern, three lis only in French arms, ropes and ornaments as 2. Rev. as 1, two saltires between the words. *EVANS.* Wt. only 103½ grs., but considerably clipped. 4. HENRIC DI × GRA × REX ×× ANGL × Z × FRANC × DNS × HIB Z AQ. No flag. Three lis only in the French arms, four ropes from stern, one from prow, ornaments on ship, lis, lion, lis, lion, lis, lion, lis. Rev. as 1, with two saltires between each word. *MB.* Wt. 118·8 grs. See Rud. ii. 6. This coin was purchased in 1848 from the Pembroke collection for £21. 5. HENRIC × DI ×× GRA ×× REX ×× ANGL ×× Z × FRANC × DNS × HIB × Z ×× AQI × No flag, three lis only in the French arms, ropes and ornaments as 2. Rev. IHC × AVTEM ××

TRANSIENS × PER × MEDIVM × ILLORVM × IBAT. Cross in second quarter above the lion's tail. (19) *EVANS.* Wt. 118¼ grs. 6. HENRIC × DI × GRA × REX × ANGL × Z × FRANC × DNS × HYB. Trefoil or quatrefoil after Hyb, trefoil? at king's wrist, trefoil at prow; three lis only in the French arms; three ropes from stern, two from prow, ornaments on side of ship, lion, two lis, lion, two lis; annulet below them; annulet? between the king's arm and his sword. Rev. IHC × AVTEM × TRANSIENS × PER × MEDIV × ILLORV × IBAT. Trefoil or quatrefoil over head of lion in second quarter. Rud. iii. 3. Wt. 113 grs. *Very rare.*

HALF-NOBLES. 1399 to 1412. We know of no specimens. In Henfrey's "Guide to English Coins," the legends are given as Henric Di Gra Rex Angl z Franc. Rev. Domine ne in furore tuo arguas me. Gold half nobles seem to be intimately connected with silver half groats, frequently having the same mint-marks, &c.; and of heavy half groats of Henry IV only one or two specimens are known.

QUARTER NOBLES. 1399 to 1412. Type as before. HENRIC . . . . . ANGL Z FRAN. French arms *semé de lys.* Crescent over shield. Rev. EXALTABITVR IN GLORIA. Pellet in centre of cross. (20) *EVANS.* Weight 30 grs. *Ext. rare.*

Throughout this reign constant complaints were made in Parliament of the want of gold and silver money, and various enactments were passed to prevent its exportation; and at last in the 13th year of the king, 1411, "because of the great scarcity of money at this time within the realm of England, and because of other mischiefs and causes manifest," the weight of all the coins was reduced, so that a pound of gold, Tower weight, which had previously been made into 45 nobles, was now to be made into 50, thus bringing down the weight of the noble to 108 grains. Its nominal value was still 6*s* 8*d*, and the fineness was the same as before. This statute came into operation at Easter, 1412, and as the king died on the 20th of March, 1412-13, the coins struck by virtue of it in his reign must all have been struck in rather less than a year, and they are accordingly rare. The great rarity of the earlier coins is easily accounted for, as they were scarce before the statute, and would naturally be melted down as soon as the weight was reduced.

A little before this reduction of weight, the number of lis in the French arms, which had hitherto been indefinite, was reduced to three by Charles VI; but the old form continued to be used on the quarter nobles of Henry IV till the end of his reign, and any light nobles or half nobles having the French arms *semé de lys* would necessarily be attributed to this second coinage; but we do not know of the existence of any of these. The new form was used by Henry V, when Prince of Wales, as early as the sixth year of his father, and seems to have been adopted upon the heavy nobles at about the same date. It is necessary, therefore, to look for some other means than the form of the French arms to distinguish the last coinage of Henry IV from that of his son, and a comparison of the gold with the silver coins of this period leads us to believe that all or almost all of the nobles and half nobles, as well as of the groats and half groats, struck in the last year of Henry IV, were marked in some part or other with a trefoil, as is the last described of his heavy nobles. The trefoil occurs also on a few coins which we attribute to the beginning of Henry V's reign, but in that case it seems to be always connected with a pierced cross at the beginning of the legend, which is a distinguishing mark of the silver coins of Henry V. These trefoil-marked coins are certainly the earliest we possess of the light coins of the three Henries, and it is very unlikely that no specimens of the coinage of 1412 should have come down to us. According to this rule, the following coins belong to Henry IV.

NOBLES, 1412. Type as before. There are only three lis in the French arms, and there is no flag at the stern of the ship. 1. HENRIC ×× DI ×× GRA × REX × ANGL × Z × FRANC × DNS ×× HIB × Z A. Three ropes from stern, one from prow. Ornaments on ship lis, lion, two lis, lion, lis.

Slipped trefoil below them on the side of the ship. Rev. IHC ×× AVTEM ×× TRANSIENS ×× PER ×× MEDIVM ×× ILLORV IBAT. Trefoil at head of lion in third quarter. (21) *MB.* Wt. 106 grs. 2. Same but FRAC, AQ, ILLORVM, annulet as well as trefoil on side of ship, trefoil in second instead of third quarter of rev., saltire between each word on obv., two on rev. *EVANS.* Wt. 108 grs.

HALF NOBLES, 1412. Type as the nobles. 1. HENRIC × DI × G × REX × ANGL × Z × FRAC × D × H × AQ. Two ropes from stern, one from prow. Ornaments on ship, lion, lis, lion, lis, lion; annulet and trefoil below them. Rev. DOMINE ×× NE ×× IN ×× FVRORE ×× TVO ×× ARGVAS ×× ME. Trefoil at head of lion in first quarter. *EVANS.* 2. Same, but trefoil in second quarter instead of first. *EVANS.* 3. Same, but trefoil in fourth quarter, two saltires after Me. (22) *EVANS.* Weight of all three about 53 grs.

QUARTER NOBLES, 1412. These are not all marked, like the nobles and half nobles, with a trefoil in the field, but nearly all of them have more than three lis in the French arms, and are distinguishable by this means from the coins of Henry V and VI. Type like the first issue, viz. Obv. a shield with the arms of France and England quarterly within a double tressure of eight arches, having a trefoil at each angle; the whole within an inner circle. MM cross patée. Rev. within a double tressure of eight arches is a cross having an annulet or lis in the centre, the extremities are foliated, and there is a lis opposite each of them, and a lion passant guardant in each angle. The whole within an inner circle. MM cross patée. 1. HENRICVS ×× DI ×× GRA ×× ANGL ×× Z FRAN. Crescent? above shield. French arms *semé de lys.* Rev. EXALTABITVR ×× IN ×× GLORIA. Annulet in the centre of the cross. Rud. i. 14. Wt. 25½ grs. 2. HENRICVS × D ×× GRA ×× REX ×× ANGL. French arms *semé de lys.* Rev. as last but a lis in centre of cross, saltire after Gloria. *MB.* Wt. 18·8 grs. 3. HENRIC DEI GRA REX ANGL. Four lis in first quarter of shield, three in fourth quarter. Trefoil after Henric, other stops doubtful. Rev. as 2, but stops doubtful, h after Gloria. *MONTAGU.* Wt. 23½ grs. 4. HENRIC ×× DEI ×× GRA ×× REX ×× ANG. Lis above the shield, slipped trefoil with annulet below it on each side of the shield; French arms *semé de lys.* Rev. EXALTABITVR IN GLORIA, lis in centre of cross, stops between words doubtful. (23) *MB.* Wt. 20·8 grs. 5. HENRIC × DI × GRA × REX × ANGL. Lis above the shield, slipped trefoil with annulet below it on each side. Three lis only in the French arms. Rev. EXALTABITVR × IN × GLORIA× Lis in centre. *MB.* Wt. 20 grs.

Henry IV appears to have struck coins in London only, and they are all rare. At Mr. Forster's sale, in 1868, a noble of the first coinage sold for £12, and one of the second coinage for £11.

TABULAR VIEW.

	Noble.	½ Noble.	¼ Noble.
1ST COINAGE, 1399-1412.			
French arms *semé de lis*, no flag	Rud.		
" " flag at stern	Rud.		
" " crescent above shield			Evans
French arms three lis, flag at stern	Evans		
" " no flag	+		
" " cross in 2nd quarter	Evans		
" " trefoil ? after Hyb, at prow, at wrist, and in 2nd quarter, annulet on side of ship and between arm and sword	Rud.		
2ND COINAGE, 1412.			
Trefoil on side of ship and in 3rd quarter	+		
Trefoil and annulet on side of ship, trefoil in 1st quarter		Evans	
" 2nd quarter	Evans	Evans	
" 4th quarter		Evans	
French arms *semé de lis*, crescent above shield, annulet in centre of rev.			Rud.
" " lis in centre of rev.			+
" " lis in centre of rev., trefoil in obv. legend			Montagu
" " lis in centre of rev. and above shield, trefoil and annulet on each side			+
French arms three lis, otherwise as last			+

Henry V, 1413 to 1422.

The coins of Henry V resemble those of his predecessor, and are of the weight established in 1412. The king's name is not distinguished by numerals on any of the coins of Henry IV, V, or VI, but the earlier coins of Henry IV may be known by their weight, and all his later ones have either a trefoil ornament in the field or more than three lis in the French arms. On Henry V's coins there are never more than three lis in the French arms, and any which have a trefoil in the field have also a pierced cross at the beginning of the legend on one side or the other, a mark which we believe never appears on coins of Henry IV, and very rarely on those of Henry VI before his restoration. On Henry V's coins no other mark than a cross ever appears at the beginning of the legend, nor is there anything but saltires between the words. The marks on the gold series correspond to a great extent with those on the silver, and this enables us to arrange the coins with much greater certainty than we could otherwise have attained.

Several complaints were made in Parliament during this reign of the clipping, filing, washing, and counterfeiting of the coins. In 1421 the gold coins are said to have been less scarce than the silver, so much so that silver money could not be obtained in exchange for a noble even of full weight; but the gold coins must have been in a very bad condition, for in this year the tax collectors, who generally received money only by weight, were ordered to accept any noble which by its weight was of the intrinsic value of 5*s* 8*d*, in full payment of the sum of 6*s* 8*d*, which was its original value; and by a statute of this same year all gold coins which were less than their lawful weight were ordered to be brought to the Tower of London to be recoined. This was the only place in England at which gold coins were struck during this reign. In June, 1420, Henry married Catherine, daughter of the King of France, and by the treaty made on this occasion he agreed to relinquish the title of King of France and adopt that of Heir of France instead, during the lifetime of Charles VI; but this agreement does not seem to have been acted upon in England, as all his coins bear the title of King of France.

NOBLES. Type as those of Henry IV. There is no flag at the stern of the ship. They all have a mullet in the field below the king's wrist, and a quatrefoil in the second quarter of the reverse, thus corresponding with the second class of the groats and half groats of Henry V.

1. HENRIC × DI × GRA × REX × ANGL × Z × FRANC × DNS × HYB. Quatrefoil after Hyb, trefoil at prow, three ropes from stern, two from prow, ornaments on side of ship lion, two lis, lion, two lis; annulet below them and between the king's arm and his sword. Rev. IHC × AVTEM ×× TRANSIENS ×× PER ×× MEDIV × ILLORV × IBAT MM cross pierced. See *Num. Chron.*, N. S., v. p. 174, No. 1. Wt. 107 grs. This is almost identical with Rud. iii. 3, the weight of which, however, shows that it was struck before 1412, whereas the pierced cross appropriates this coin to Henry V. 2. Obv. legend as last, but DNS ×××, quatrefoil after Hyb, two ropes from stern, one from prow, ornaments on ship, lion, two lis, lion, two lis (?), annulet below them. Rev. legend and MM as last, trefoil in first quarter. *MB.* 3. Same as 2, with broken annulet (?) between the king's arm and his sword. Ornaments on ship, lis, lion, lis, lion; pellet instead of trefoil in first quarter. (24) *MB.* 4. Same as 1 without the quatrefoil after Hyb, the trefoil at prow, and the annulet between the king's arm and his sword; the annulet on the side of ship is broken. *MB.* 5. Same as 1, but without the trefoil at prow and the annulet between the arm and the sword; slipped trefoil and broken ? annulet on side of ship, ornaments and ropes as 1. Rev. MM cross and pellet. *MB.* Wt. 106·3 grs. 6. Same as 1 but : after Z and Dns, no trefoil at prow, no annulets. Rev. MM plain cross and pellet. *MB.*

HALF NOBLES. Type like the nobles. They all have a mullet over the shield on obv. 1. HENRIC × DI × GRA × REX × ANGL × Z × FR × D × HYB. Mullet over shield, three ropes from stern, two from prow. Ornaments on ship, lion, two lis, lion, two lis; broken annulet below them. Rev. DOMINE × NE × IN × FVRORE × TVO ×× ARGVAS ×× ME MM plain cross, broken annulet in first quarter. (25) *MB.* Wt. 52·8 grs. 2. Same, but H for Hyb, broken annulet in second quarter instead of first. *EVANS.* 3. As 1, but reading F × DN × HY, two ropes from stern, one from prow, no annulet visible on side of ship, pellet in first quarter, annulet, not broken, in second; no trefoils in spandrils on rev. *MB.* 4. As the last, but reading D HY ×, and omitting the last two lis. Rev. MM pierced cross, trefoils in spandrils. *EVANS.*

QUARTER NOBLES. Type similar to the former ones, obv. a shield with the arms of France and England quarterly, those of France being three lis only, within a double tressure of eight arches, the whole within an inner circle. All of them have a lis above the shield. Rev. within a double tressure of eight arches is a cross having a lis in the centre within a compartment of four arches and four angles, the limbs are foliated, and there is a lis opposite each of them, and a lion passant guardant in each angle. The whole within an inner circle.

1. Legends transposed, EXALTABITVR ×× IN ×× GLORIA being placed on the shield side of the coin. MM pierced cross, lis above shield, trefoil? and annulet on each side, two annulets below; annulet at each angle of tressure. Rev. HENRIC REX ANG Z FRAN, MM pierced cross, one or two saltires between the words. *EVANS.* 2. HENRIC × REX × ANGL × Z × FRANC. MM pierced cross, lis above shield, trefoil on one side, mullet on the other, annulet at six angles of the tressure. Rev. EXCVLTABITVR ×× IN ×× GLORIA, MM pierced cross. (26) *MB.* 3. Exactly the same, but only one saltire between words on rev. *MB.* 4. HENRIC × REX × ANGL × Z × FRANC. MM pierced ?

cross, lis above shield, broken annulet on one side, mullet on the other, annulet at six angles of the tressure. Rev. EXALTABITVR ×× IN ×× GLORIA. MM cross pierced. *MB.* See Rud. i. 17, where the MM on both sides is a plain cross, and the stops on the obverse are represented as trefoils. 5. HENRIC × REX ×× ANGL Z × FRACIE MM plain cross, lis above shield, broken annulet ? at each side, annulet at each angle of the tressure. Rev. as the last, but only one saltire after each word, MM plain cross. *MB.* Wt. 20 grs.

TABULAR VIEW.

	Noble.	½ Noble.	¼ Noble.
MM pierced cross; mullet, trefoil, and annulet in field; annulet on ship; quatrefoil in legend and in 2nd quarter	*Nm. Chr.*		
,, ,, mullet in field; annulet on ship; quatrefoil in legend and in 2nd quarter; trefoil in 1st quarter	+		
,, ,, mullet and broken annulet in field; annulet on ship; quatrefoil in legend and in 2nd quarter; pellet in 1st quarter .	+		
,, ,, mullet in field; broken annulet on ship; quatrefoil in 2nd quarter . . .	+		
MM plain cross and pellet; mullet in field; trefoil and broken annulet on ship; quatrefoil in legend and in 2nd quarter	+		
,, ,, mullet in field, quatrefoil in legend and in 2nd quarter	+		
MM plain cross; mullet in field; broken annulet on ship and in 1st quarter .		+	
,, ,, ,, broken annulet on ship and in 2nd quarter .		Evans	
,, ,, ,, pellet in 1st quarter, annulet in 2nd . .		+	
MM pierced cross; other marks as last		Evans	
,, ,, lis above shield; trefoil and annulet each side, two annulets below . . .			Evans
,, ,, lis above shield, trefoil and mullet at sides . .			+
,, ,, lis above shield, broken annulet and mullet at sides .			+
MM plain cross; lis above shield; broken annulet each side . .			+

Henry VI, 1422 to 1461.

Henry VI's coinage, until his deposition in 1461, was conducted on the same principles as that of his father. The noble continued to weigh 108 grs., and to be of the nominal value of 6*s* 8*d*, and the type remained exactly the same, so that, as his name was not distinguished by numerals from that of his father, their coins can only be known apart by the various small marks which appear in the field or within the legend, and which were used by the mint for the express purpose of distinguishing the various coinages. Of these marks the most conspicuous on Henry VI's gold coins is a lis, which was used as a mint-mark at the beginning or end of the reverse legend on nearly all struck by him before his deposition in 1461, whereas nothing but a cross was ever used in that place by his father or grandfather. The coins struck during his short restoration in 1470 were of a different type, weight, and value, and will be described afterwards.

The coins struck before the deposition may be divided into four classes, of which the distinguishing marks are respectively, annulets, rosettes, pinecones, and trefoils, corresponding with the first four issues of silver coins. But of the first and third of these, very few coins seem to have been struck.

NOBLES. None of these have any mint-mark at the beginning of the legend on the obverse, and they all have two ropes from the stern, one from the prow.

Of the first, or *Annulet Coinage*, no nobles are known.

Class II. Rosette Coinage. 1. HENRIC DI GRA REX ANGL Z FRANC DNS HYB. Rosette after every word. Flag at stern. Ornaments on ship lis, lion, lis, lion, lis. Rev. IHC × AVTEM ×× TRANSIENS ×× PER ×× MEDIV × ILLORV × IBAT MM plain cross. Rud. ii. 10. 2. Obv. as last with lis below the king's wrist. Rev. IHC AVT TRANSIENS PER MEDIVM ILLORV IBAT. MM lis,

lis over head of lion in second quarter, mascle after Per, rosette between the other words. (27) *MB.* 3. As last, but no flag on obv., and rev. legend IHC AVT TRANCIENS PER MEDIVM ILLOVR IBAT. *MB.* A mascle after certain words of the legend is a distinguishing mark of the second and third issues of silver coins.

Class III. Pine-cone coinage. 4. Obv. legend as 1, but HIB. No flag. Lis below king's wrist, mascle after Rex, rosette after every other word. Ornaments on ship as No. 1. Rev. IHC AVT TRNCIENS PER MEDIVM ILLORV IBAT. MM lis, lis in third quarter, mascle after per, pine-cone after every other word. The h in the centre is upside down. *Num. Chron.*, N. S., v. 175, No. 4. The weight of this coin is said to be 111 grs., which is 3 grs. more than the proper full weight. The rosettes and cones, the characteristics of the second and third coinages, both appear on this piece. 5. Same as the last, but HYB, rosette instead of mascle after Rex. Rev. as last, but TRANCIENS, lis in second instead of third quarter, h placed correctly. *EVANS.* 6. Obv. legend as 1, but HIYB. Mascle after Rex, cone between the other words except on each side of Z. Ornaments on ship as 1. Rev. IHC AVT TRANCIES PER MEDIVM ILLORVM IBAT. MM lis, lis in second quarter, mascle after per, cone between the other words. (28) *EVANS. Num. Chron.*, N. S., v. 175, No. 5. 7. Obv. legend as No. 1, but HY. Pellet each side of the h in Henric, two after Henric, annulet after Di, Gra, Rex, and Franc, saltire each side of Z, lis between cone (?) and annulet under the shield. Ornaments on ship as 1. Rev. IHC × AVT × TRANSIENS PER MEDIVM ILLORV IBAT. MM lis, the h in the centre upside down. *EVANS. Num. Chron.*, N. S., v. 175, No. 6. The annulets on this piece connect it with the next coinage.

Class IV. Trefoil coinage. 8. Obv. legend as No. 1, but FRAN, HY. Annulet at king's wrist, trefoil after every word. Ornaments on ship, lis, lion, lis, lion, lis. Rev. IHC AVT ° TRANSIENS ° PER ° MEDIVM ° ILLOR ° IBAT.

MM lis, trefoil after Ihc, annulet instead of trefoil in one spandril. *MB.* 9. As 8 but legend as 1, no trefoil after Hyb. Rev. as 8 but ILLORV, mullet after Ihc, trefoil in second quarter near lion's head. *THORBURN.* 10. Obv. legend as No. 1, annulet at king's wrist, lis after Henric, trefoil between the other words. Ornaments on ship, lion, two lis, lion, one lis. Rev. IHC AVT ° TRANSIENS ° PER ° MEDIVM ° ILLORV ° IBAT. MM lis, mullet after Ihc, annulet instead of trefoil in one spandril. *MB.* Rud. i. 15, where, however, a trefoil is represented in every spandril. 11. Same as the last, but reading HIB. *MB.* 12. Same as 10, but with a flag in the stern of the ship, ornaments as 8. Rud. ii. 7. *MB.* 13. Same as 10, but with a lis over the stern of the ship, ornaments as 8. *MB.* Rud. ii. 9, where, however, a trefoil is represented in every spandril.

CALAIS. 14. Exactly like 12, but with C inclosing a pellet, instead of h, in the centre of the reverse. *MB.*

HALF NOBLES. These seem to belong to the rosette and trefoil coinages only; but as the characteristics of both classes occasionally appear on the same coin, there was probably no great interval of time between the two, and rosettes may have continued to be used on the smaller pieces after they had been discontinued on the nobles. The smaller coins with rosettes, however, are not numerous, and accordingly in 1423 we find the Commons complaining to the king that "little or nothing of small coins was struck, but only nobles and groats, to the great harm of the people and the singular advantage of the master of the mint," who was paid according to the weight of money coined, and to whom it therefore answered better to coin large pieces than small ones, as the expense and trouble of coining would be greater in proportion to their weight for small than for large coins. The type of the half nobles remained exactly the same as before, and like the nobles.

Class II. Rosette coinage. 1. HENRIC DI GRA REX ANGL Z FRANC. Lis at king's wrist, rosette after every word. Rev. DOMIN NE IN FVRORE TVO ARGVAS ME. MM lis, rosette between each word. Rud. iii. 2. This is the only specimen we know of this class.

Class IV. Trefoil coinage. 2. Obv. legend as No. 1, annulet at king's wrist, lis after Henric, trefoil after every other word; ornaments on ship, lis, lion, lis, lion, lis. Rev. legend as No. 1, but DOMINE. MM lis, mullet after Domine, annulet between the other words, annulet instead of trefoil in one spandril. Rud. ii. 8. *MB.* 3. Same as the last, with a flag at the stern of the ship. Rud i. 16. 4. Same as No. 2, but with a lis over the stern of the ship. (29) *MB.*

CALAIS. 5. Exactly the same as No. 3, but with C instead of h in the centre of the reverse. *MB.* Another, said to have a star over the shield, was sold at Mr. Cuff's sale for £2. 3*s.* These four half-nobles Nos. 2 to 5, correspond exactly with the nobles Nos. 10, 12, 13, and 14.

QUARTER NOBLES. Type exactly like those of Henry V.

Class I. Annulet coinage. 1. HENRIC DI ° GRA ° REX ° ANGL. MM pierced cross, lis above shield, mullet after Henric. Rev. EXALTABITVR IN ° GLORIA. MM pierced cross, mullet before IN. *MB.* The pierced cross mint-mark, and one or more annulets in the legends, are the distinguishing marks of the first silver coinage of Henry VI. The pierced cross was soon discontinued, and not revived for about forty years. This coin, which closely resembles the other quarter nobles of the same reign, is extremely rare. Mr. Montagu has another specimen.

Class II. Rosette coinage. 2. Legends as the last, MM on both sides lis, lis above shield, rosette at each side of shield and between each word on both sides. (30) *MB.*

Class III. Pine-cone coinage. None known.

Class IV. Trefoil coinage. 3. Same as 1, but MM on both sides lis, lis after Henric, trefoil between the other words on obv. Rud. iii. 1. *MB.* 4. As the last, but reading ANGLI, and with a trefoil below the shield. (31) *MB.*

5. As 3, with lis at each side of shield, annulet instead of trefoil after DI. *MB.*

Coinage of the Restoration, 3 Oct. 1470 to 14 Apr. 1471.

In the interval between 1461 and 1470, while Edward IV was on the throne, two changes had been made in the weight and value of the nobles, and a new coin, called from its device an angel, had been introduced. At the restoration these alterations were adopted, and an indenture was made on the 7th of March, 1470-71, with Sir Richard Tonstall, master of the mint, in the same terms as those of the fifth year of Edward IV. According to this the nobles were now to weigh 120 grains each, as they had done before the reduction of their weight in 1412, but they were to be current, not for 6*s* 8*d* as before, but for 10*s*. The angel was to be current for 6*s* 8*d*, and was to weigh 80 grains. Half and quarter nobles were also authorized, and angelets, or half angels.

No nobles or half nobles of this coinage have yet been discovered.

ANGELS. These have for type, obv. the Archangel Michael, with a glory round his head, and expanded wings, trampling with his left foot on the dragon, and piercing him through the mouth with a spear, the other end of which ends in a cross-crosslet which marks the termination of the legend. Rev. upon a ship, with two ropes to the mast from the stern, one from the prow, and concealing part of the side of the ship, is a shield bearing the arms of France and England quarterly, surmounted by a large broad cross, which conceals the lower part of the mast, at the top of which is the topcastle, and, above that, a cross-crosslet; h to left of cross, lis to right. This type is the same as that which had been introduced by Edward IV, except that h and a *lis* are substituted in the field of the reverse for E and a rose; and the topcastle and cross-

crosslet take the place which on Edward IV's earliest angels is occupied by the rays of the sun, his own peculiar badge. The angels of Henry VII are distinguished from those of Henry VI by having h and a *rose* in the field, and also by their mint-marks. The Rs in the legends of Henry VI's angels often look more like Bs. The legend is an abbreviation of *Per crucem tuam salva nos Christe redemptor*.

1. HENRICVS DI GRA REX ANGL Z FRANCIE. Small trefoil before Henricus and after every word. Rev. PER CRVSE TVA SALVA NOS XPC REDE'T. MM pierced cross at beginning of legend, two small trefoils after Per, one after Nos. *MB*. 2. Legends as the last but FRANC, REDE'TOR. Trefoil between words on both sides, MM on both sides, at end of legend, pierced cross. *MB*. 3. Legends as the last but CRVCSE. Trefoil between words on both sides except after Per, and one before Henricus and between E and T in Rede'tor. MM pierced cross at end of obverse legend. *MB*. 4. HENRIC DI GRA REX ANGL Z FRANC. Trefoil before Henric and after every word. Rev. as 2. *MB*. 5. Same as the last, but no trefoil after Di, nor after Per, Tua, or Salva; MM plain cross at beginning of legend on rev. Rud. n. 14. 6. Obv. as 4. Rev. PER CRVSE TVA SALVA NS XPC REDEMTOR. MM plain cross at beginning of legend, trefoil after Cruse and Ns. *MB*.

Bristol. 7. Legends as 1 but DEI, FRANC. Small trefoil before Henricus and after every word on obv. except Rex, two after Franc. Rev. MM pierced cross before legend, two dots after Per, trefoil after Nos, trefoil at each side of shield, B, for Bristol, under the ship. (32) *MB*. 8. Obv. as last but legend HENRICV DI GRA REX ANGL Z FRANC DNS. Rev. PER CRVCE TVA SALVA NOS XPC REDE TOR. No MM, trefoil after Cruce, Tua, Nos, and Rede, nothing at sides of shield, B under the ship. *EVANS*. The mint at Bristol, which had been disused for a long time, was re-established by Edward IV about the year 1465. See *post*, p. 68. *Very rare.*

ANGELET. Type as the angels. HERIC DEI GRA REX ANGL Z FR. Trefoil between words except after Dei. Rev. O CRVX AVE SPES VNICA. Trefoil each side of the X in crux, and after ave, two after unica, three between the V and N in unica. MM lis at end of legend. (33) Rud. iii. 16. *MB. Ext. rare.*

QUARTER NOBLE. We assign to this coinage the following quarter noble, because it has for MM a crown, a MM which is found upon no other coin, gold or silver, of any of the Henries, but which occurs on several coins, both of gold and silver, of Edward IV struck after his fourth year, and probably about the time of Henry's short restoration. It also differs from the other quarter nobles of Henry VI by having a pellet instead of a lis in the centre of the reverse, and by having the French title in the obverse legend, which title also appears on several of the quarter nobles of Edward IV. Except in the particulars mentioned its type is the same as that of the previous quarter nobles of Henry VI, and different from those of Edward IV, but the reason of this is obvious. Henry, upon his restoration, adopted the devices upon Edward's angels, in which there was nothing peculiarly appropriate to the Yorkist as distinguished from the Lancastrian faction; but the device which Edward had placed upon the reverse of his nobles and half and quarter nobles consisted of his own badge, the rose and sun united. It was impossible, therefore, for Henry to adopt this; and if nobles were to be coined at all, as by the indenture with Sir R. Tonstall they were directed to be, it was necessary to recur to the old type; and the following coin proves that this was actually done. Obv. HENRIC × DI × GRA × REX × ANGL × Z × FRA × No MM. Rev. ×× EXALTABITVR ×× IN ×× GLORIA ×× MM crown. Pellet in centre of cross. (34) *MB.* Weight 25 grs. The proper weight of a quarter noble at this time was 30 grains. Before the fifth year of Edward IV, the proper weight was 27 grs., but this coin seems to have lost decidedly more than 2 grains by wear. *Ext. rare.*

Henry VI, like his predecessors, used no mint but those of London and Calais for his coins of the English type, except during his short restoration, when a few coins were, as we have seen, struck at Bristol. Some of his earlier coins are common, but those of the restoration are very rare. At Capt. Murchison's sale, in 1864, a Bristol angel was sold for £10, and the angelet for £30. 10*s*.

Tabular View.

	Noble.	½ Noble.	¼ Noble.
1st Coinage, *with annulets.*			
MM pierced cross, mullet and annulets in legends, lis above shield . .			+
2nd Coinage, *with rosettes.*			
MM plain cross, rosettes in obv. legend, flag at stern	Rud.		
MM lis, rosettes in legends, lis at king's wrist and in 2nd quarter of rev., mascle after Per ; flag at stern .	+		
„ as last, without flag. The mascle, and the lis in 2nd quarter, are also omitted on the ½ noble .	+	Rud.	
„ rosettes in legends and at each side of shield, lis above shield .			+
3rd Coinage, *with pine cones.*			
MM lis, lis at king's wrist and in 3rd quarter of rev., rosettes and mascle in obv. legend, pine cones and mascle in rev. legend . . .	*Num. Chr.*		
„ „ „ 2nd quarter of rev., rosettes in obv. legend, pine cones and mascle in rev. legend	Evans		
„ lis in 2nd quarter, pine cones and mascles in legends . .	Evans		
„ cone, lis, and annulet under shield on obv., pellets and annulets in obv. legend . . .	Evans		

TABULAR VIEW—*continued.*

	Noble.	½ Noble.	¼ Noble.
4TH COINAGE, *with trefoils.*			
MM lis, trefoils in obv. legend, trefoil and annulets in rev. legend, annulet at wrist and in one spandril on rev.	+		
,, same but mullet instead of trefoil in rev. legend, trefoil in 2nd quarter.	Thorburn		
,, lis and trefoils in obv. legend, mullet and annulets in rev. legend. (The nobles and half nobles have also an annulet at the king's wrist and in one spandril on rev., and the ¼ nobles have a lis above the shield) . .	+	+	+
,, same as last, with flag at stern of ship	+	Rud.	
,, same as last but one, with trefoil below shield on obv. . .			+
,, same as last but two, with lis over stern of ship on nobles and ½ nobles, and with lis at each side of shield, and annulet after Di, on ¼ nobles	+	+	+
CALAIS, *with C in centre of reverse.*			
MM lis, lis and trefoils in obv. legend, mullet and annulets in rev. legend, annulet at king's wrist and in one spandril on rev., flag at stern .	+	+	
COINAGE OF THE RESTORATION.	Angel.	½ Angel.	¼ Noble.
MM pierced cross, trefoils in legends .	+		
MM plain cross, trefoils in legends .	+		
MM lis, trefoils in legends . .		+	
MM crown, pellet in centre of cross on rev.			+
BRISTOL, *B under ship.*			
MM pierced cross, trefoils in legends and at each side of shield . .	+		
No MM, trefoils in legends . .	Evans		

EDWARD IV, 1461 TO 1483.

No indenture with the master of the mint during this reign has been preserved, earlier than one with William Lord Hastings, dated the 13th of August, 1464, in the king's fourth year, by which the weight of the silver coins was reduced, and the gold coins, though their weight was to remain as before, were raised in nominal value, so that a noble, which had hitherto been current for 6*s* 8*d*, was now to pass for 8*s* 4*d*. Silver coins of Edward IV were certainly struck before this depreciation of the currency, but whether gold ones were or were not, we have no means of knowing. The two following nobles, however, were certainly struck before 1465, when another alteration in the gold coins was made. They are of the same type as those of the preceding kings. 1. EDWARD DI GRA × REX ANGL Z × FRANC × DNS. HYB. No MM. Pellet to left of king's crown, lis under the shield, no flag or rudder to the ship, the ornaments on which are lis, lion, lis, lion, lis, as on most of Henry VI's nobles. Rev. IHC AVT TRANSIENS PER MEDIVM ILLORV × IBAT. MM lis. There is an E in the centre of the cross, but it appears to have been stamped over an h which has been placed upside down, as on Henry VI's nobles, Nos. 4 and 7. Wt. 107½ grs. *Num. Chron.* xvi. 38. *EVANS.* 2. Same as the last but from a different die, pellet each side of crown. Wt. 107¼ grs. (35) *Num. Chron.* xix. 8. *EVANS.* These two nobles are the only specimens known of gold coins of Edward IV, struck before his fifth year, 1465. The first was found with one of Henry VI's latest nobles, No. 13. They are both in the collection of Mr. J. Evans.

In the king's fifth year, 1465, by another indenture with Lord Hastings, the gold coins were again altered, and it was ordered that 45 nobles only, instead of 50 as in the last two reigns, were to be made of a pound of gold. This brought back the weight of the noble to 120 grs., as it had been from 1351 to 1412, but its value was raised to ten shillings. At the same time new coins impressed with angels were ordered to be made, 67½ to be struck from a pound of gold, and each to be of the value of 6*s* 8*d*, that is to say, the new angel which weighed 80 grs. was to be of the same value as the noble had been which weighed 108 grs. The new nobles, to distinguish them from the old ones, were called rose nobles, from the rose which is stamped on both sides of them, or ryals, or royals, a name borrowed from the French, who had given it to a coin which bore the figure of the king in his royal robes, which the English ryals did not. Notwithstanding its inappropriateness, however, the name of ryal was given to these ten-shilling pieces, not only by the people but also in several statutes of the realm, and by that name, instead of noble, we shall designate them. The new six and eightpenny pieces were named, from their device, angels, and were sometimes called "noble angels," as being of the value of the former nobles. Half and quarter ryals were also coined, and angelets, or half angels.

RYALS, or ROSE NOBLES. Obv. the king standing in a ship, crowned, holding a sword in his right hand, a shield bearing the arms of France and England in his left. The ship has three ropes from the stern to the mast, one from the prow, at the stern is a flag marked with the letter E, and on the side of the ship is a rose, with a lion and lis on each side of it. Rev. within a double tressure of eight arches, having a trefoil in each spandril, is a cross, the centre concealed by a rose upon a sun, the extremities corniced and ending in a lis between two cartouches; a lion, and a crown above him, in each quarter; the whole within an inner circle. The rose on the side of the ship, and the rose and sun on the reverse, are the badges of Edward IV, who is said to have adopted the sun in consequence of the appearance of three suns in the heavens immediately before his first battle, that of Mortimer's Cross in 1460, in which he was successful. The white rose was the well-known badge of his family. 1. EDWARD DI GRA REX ANGL Z FRANC DNS IB. Trefoil after every word and between I and B; one after Ed, two after Di; lis after Franc and IB. Rev. IHC AVT TRANSIENS PER MEDIVM ILLORVM IBAT. MM. Rose. Trefoil after Aut, Transiens, and Illorum, and between I and B in Ibat, two between I and E in Transiens and after Medium. *MB.* This coin in the British Museum is counter-marked with a double cross, surmounted by a crown, being the arms of Dantzic, which were doubtless stamped upon the coin in order to make it current in that town. 2. Obv. as the last. Rev. legend as last. MM sun, trefoil after every word and between I and B in Ibat, two after Transiens and Medium. (36) *MB*. 3. Legends as 1, but HIB, HIBAT. MM sun on both sides. Trefoil between all the words except after Franc and Per, two after Di, Transiens, Medium, and Illorum, one between I and B in Hib. *MB*. The difficulty of the aspirates was evidently felt 400 years ago. The maker of these coins found it necessary either to leave out the H in Hiberniæ, or to add it to Ibat! 4. Legends as 1. MM sun on both sides. Trefoil after every word except Franc and Ibat, two after Di, Transiens, and Medium, one between I and B in IB, each side of the I in Transiens, and after the I in Illorum. *MB*. 5. Legends as 1, but TRANNIENS. MM sun on both sides. Trefoil after every word except Per and Ibat, before Dns, and after I's in Ib and Ibat, quatrefoil also after Franc, two trefoils after Tranniens, Medium, and Illorum. *MB*. 6. Legends as 1, but DEI. MM sun on rev. only. Trefoil after last six words on obv., before Dns, and between I and B, two after B; one after every word on rev. and between I and B in Ibat, two after Illorum and Ibat. *MB*. This coin in the Museum is countermarked as No. 1. 7. Legends as 1, but ILLORV. MM sun on rev. only. Trefoil after every word except Per and Ibat, before Dns, and after Ed in Edward and the I's in IB and Ibat, two after Di, Medium, and Illoru. *MB*. 8. Legends as 1, but FRAN, ILLORV. MM crown on rev. only. Trefoil after Ed in Edward and after every word except Ihc, one also before Dns. *MB*. 9. Same as last, with trefoil after Ihc. *MB*. This coin in the Museum is countermarked with a shield on the breast of a double-headed eagle, being the arms of the towns of Groningen and Cambrai. 10. Legends as 1, but TRANSIES. MM crown on rev. only. Nothing after Di, Dns, Ib, or Illorum, two trefoils after Ibat, one after every other word, before Dns, and between I and B in Ibat. The trefoils in the spandrils are formed by three pellets. *MB.* Rud. iii. 4, where however the trefoils are arranged differently. 11. Legends as 1 but MEDVM. MM cross fitchee on rev. only. Trefoil after every word except Edward and Ibat, one before Dns and after the I's in IB and Ibat, two after Ed in Edward. Trefoils in spandrils formed by three pellets. *MB.* This last is the only ryal which appears to have been struck after 1470, the year of the restoration of Henry VI, when the crown MM was in use. After this, few coins except angels and half angels were issued.

BRISTOL. With B under the ship. 1. Obv. legend as the first London ryal. Trefoil after every word except Gra, two after Di and Ib, one before Dns, and between I and B in Ib. Rev. IHC AVT TRANSIENS B MEDIVM ILLORVM IBAT. MM sun. Rose after Illorum, trefoil after every other word, and between I and B in Ibat, two after Transiens. *MB.* 2. Obv. same as last, Rev. legend as last, but PER instead of B, MM sun, trefoil after every word, and between I and B in Ibat, two after Illorum and Ibat. *MB.* 3. Obv. as the others, Rev. as last, but MM crown, and no trefoils after Ibat. *MB.* See Rud. Suppl. vi. 22, obv. only.

COVENTRY. With C under the ship. EDWARD DI GRA REX ANGL Z FRNC DNS IB. Trefoil after every word except Rex, and between I and B in Ib. Rev. IHC AVT TRANSENS B MEDIVM ILLORVM IBAT. MM sun. Rose after Illorum, trefoil after every other word and between I and B in Ibat, two after Ibat. Rud. iii. 5. *MB.*

NORWICH. With N under the ship. Obv. legend as the Coventry coin. Trefoil after Edward, Gra, Rex, Angl, and Z, before Dns, and between I and B in Ib; two after Di, quatrefoil after Frnc. Rev. legend as the first London ryal, MM sun, trefoil between every word and between I and B in Ibat, two after Medium. *MB.* See Rud. Suppl. vi. 24, obv. only.

YORK. With E (for Eboracum) under the ship. Legends as first London ryal. MMs, on rev. only, sun and lis, with two trefoils between them. Trefoil after every word except Dns and Per, one before Dns, two after Medium, Illorum, and Ibat, and between I and B in Ibat, trefoil and quatrefoil after IB on obv. *MB.*

ANGELS. The type of these has already been described by anticipation under the reign of Henry VI, who in his short restoration copied the current coins of Edward IV. On the earliest angels, however, Edward placed over the mast of the ship his own badge, the rays of the sun, and this seems to have continued till it was removed by Henry VI in 1470. In the field, on each side of the cross on the reverse, are a rose and a sun, both being emblems or badges of Edward and his family. 1. EDWARD × DI ⁑ GRA × REX × ANGL × Z × FRANC × DNS × I × B × Rev. PER CRVCEM TVAM SALVA NOS XPC REDEMPTOR. No MM on either side, crown with rays descending from beneath it over the mast, sun to left, rose to right of cross; trefoil after Per, Salva, and Nos, two after Crucem and Tuam. (37) Rud. iii. 13, rev. only. *MB.* 2. Same but CRVCE TVA, small rosette before rev. legend, rays as on the last but no crown above them, rose to left, large sun to right of cross, small trefoil above the ropes on each side. Trefoil between all the words except after Z, Per, and Cruce, one between I and B in Ib, and before D in Redemptor, two after Di, Angl, and Nos; two pellets after Per. See Rud. Sup. vi. 23. *MB.*

These are the earliest angels, and were doubtless struck before 1470. The mint-mark then in use was a crown, as is proved by its adoption on the quarter noble struck in that year by Henry VI. Neither this nor any previous mint-mark appears on Edward IV's angels, but the annulet enclosing a pellet, which on the silver series immediately succeeded the crown, does. We conclude, therefore, that the angels with the sun's rays, and with no mint-mark, were the only ones issued before Henry VI's restoration. Afterwards, the regular series of mint-marks, the same as on the other coins, was adopted, and the sun's rays, which had been removed by Henry VI, were not replaced. Instead of them, there is the topcastle on the top of the mast, surmounted by a cross-crosslet, which was introduced by Henry VI; and E and a rose in the field; except on the first coin now to be described.

3. EDWARD DEI GRA REX ANGL Z FRANC. Rev. PER × CRVCEM × TVA × SALVA × NOS × XPE × REDEMPT. MM annulet enclosing pellet on both sides, no crown or rays above the mast, but instead of them an object, possibly intended for a topcastle. E to left, sun to right of cross. Trefoil after the first four and last words on obv. *MB.*

The rest all have a topcastle above the mast, surmounted by a cross-crosslet, and E to the left, a rose to the right of the cross.

4. EDWARD DEI GRA REX ANGL Z FRANC. Rev. PER CRVSE TVA SALVA NOS XPC REDEMTOR. MM annulet on obv. only. Trefoil between all the words except after Dei, Tua, and XPC. *MB.* 5. Same but REDETO, trefoil between all the words except after Gra and XPC, one after Franc. *MB.* 6. As 4, but MM to left instead of right of the angel's head, trefoil before Edward and after first four words on obv., and after Cruse, Salva, Nos, and XPC on rev. *MB.* 7. As 4 but DI, REDETOR. Trefoil after Di and last four words on obv., and after Cruse, Salva, and XPC, and between E and T in Redetor on rev. *MB.* 8. Legends as last. MM cross pierced on obv. only. Trefoil after every word on obv., no stops on rev. *MB.* 9. Obv. legend as 4. Rev. PER × CRVCEM × TVA × SALVA × NOS × XPC REDEMPT MM on each side a cross pierced. Saltire after Rex, Angl, and Z, three after Franc. 10. Legends as last, MM on each side a cross pierced with a pellet in one angle, saltire after every word on obv., four after Franc, two after Crucem and Tua, one after Salva and Nos. *MB.* 11. Same but one saltire between each word on rev., none after Franc. *MB.* 12. Legends as 9, MM

on each side a cross with a pellet in each angle. Saltire after every word on obv. except Dei, two saltires, a trefoil, and another saltire after Franc. No stops on rev. *MB.* Rud. iii. 11, where the pellets in the obv. MM are omitted. 13. Legends as 9, but REDEMP. MM on both sides heraldic cinquefoil. Saltire after every word on obv. except Z, no stops on rev. *MB.* 14. Same as the last but REDEMT, two saltires after Franc and Crucem, one after Tua and Salva. *MB.* 15. Same but saltire only, on obv., after Edward, Gra, and Angl, two after Dei. Rev. same as last. *MB.* 16. Same as last with no saltires after Dei, four after Franc. *MB.* 17. Legends as 9, MM as 13. Saltire after Edward, Dei, and Angl, two after Franc, one after each word on rev. except the first and last. (38) *MB.* 18. Same with saltire after Edward, Rex, and Angl, two after Dei and Gra. *MB.* 19. Legends as 9, MM on both sides rose and sun united. Saltire after first four words on obv. and two after Franc, one after Crucem, Tua, Salva, and XPC. *MB.* A similar coin, having R instead of E in the field on the reverse and therefore struck for Richard III, will be found described under his reign. Coins with MM rose and sun are sometimes attributed to Edward V, and therefore fetch high prices. Mr. Sheppard's was sold in 1861 for £10.

BRISTOL. With B under ship. Legends as 4 but REDETOR. MM annulet on obv. only. No stops on obv., but two trefoils after Franc; trefoil after Cruse, Salva, Nos, and XPC, two after Per. *MB.* We know of no provincial angels other than these, which are very rare. The Museum specimen was bought at Mr. Cuff's sale for £12.

HALF-RYALS. Type same as the ryals. None of them appear to be later than 1470. 1. EDWARD DI GRA REX ANGL Z FRANC. MM sun, followed by two trefoils and a quatrefoil. Trefoil between every word, two between F and R in Franc. Rev. DOMINE NE IN FVRORE TVO ARGVAS ME. MM crown, trefoil after the first five words.

MB. 2. Same but no MM on obv., nothing after Franc or between F and R, two trefoils after DOMINE. *MB*. 3. Same as 1 but FRAN, no MM, nothing after Z or Fran, or between the F and R, no trefoil after Furore. *MB*. 4. Legends as 1, lis under the ship in the same place as the distinguishing letter on the provincial coins; MM obv. rose, rev. crown, quatrefoil after the rose, trefoil after Edward, Gra, Rex, Angl, and Z, and after Domine, Ne, Furore and Tuo, two between the R and A in Franc. (39) *MB*. The lis on this coin looks as if it was intended to denote some mint other than that of London.

No coins are known to have been struck at Calais in this reign; but the Statute 3 Edward IV, c. 1, enacts that any "plate or bullion of silver or gold" received by merchants in Calais in payment for wool sold there, shall be taken to be coined at the mint of Calais. Whether this enactment was ever carried out is doubtful. But though there are no coins in existence bearing the name of that mint, yet there are a few silver groats which, with the name of London on the reverse, have on the obverse the marks generally used under Henry V and VI at the Calais mint. These were struck before the reduction of the weight of the silver coins in the king's fourth year. The half-ryal with the lis under the ship cannot have been struck before the fifth year, and the crown mint-mark is probably three or four years later than this; but as it is evident that in the king's third year there was an intention to strike coins at Calais, it is not unlikely that during the next year or two dies for this purpose were prepared at the Tower, and that some of them, not being required at Calais, were used at the Tower for the obverses of the gold and silver coins in question.

Bristol. With B under the ship. 1. Legends as London No. 1, but ARGVS, trefoil after every word except Di, Gra, In, and Me, after Ed in Edward and before Franc, two after Tuo and Argus. MMs on rev. only, a rose and a sun separated by two trefoils. *MB.* 2. Legends as London No. 1, trefoil after first three words on obv. and after Franc, lis each side of Z, trefoil after Ne, Tuo, and Arguas, two after Domine, quatrefoil and two trefoils after Me. MM crown on rev. only. Rud. iii. 7, obv. only. *MB.*

Coventry. C under ship. Legends as London No. 3 but ARGVS. Trefoil between all the words except after In, and one also before Fran, two after Di, Rex, Tuo, and Arguas. MMs as Bristol No. 1. The trefoils in the spandrils, all except three, are omitted. *MB.*

Norwich. N under ship. Legends as London No. 1, trefoil after Franc, Ne, and In, two after Domine, Tuo, and Me. MM rose on rev. only. *MB.* It is doubtful whether there are any stops between the words on the obverse of this coin, and it differs from other half-ryals in having no lis on the side of the ship.

York. E under ship. Legends as London No. 1. 1. Small cross after each word on obv., and before Franc, two after Rex. Trefoil after each word on rev. except Ne and Me, two after Tuo. MMs rose and lis on rev. only. *MB.* 2. Trefoil between all the words on obv. and before Franc, two after Di; one after Domine and Ne, two after Tuo and Arguas. After Me are two trefoils, a quatrefoil, and the MM, a lis. There are no trefoils in the spandrils. *MB.* 3. Trefoil after every word on obv. except Rex, one after E in Edward and before Franc; two after Domine, one after In and Furore. MM sun on rev. only. Rud. iii. 6. *MB.*

ANGELETS. Type same as the later angels, and as the angelets of Henry VI. 1. EDWARD DI GRA REX. ANGL ⁘ Rev. O ⁘ CRVX AVE SPES VNICA. MM annulet on both sides, rose after Crux, trefoil after Ave, Spes, and Unica. *MB.* 2. A coin with the same obverse as this, except that it has a small cross instead of a pellet after Rex, has on the reverse the king's titles, EDWARD DI GRA REX. ANGL. Z. FR, instead of any other legend, with no MM. *MB.* 3. On another coin the legends are transposed, so that it has on the obv., with the figure of St. Michael, the legend O CRVX AVE SPES VNICA, with a pierced cross for MM., and on rev. EDWARD DI GRA REX. ANGL. Z. FRA, with no MM. Trefoil after Crux, Ave, Spes, and Unica, and after the first letter in Unica. (40) *MB*. 4. Legends as 1, MM obv. pierced cross, rev. pierced cross and pellet. Saltire after every word on obv., two before O and after O, Crux, and Spes, rose after Ave, sun after Unica. *MB*. 5. EDWARD × DEI GRA REX × ANGLE × Rev. legend as 1, MM plain cross on a circle. Small cross after Spes, two before O and after O and Unica, rose after Ave. *MB*. 6. Legends as last but ANGL. MM plain cross on rev. only. No stops on obv., saltire after every word on rev., two each side of O. Rud. iii. 12. 7. As 6 but MM cinquefoil on both sides, rose after Crux and Spes. *THORBURN*. 8. Legends as 1 but MM rose and sun united on both sides. Saltire after Edward and Di, and after Spes and Unica, two each side of O. It is doubtful whether there are any marks on either side of Ave. *MB*. There are no provincial half angels.

QUARTER RYALS. 1. Within a double tressure of eight arches, having a trefoil at each angle, is a shield with the arms of France and England quarterly, a rose above it, the whole within an inner circle. EDWARD × DI × GRA × REX × ANGL Z F. MM sun. Rev. Within a double tressure of eight arches is a cross, the centre concealed by a rose upon a sun, each limb ending in a lis between two cartouches, a lion passant guardant in each angle. EXALTABITVR IN GLORIA. Trefoil after Exaltabitur and Gloria, two after In. MM rose. Rud. iii. 10, obv. only. *MB*.

The type of all the rest is, obv. within a tressure of four arches, having a trefoil in each spandril, is a shield bearing the arms of France and England quarterly, the whole within an inner circle. Rev. type as No. 1. 2. EDWARD DI GRA REX ANGL FR or ANGLIE (the last two letters are doubtful). E above shield, lis below, sun to left, rose to right. MM rose. Lis after Edward, trefoil after Di, two after Gra. Rev. EXALTABITVR IN GLORIA CN. MM sun. Two trefoils after Exaltabitur, In, and Cn. (41) *MB*. It does not appear what Cn. stands for. 3. EDWARD DI GRA REX ANGL. Trefoil after Edward and Gra, two after Di and Rex; MM sun; otherwise as 2. Rev. EXALTABITVR IN GLORIA. MM crown, trefoil between the words. *MB*. 4. As the last, but two trefoils also after Gra, EXATABITVR, rose after each word on rev. Rud. iii. 8, obv. only. *MB*. 5. Legends as 3; E above shield, lis below, rose to left, sun to right; MM obv. crown, rev. rose and crown; trefoil after Edward Di and Rex and on each side of In. There is no lis at the extremity of the right hand limb of the cross upon this coin. *MB*. 6. Obv. as 5; rev. legend same, but lis before, rose after In, MM clipped off. *THORBURN*. 7. Same as 5, but no trefoils in the spandrils or between words on obv., rev. MM crown only, two trefoils between each word, lis at each extremity of cross. *MB*. 8. Same as the last, with Z after Angl, a small cross after Di, and a lis instead of trefoils after each word on rev. *MB*. 9. EDWARD DI GRA RE A. MM crown on obv. only, ornaments round shield as 5, two or three dots instead of trefoil in each spandril, rev. legend as 3, the word Gloria blundered, a star, apparently, before the R; no stops between the words. *MB*. This is a very rudely executed coin. 10. EDWARD DI GRA REX ANGL Z. MM cross fitchee, trefoil after Z, ornaments round shield as 2. Rev. legend as 3, MM rose and cross fitchee, trefoil between each word. *MB*. 11. Legends as last, MM obv. plain cross (perhaps intended for cross fitchee), rev. rose, E above shield, nothing below, rose to left, sun to right, trefoil (?) after each word. Rud. iii. 9. 12. EDWARD DI GRA REX ANGL Z FR. MM lis, trefoil after first three words, ornaments round shield as 5. Rev. legend as 3, MM lis? trefoil before each word, saltire after Gloria. *MB*. The lis does not appear as a MM on any silver coins of Edward IV except those struck at York, of which mint it is a common mark; and as all the other

MMs on the London gold coins occur also on the silver ones of the same place, and as we have no quarter ryals marked with an E like the ryals and half-ryals to denote that they were struck at York, it is possible that this coin may be from that mint.

Edward IV was the first English king who struck gold coins at any place in England, except London. His provincial mints, which were at Bristol, Coventry, Norwich, and York, were probably established in or about the year 1465, to assist in the great recoinage then taking place, and those at Bristol and York were made use of by Henry VI in 1470; but they seem to have been discontinued after a short time, as none of the later mint-marks appear on the provincial coins; and their coinage of gold seems to have been almost confined to ryals and half-ryals. No coins are known to have been struck at Calais during this reign, though it was at one time intended to do so, and some dies appear to have been made for the purpose. See ante, p. 64.

From a comparison of the numerous silver coins of this reign, it appears that the mint-marks followed each other in the order in which they are here arranged. The approximate date of each coin may be thus ascertained.

TABULAR VIEW.

	Nobles				
1st COINAGE.					
MM lis, lis under shield on obv., pellet to left of crown .	Evans				
" " pellet each side of crown . .	Evans				
2nd COINAGE, 1465.	Ryals	Angels	½ Ryals	½ Angels	¼ Ryals
MM rose. Lis after Franc and Ib, trefoils in legends .	+				
MM sun. As the last . .	+				
MM sun, rev. rose. Tressure of 8 arches on obv., rose above shield, trefoils in rev. legend . . .					+
MM rose, rev. sun. E above shield, lis below, sun to left, rose to right. Lis after Edward, trefoils in legends.					+

TABULAR VIEW—*continued.*

	Ryals	Angels	½ Ryals	½ Angels	¼ Ryals
MM sun. Trefoils in the legends . . .	+				
,, ,, quatrefoil after Franc . . .	+				
MM sun, rev. crown. Trefoils in the legends, two trefoils and a quatrefoil after obv. MM			+		
,, ,, Trefoils in the legends, E above shield, lis below, sun to left, rose to right					+
,, . As the last, but rose after each word on rev.					+
MM crown, rev. rose and crown. Trefoils in the legends, E above shield, lis below, rose to left, sun to right					+
MM crown. Trefoils in the legends . . .	+		+		
MM crown. E above shield, lis below, rose to left, sun to right. Trefoils in obv. legend, lis and rose in rev. .					Thorb.
,, As last, but trefoils in rev. legend, none in obv. .					+
,, As last, but no trefoils, lis after each word on rev. .					+
,, As last, but no trefoils or lis on rev., star? in rev. legend . . .					+
No MM. Trefoils in legends			+		
,, Trefoils in rev. legend, sun to left, rose to right of cross		+			
,, Trefoils in legends and in field on obv., rose to left, sun to right of cross .		+			
MM annulet enclosing pellet. Trefoils in obv. legend, E to left, sun to right of cross .		+			
MM annulet. Trefoils in legends . . .		+			
,, Trefoils in rev. legend, rose after Crux .				+	
,, King's titles on both sides . . .				+	
MM cross fitchee. Trefoils in legends . . .	+				
,, ,, Rev. rose					

TABULAR VIEW—*continued.*

	Ryals	Angels	½Ryals	½Angels	¼Ryals
and cross fitchee. Trefoils in legends. E above shield, lis below, sun to left, rose to right					+
MM cross, rev. rose. Trefoils in legends, E above shield, rose to left, sun to right. . .					Rud.
MM cross pierced. Trefoils in obv. legend . . .		+		+	
„ „ no trefoils		+			
„ „ rev. cross pierced with pellet in one angle. Rose after Ave, sun after Unica . . .				+	
MM cross pierced with pellet in one angle . . .		+			
MM cross with pellet in each angle : trefoil after Franc .		+			
MM plain cross upon a circle. Rose after Ave . .				+	
MM plain cross . . .				Rud.	
MM heraldic cinquefoil .		+		Thorb.	
MM rose and sun united .		+		+	
MM rose, rev. crown. Quatrefoil after obv. MM, trefoils in legends. Lis under ship. (*Calais ?*) . . .			+		
MM lis. E above shield, lis below, rose to left, sun to right. Trefoils in legends (*York ?*) .					+
BRISTOL. B under ship. MM rose and sun. Trefoils in legends . . .			+		
„ „ MM sun. Trefoils in legends, rose after Illorum . .	+				
„ „ MM sun. Trefoils in legends .	+				
„ „ MM crown. Trefoils in legends .	+				
„ „ MM crown. Trefoils in legends, lis each side of Z, quatrefoil after Me . . .			+		
„ „ MM annulet. Trefoils in legends .		+			
COVENTRY. C under ship. MM rose and sun. Trefoils in legends . . .			+		
„ MM					

TABULAR VIEW—*continued.*

	Ryals	Angels	½Ryals	½Angels	¼Ryals
sun. Trefoils in legends, rose after Illorum .	+				
NORWICH. N under ship. MM rose. Trefoils in legends .			+		
" " MM sun. Trefoils in legends, quatrefoil after Frnc . .	+				
YORK. E under ship. MM rose and lis. Trefoils in rev. legend			+		
" " MM sun and lis. Trefoils in legends, quatrefoil after Ib. . .	+				
" " MM lis. Trefoils in legends, quatrefoil after Me . . .			+		
" " MM sun. Trefoils in legends . .			+		

EDWARD V, APRIL 9 TO JUNE 26, 1483.

On the 20th of May, after Edward IV's death, Sir William Hastings was appointed Master and Worker of the Mint, and also Warden of the Exchange, for life, with all the profits of the office and without paying any rent to the king, according to the form of an indenture to be made between the king and him. This indenture was never executed; but Ross of Warwick, who wrote early in Henry VII's reign, says, in a passage quoted by Ruding, "In the new king's name the laws were, as usual, administered, the money then made was struck and fashioned in his name, and in his name all the usual forms were observed which his dignity as king required." It seems therefore that money was actually struck in his name; and even had this passage not existed, it would perhaps have been reasonable to attribute to him certain very rare angels and groats of the same type as his father's but having for MM the boar's head, which is well known as the badge of the Protector

Gloucester, afterwards Richard III, but which is not known to have been used by any other of the descendants of Edward III, by whom it had been originally adopted. Gloucester was never in such power or favour at his brother's court as to make it likely that his badge should be placed upon his brother's coins, whereas none would have been more likely to have been placed on those of his nephew during his own protectorate.

The only angel we know with this MM is of identically the same type as the later ones of Edward IV, and reads EDWARD × DI × GRA × REX · ANGL × Z × FRANC ×× ×× Rev. PER CRVCEM TVA SALVA NOS XPC REDEMP ×× MM obv. boar's head, rev. rose and sun united. (42) *MB.*

No other denominations of gold coins with the boar's head MM are known. All those which have the rose and sun MM are sometimes attributed to Edward V, but the rose and sun was the well-known cognizance of Edward IV, and is therefore as likely as the boar's head is unlikely to have been placed on his own coins; and though the dies of Edward IV, with his last MM, are very likely to have been used, as on the above coin, in conjunction with the new ones of Edward V, and also, as we shall see was the case, with those of Richard III, it is very improbable that more than one new MM can have been authorized for the coinage during the very short reign of Edward V.

Richard III, 1483 to 1485.

The only gold coins known to have been struck by Richard III are angels and angelets, and they are all very rare. They are of exactly the same type as those of Edward IV, but have R to left, rose to right of the cross on rev. They were struck at London only, by Robert Brakenbury, "Master Worker of the Money in the Tower."

ANGELS. 1. Obv. from a die of Edward IV, MM rose and sun united. EDWARD × DI × GRA ×× REX × ANGL ××

Z FRANC. Rev. PER CRVCEM × TVA × SALVA NOS XPC REDEMPT, MM rose and sun united. *MB*. 2. RICAD × DI × GRA × REX ANGL × Z FRANC ⁝ Rev. as last, but CRVCE× saltire also after XPC. MM, on both sides, rose and sun united. *MB*. Or RICARD. Rud. iv. 1. *EVANS*. 3. Same as last, but CRVSEM, rev. MM boar's head. *MB*. 4. RICARD × DI ⁝ GRA × REX ANGL × Z FRANC ⁝ Rev. PER CRVCE × TVA × SALVA NOS XPC × REDEMP. MM obv. boar's head, rev. rose and sun united. *MB*. 5. Same, but only one saltire after Franc, and reading REDEDMT. *MB*. 6. MM boar's head on both sides, legends as 4 but no saltire after Franc or XPC, one after Salva and Nos. (43) *MB*. Or legends as 4 but REDEMPT. *EVANS*. 7. Obv. legend as 4, rev. as 3, MM boar's head both sides. Saltire after every word on obv. except Rex and Z, two after Franc, one after Salva and XPC. Rud. iii. 17. 8. MM boar's head on both sides, legends as 4 but TVAM, REDE, saltire after every word except Gra, Franc, and Per, two after Rede. *THORBURN*.

ANGELET. 1. RICARD × DI × GRA × REX × ANGL Rev. O CRVX × AVE × SPES × VNICA ×. MM rose (no doubt a mistake for rose and sun united) on both sides. Rud. iii. 18. 2. Same, but MM on both sides a boar's head. Rud. iv. i. 3. Legends as 1 but ANG, MM boar's head on both sides, no saltire after Rex or Unica, two each side of O. (44) *MB*.

TABLE OF MINT MARKS.

	Angels	½ Angels
Rose and sun united. Obv. from die of Edward IV	+	
Rose and sun united	+	Rud.
„ „ rev. boar's head . .	+	
Boar's head, rev. rose and sun united . .	+	
Boar's head	+	

Henry VII, 1485 to 1509.

The coins of Henry VII were of the same weight, fineness, and value as those of Edward IV, but some changes were introduced in the type during his reign, and he struck coins both in gold and silver, namely sovereigns and shillings, of a larger denomination than had ever been struck before. In his first year Sir Giles Daubeney and Bartholomew Reed were appointed joint masters and workers of the mint, to coin pieces of the same description as had been coined under Edward IV; and in 1489 the same persons—Sir Giles having now become Lord Daubeney—were ordered to make a new money of gold according to the print and form of a piece of lead annexed to the Letters Patent. The new money was to be of the standard fineness, to be double the weight of the ryal, and to be called the sovereign, and was to be current for 20*s*. Out of every pound weight of gold to be coined in the Tower, two of these pieces, and no more, were to be made, unless the king should command the contrary. Sovereigns are again mentioned in a statute of the year 1504, and also half-sovereigns, but the latter are not mentioned in this indenture.

SOVEREIGNS. Of these there are four distinct types, which are here described in the order in which they appear to have been issued.

1. The king, front-faced, robed and crowned, holding the sceptre in his right hand, the orb in his left, seated on a throne, the back of which is concave, and reaches about halfway up the king's head. The base of the throne is solid, without legs, and the seat is a wide one, part of it being visible on each side of the king; it has arms, and at each corner is an ornamented pillar, the pillars in front of the arms being surmounted by a slender ornament, which may be a lis. There are no ornaments in the field. The king's crown is arched, the principal arch being surmounted by a globe and cross, and supported by two lower arches which cross each

other at right angles. All the arches are ornamented. There is a trefoil after every word, two after Trancies and Ibat. MM heraldic cinquefoil. HENRIC DI GRA REX ANGL FRANC Z DNS IBARNE (for Hiberniæ). Rev. upon a large double rose, which fills the whole field, is a shield bearing the arms of France and England, surmounted by a large crown with a double ornamented arch, the globe and cross on the top of which extend to the edge of the coin. MM a cinquefoil. IHS AVTE TRANCIES PER MEDIV ILLORV IBAT. (45) *EVANS.* Rud. iv. 11. The MM and legend on the obverse are not quite accurate on this plate.

2. Similar to the last, but the throne has a low straight back of the same height as the arms, and at each corner of it is a slight unornamented pillar. The lower arches of the crown are plain. The field is chequered and covered with lis. HENRICVS × DI ⁑ GRACIA × REX × ANGLIE × ET × FRANC × DNS I × BAR. Rev. like the last, but with no crown over the shield; the rose is not so large, and is enclosed within a double tressure of ten arches, having a small lion and lis alternately in each arch, and a trefoil in each spandril. The whole within the inner circle. MM cross fitchee. IHC AVTEM TRANSCIENS PER MEDIVM ILLORVM IBATHE. Trefoil after first, third, and fourth words, two after second, fifth, and sixth. (46) Rud. iv. 3. *MB.* What the two last letters on the reverse mean is not clear. Possibly they were copied by mistake from the obverse of the last coin, as the spelling of "Transciens" shows that the artist was a blunderer.

3. Similar to No. 1, but the back of the throne is lower and there is a canopy of three ornamented arches, the centre one being over the king's head. The seat projects beyond the base, and the arms are very low and far away from the king, and there are two small ornamented pillars in front of each. The field is strewn with lis, but is not chequered. The king's crown has only one arch, which is surmounted by a globe and cross. MM lis. HENRICVS ×

DEI × GRA × REX × ANGL × ET × FRAN × DNS × HIBN. Rev. like the last but both rose and shield considerably smaller, and two saltires instead of trefoil in each spandril. MM dragon. ⁑ IHESVS ⁑ AVTEM ⁑ TRANSIENS ⁑ PER ⁑ MEDIVM ⁑ ILLORVM ⁑ IBAT. Four saltires and a rosette after Ibat. (47) Rud. iv. 4. *MB.*

4. Like the last, but the throne is highly ornamented, the back is high and in three divisions, but with no arch over the king's head. The seat is entirely covered by the king's robes, the arms are curved and rather high, and in front of each is a thickish pillar, that on the king's right being surmounted by a greyhound, that on his left by a dragon. The principal arch of the king's crown is supported by a plain arch at right angles to it. MM dragon. Legend as 2 but DEI, FRANCIE, the letters being large and mostly of the Roman form, instead of, as on all the others, the old English; two mullets, or stars with five points, after the first, second, seventh and eighth words, one after the third, fourth, and fifth. Rev. like the last, but the letters larger and coarser, nothing in the spandrils, mullet before Ihesus and after each word, two after Per and Illorum, four after Ibat. (48) Rud. iv. 5. *MB.*

RYAL. Obv. the king, nearly full face, with crown with upper and two lower arches all plain, standing in a ship, holding a sword in his right hand, a nearly square shield with the arms of France and England in his left. The upper part of the side of the ship is ornamented with lions and lis; there are three ropes from the stern and two from the prow, and at each end of the ship is a flag, that at the stern bearing a dragon, that at the prow an h. No MM. HENRIC DI GRA REX ANGL Z FRANC DNS IBAR. Trefoil between every word, one before R in Henric. Rev. spade-shaped shield bearing arms of France only upon a large double rose, within a tressure of ten arches, a trefoil at the point of each arch and in four spandrils; the whole within inner circle. MM cross fitchee.

IHC AVTEM TRANSIENS PER MEDIV ILLORV IBAT. Trefoil between the words, except after Per. (49) Rud. iv. 6. *MB.* This is doubtless the coin mentioned as a half-sovereign in the statute 19 Henry VII, c. 5, with respect to clipped coins. It must have been struck by virtue of the authority to strike ryals, which were of exactly half the value of the sovereign, because the indenture for striking sovereigns contains no mention of half-sovereigns, nor is there any other authority known for the issue of half-sovereigns. It is, therefore, properly called a ryal, and its obverse is similar in general design to the ryals of Edward IV, but as the reverse is unlike the ryals and the same as that of the sovereigns, it would very likely be popularly called a half-sovereign. The alteration of type was made necessary by the fact that the rose and sun combined, which had formed the type of the former ryals, was the peculiar badge of Edward IV, and, therefore, could not be used by Henry VII, who claimed to represent the Lancastrian family.

ANGELS. *First coinage.* Type like those of Henry VI, but with a rose instead of a lis to the right of the cross. The obverse legend is always HENRIC DI GRA REX ANGL Z FRANC. Mr. Evans, however, has one which differs from all the others in adding DNS, apparently, to this legend, and in having three instead of two ropes from the stern of the ship. The MM is doubtful. The reverse legend is PER CRVCE TVA SALVA NOS XPC REDETOR. 2. MM rose, saltire between every ? word, two after Franc. Rev. PER CRVSE TVA SALVA NOS XPC REDEMPT. *MB.* ˙3. Same but MM lis upon rose, CRVCEM, REDET, two saltires after Di, none on rev. *MB.* 4. As last but REDEM. *MB.* 5. Obv. MM heraldic cinquefoil, trefoil after every word. Rev. no MM, PER CRVC TVA SALVA NOS XPC REDETOR. Trefoil after every word except the first and last. *MB.* 6. No MM. Rev. legend as on the ryals, IHC AVTE TRANSIENS

PER MEDIV ILORV. Saltire before Henric, trefoil after every? word except Per and Mediu. (50) *MB*. 7. MM obv. heraldic cinquefoil, rev. escallop, rev. legend like the last, IHC AVT TRANSIENS PE MEDIV ILLOR IB. Stops doubtful. *MB*. 8. MMs as last, trefoil after every word on obv. Rev. PER CRVCE TVA SALVA NOS XPE REDE. Two rosettes between each word. The shield on the reverse of the last two is broader and rounder than on previous ones, and rests on the top of the side of the ship instead of being in front of and hiding part of it; as on the angels of the second coinage. *MB*.

Second coinage. The type of these is somewhat different from that of the previous angels. Obv. the Archangel Michael, with a glory round his head, and expanded wings, both knees bent, both heels resting on the Dragon, to whom his back is half turned, while he is piercing him through the mouth with a spear, the handle of which is generally shaped like a cross-crosslet and marks the termination of the legend. Rev. upon a ship, with two ropes to the mast from the stern, one from the prow, and filling up the whole space within the ship, but not concealing any part of its side, is a shield bearing the arms of France and England quarterly, surmounted by a large broad cross which conceals the lower part of the mast, at the top of which is a top-castle; h to left of cross, rose to right. 9. MM on both sides escallop shell. HENRIC DI GRA REX ANGLI Z FRANC. Rev. Legend like that on the ryals, IHC AVTE TRANSIES PE MEDIV ILLOR IB. Rosette between words on both sides. The Es in the legend are peculiar, and more like reversed 3s. *EVANS*. 10. MM escallop shell. HENRIC DI GRA REX ANGL Z FRAN. Rev. PER CRVCEM TVA SALVA NOS XPE REDEM. Rosette between each word. The Es on the reverse are like those on the last coin. (51) *MB*. 11. MM cinquefoil. Obv. legend as last but FR, rev. PER CRVC TVA SALVA NOS, etc. (the last two words illegible). Rosette between each word. *MB*.

12. Same but ANGLI Z FRACI, XPE REDE. Saltire between each word on obv., rosette after every word on rev. *MB*. 13. MM cinquefoil, obv. legend as 10 but FRANC. Saltire between the words. Rev. PER ⁑ CRVC× TVA × SALVA ⁑ NOS × XPE ⁑ RED. *MB*. 14. Same but AGLIE Z FRA, two saltires after Gra, Rex, and Z. *MB*. 15. MM greyhound's head. HENRIC DI GRA REX AGL Z FRA. Rosette between each word. Rev. PER × CRVCE × TVA × SALVA × NOS × XPE × RED. *MB*. Rud. iv. 10 differs only in reading R instead of Red. 16. MM same, and legends same but HENRI, FR, CRVC, and omitting RED. Saltire after every word, two after Per and Nos. *MB*. 17. Same but HENRIC, DEI, ANGL, CRVCE, XP; no saltire at ends of legends. *MB*. 18. MM obv. greyhound's head, rev. anchor. Legends as 15 but F, CRVC, SALV; saltire after every word except Red, two after Rex. *MB*. 19. MM obv. anchor, rev. greyhound's head. Legends as 15 but REDE. Saltire between each word, two after Per and Nos. *MB*. 20. MM anchor. Legends as 15 but CRVC, SALV, REDE. Saltire between each word. *MB*. 21. Same but CRVCE, SALVA. *MB*. 22. Same as 20 but CRVCE, SALVA, RE, two saltires after Per, one after Re. *MB*. 23. MM anchor. Legends as 15 but AGLIE. Saltire between each word except after Z. *MB*. 24. MM pheon. Legends as 15 but FR. Saltire between every word, two after Fr, Per, and Nos. *MB*. 25. Same but AGLIE Z FR, only one saltire after Per and Nos, one after Red. *MB*. 26. As 24 but ANGL, R' D', only one saltire after Nos. *MB*. 27. MM pheon. Legends as 15 but ANGL, REDE. Saltire between every word, two after Rex, Per, Cruce, Tua, and Nos, three after Fra. *MB*. See Rud. iv. 7, which differs only in the arrangement of the saltires. 28. Same but RED, two saltires after Henric, Rex, Angl, Z, Per, Salva, and Nos, one between the other words, four after Fra. *MB*. 29. MM pheon. Legends as 15 but ANGL Z FR. Two saltires after Henric, Rex, and Z, and between each word on rev.,

one after Di Gra and Angl, three after Fr. *MB.* 30. Same with two saltires between each word, except that there is one only after Cruce and XPE. *MB.* The specimens of the two last coins in the British Museum are countermarked with the arms of Holland. 31. MM obv. pheon, rev. cross-crosslet. Legends as 15 but AGLIE. Two saltires after first four words on obv. and after Fra and Red. Arrow head followed by saltire at end of legend on rev. *MB.* 32. MM cross-crosslet. As last but saltire before obv. MM, only one between the words, arrow head also after Fra. *MB.* 33. MM cross-crosslet. Legends as 15 but AGLI, saltire between every word, two after Rex. *MB.* 34. Same but RE for Red, no saltire after Cruce, one between every other word. *MB.* 35. MM cross-crosslet. Legends as 15 but ANGL, two saltires after first four words on obv. and first five on rev., one after Angl and XPE, three after Fra. *MB.* 36. Same but ANGLIE, two saltires after Henric and Di, one after every other word except Red. *MB.* 37. MM cross-crosslet. Legends as 15 but FR, × after Agl, Cruce, and Tua, none after Z or Red, two saltires after the other words. *THORBURN.* 38. MM Portcullis, HERIC (?) × VII × DI × GRA × REX × AGL × Z. FR. Rev. legend as 15. *MB.* If this is a coin of Henry VII it is very curious, as being the only gold coin of his with numerals; but the numerals are not very distinct and may perhaps be intended for VIII, the coin being very like some of Henry VIII with the same mint-mark.

ANGELETS. *First coinage.* Type like the angels of the first coinage. MM, on both sides, rose and sun united. Legends HENRIC × DI GRA × REX ANGL. Rev. ×× O ×× CRVX × AVE ×× SPES ×× VNICA. (52) *EVANS.* Wt. $38\frac{1}{4}$ grs. This is the only specimen of angelets of the first coinage which we have seen. The MM is a badge of Edward IV and Richard III, and occurs on no other coins of Henry VII, so that this piece was no doubt struck at the very beginning of his reign.

Second Coinage. Type like the angels, with some slight variations. The reverse legend is always O CRUX AVE SPES VNICA. 1. MM cinquefoil. HENRIC DI GRA REX ANGLI. Rosette between each word on obv., one before, two after, O, two after Crux, one or two after Ave and Spes, three after Unica. (53) *MB.* 2. MM cinquefoil. HENRIC DI GRA REX AGL Z F (apparently, but this specimen is double struck). Saltire between each word on obv. and before O, two after every word on rev. *MB.* 3. No MM on obv., greyhound's head? to left of mast on rev. Legends as last. Trefoil between words on obv. and after Ave, two after Spes and Unica. The mast on this coin seems to be surmounted only by a plain cross, with no top-castle. *MB.* 4. MM pheon. HENRIC DI GRA REX AGL Z. Two saltires between the words on both sides, one after Unica. *MB.* 5. MM pheon. Legend as last omitting Z, one saltire after each word on obv., two after each on rev., a cross instead of a rose to the left of the mast on rev. Rud. iv. 8. 6. MM Portcullis. Legend as 4, saltires as last. Rud. iv. 9. *MB.*

Henry VII's sovereigns are very rare, a specimen having several times fetched £27 or £30; the ryal is almost unique, but the other coins are common. They were all struck at the Tower of London.

Table of Mint Marks.

	Sovereign	Ryal	Angel	Angelet
Rose and Sun united . .				Evans
Doubtful mint-mark, 3 ropes from stern			Evans	
Rose			+	
Lis upon rose . . .			+	
Heraldic cinquefoil, . .	Evans		+	
Cross fitchee . . .	+	+		
Lis, rev. dragon . . .	+			
Dragon, mullets between the words	+			
No MM, rev. legend as ryals .			+	
Heraldic cinquefoil, rev. escallop, rev. legend as ryals . .			+	
Heraldic cinquefoil, rev. escallop, rosettes between the words on rev.			+	
Escallop, rev. legend as ryals, rosettes between the words .			Evans	
Escallop, rosettes between the words			+	
Cinquefoil, rosettes between the words			+	+
Cinquefoil			+	+
Greyhound's head, rosettes between the words on obv.. .			+	
Greyhound's head . . .			+	+
Greyhound's head, rev. anchor .			+	
Anchor, rev. greyhound's head .			+	
Anchor			+	
Pheon			+	+
Pheon, rev. cross-crosslet, arrow head on rev.			+	
Cross-crosslet, arrow head on both sides			+	
Cross-crosslet			+	
Portcullis			+	+

Henry VIII, 1509 to 1546.

The gold coinage of Henry VIII may be divided into five classes, differing from each other in various particulars of type, weight, and fineness of metal. The first class began at the beginning of his reign; the second in his 18th year, 1526; the third in his 35th year, 1543; the fourth in his 36th year, 1544; and the fifth in his 37th year, 1545.

FIRST COINAGE. This was made by virtue of an

indenture with Lord Mountjoy in the first year of the reign, and was similar in all respects to that of Henry VII, consisting of sovereigns, ryals, angels, and angelets, of the standard fineness, viz., 23 cts. 3½ grs. fine gold to ½ gr. of alloy. A few double sovereigns also exist, but were probably patterns never issued for circulation. The king's titles are King of England and France, and Lord of Ireland.

DOUBLE SOVEREIGN. Probably a pattern. Obv. the king crowned and robed, with long locks, beardless, holding sceptre and globe, seated on a high throne with straight back ornamented with chequers. At the end of each arm is a pillar surmounted by a cross with an ornamental base. Under the king's feet, and dividing the inner circle and the legend, is a portcullis (the well-known badge of the Tudor family), to which is attached a chain ornamented with lis, which surrounds the field. MM lis. Legend HENRICVS ⁑ DEI ⁑ GRACIA ⁑ REX ANGLIE ⁑ ET × FRANC × DNS × HIB × Rev. plain shield bearing the arms of France and England, upon a large double rose, within an ornamented tressure of ten arches, within the inner circle. MM cross-crosslet. IHESVS ⁑ AVTEM ⁑ TRANSIENS ⁑ PER ⁑ MEDIVM ⁑ ILLORVM ⁑ IBAT ⁑ Rud. v. 1. Weight 480 grs. A specimen weighing 788·6 grs. is in the British Museum. Another, weighing 476 grs., was sold at Mr. Dimsdale's sale for £40, and at Mr. Thomas's, in 1844, for £30.

SOVEREIGN. *Value* 20*s*. *Weight* 240 *grs*. 1. Exactly like the double sovereign. *MB*. 2. Same but MM portcullis crowned, and reading TRANCIENS; a plain double tressure of ten arches, the inner one beaded, round the rose on rev., a lion and lis alternately in each arch, two small crosses in each spandril; two saltires after Et and Dns, none after Ibat. (54) *MB*. Both the portcullis and cross-crosslet mintmarks occur on Henry VII's coins, and the former also on the early silver ones of Henry VIII. For this reason we attribute these sovereigns, as well as the double sovereign, to this period; and we give them to Henry VIII, because they resemble his other sovereigns more than those of his father, because we have no other sovereigns to attribute to this coinage, and because the portcullis under the king's feet is common on the coins of Henry VIII, but unknown on those of his father. *Very rare.*

RYAL. *Value* 10*s*. *Weight* 120 *grs*. Obv. king standing, with sword and shield, in a ship, the mast to his right, at right angles to which stretches a yard-arm immediately over his head, three ropes from it to stern, one from mast to prow. A bowsprit extends from the prow to the edge of the coin. The upper part of the side of the ship is ornamented with lions and lis, on the centre of it is a rose, at the stern a banner with the letter h. Legend HENRIC × VIII × DI × GRA × REX × ANGL × Z × FRANC DNS × I × B. Rev. Same type as Edward IV's ryals, MM portcullis crowned, legend IHC × AVT × TRANSIENS ⁑ PER ⁑ MEDIVM ⁑ ILLORVM ⁑ IBAT. (55) *MB. Ext. rare.*

Henry VIII had not the same objection to tracing his title to the throne through his mother, a daughter of Edward IV, as Henry VII had to being thought to depend for a title on his wife, and consequently the son placed the badge of Edward IV, the rose and sun, upon his coins although the father would not. The portcullis MM shows that this coin must belong to this period of his reign.

ANGELS. *Value* 6*s* 8*d*. *Weight* 80 *grs*. Type as the second coinage of Henry VII. One coin, however, omits the rose to the right of the cross on the reverse. 1. MM portcullis crowned. HENRIC × VIII × DI × GRA × REX × AGL × Z × FR.× Rev. PER × CRVCE × TVA × SALVA × NOS × XPE × REDET. *MB.* 2. Same, but omitting the rose at the side of the cross on the reverse, two saltires after Fr, Per, and Cruce. Rud. v. 5. *MB.* 3. Same as 1, but REDE, two saltires after Fr. *MB.* 4. Same as the last, with small annulet also after Fr. *Num. Chron.*, N. S., xii. 187. 5. Same as 1, but FRA, REDE, two saltires after Fra, one before obv. MM, and after Rede. Rud. v. 6. *MB.* 6. As 1, but F, REDE. *MB.* This specimen is countermarked with the arms of Zealand. 7. As 1, but RED, two saltires after Fr. *MB.* 8. As 1, but FRA, RED, saltire before MM on obv. *MB.* 9. Same as last, with saltire also after Red. *MB.* 10. MM castle. Legends as 1, saltire between every word, two after Rex, Fr, Per, and Nos. *MB.* 11. Same, but REDE, only one saltire after Rex, four after Fr, two after Cruce. *MB.* 12. As last, with only two saltires after Fr, one after Salva, two between all the other words on rev. *MB.* 13. As 10, but FRA, REDE, saltire between every word, two after Z and Fra. *MB.* 14. Same as last, with two saltires also after Gra, Rex Per, and Nos, one after Rede. *MB.* 15. As 10, but FRA RED, saltire after every word. *MB.* 16. As 10, but F, REDE, two saltires after F, Per, Nos, and XPE, one after every other word. *MB.* 17. As 10, but ANGL Z F, RED, saltire between each word, two after F and the first five words on rev. *MB.* 18. As 10, but REDE, annulet after Fr, two after Henric, saltire after every other word on obv. and after Salva, two after Fr and between the other words on rev. *Num. Chron.*, N. S., xii. 187. 19. Same, but F, RED, saltire after Red. *Ib.*

These two mint-marks, the portcullis and the castle, both occur on the silver coins of the first coinage, before 1526.

ANGELETS. *Value* 3*s* 4*d.* *Weight* 40 *grs.* Same type as the angels. 1. MM portcullis crowned. HENRIC × VIII × DI × GRA ×REX × AL Z. Rev. O ×× CRVX ×× AVE ×× SPES ×× VNICA. *MB.* 2. MM castle. As 1, but REX× AN, omitting Z, only one saltire after O, two after Unica. Rud. v. 7. 3. MM castle, HENRIC DI GRA REX AGL Z. Saltire after every word on obv. Rev. as 1, two saltires after Unica. (56) *MB.*

SECOND COINAGE, 1526 to 1543. In the years 1522 and 1525, in consequence, it must be presumed, of the insufficiency of the English coinage, several foreign coins both of gold and silver were proclaimed current in England at certain declared values, and it was made penal to refuse them. The gold coins so made current in 1522 were "every ducat large of gold" at 4*s* 6*d*, and "every crown of gold not soleil (*i.e.* not being a French crown of the sun) nor clipped" at 4*s*; and in 1525 were added "every crown soleil, of weight, 4*s* 4*d*; and other crowns named Porpynes, and all other crowns being of like fineness, of weight, as the crowns of the sun be, at 4*s* 4*d* sterling; every piece of fine gold named a Carolus, keeping weight, at 6*s* 10*d*; every piece of base gold, named a florin, keeping weight, at 3*s* 3*d*; every piece of base gold of less quantity, named also a florin, keeping weight, at 2*s* 1*d*." Notwithstanding these proclamations it appears that the amount of gold coin in the kingdom was still insufficient for its wants; and on the 24th July, 1526, a writ was issued to Wolsey, then Lord Chancellor, commanding him to make such alterations in the king's money as might reduce it to an equality with that of foreign countries. The reason of this reduction was stated, in a proclamation of August 22nd, to be that, notwithstanding the law to the contrary, gold was continually transported by the merchants to Flanders and France because it was rated at a higher value there than here. By this proclamation it was ordered that thenceforth the sovereign should be current for 22*s*, the Ryal for 11*s*, the noble (angel) for 7*s* 4*d*, and the fortypenny-piece (angelet) for 3*s* 8*d*; and a new coin, to be called the "Crown of the Rose," introduced in imitation of the French "Crown of the Sun," and of the same fineness and value, was made current for 4*s* 6*d*, to which rating the crown soleil itself was raised. The "single ducat large" of fine gold and due weight was also raised to 4*s* 8*d*, and the double ducat in proportion. These values, however, did not last long, for it was found that the exportation of coin rather increased than diminished, and, as it was thought that this exportation would be stopped by a further increase in the nominal value of the coins, another proclamation was issued on the 5th of November, 1526, by which the sovereign was made current for 22*s* 6*d*; the ryal for 11*s* 3*d*, and the half and quarter in proportion; the angel noble for 7*s* 6*d*, and the half angel for 3*s* 9*d*. Besides the angel noble, there was also ordered to be made another noble, to be called the George noble, which was to be current for 6*s* 8*d*, and a half George noble in proportion; and whereas the "Crown of the Sun," not being an aliquot part of a pound, was inconvenient for calculation, another crown, called the "Crown of the Double Rose," was to be made which should be current for 5*s*; and its half for 2*s* 6*d*. No alteration was made in the values of the Crowns of the Sun and others of the same weight and fineness, but all other foreign gold coin was to cease to be current except as the payer and receiver should agree. By the same proclamation the Tower pound, consisting of 5400 grs., which had always hitherto been used in all Mint calculations, was abolished, and the pound troy, of 5760 grs., substituted for it.

The weight, fineness, and type, therefore, of the gold coins hitherto in use, namely, the sovereign, ryal, angel, and angelet, were to remain as they had been before 1526, the only alteration being that the nominal value of every coin was increased. Of the new coins, the George noble and half noble were to correspond in weight and fineness with the old coins; but the crowns and half-crowns, in order that they might the more nearly resemble the French "crowns of the sun," were to be made of gold of 22 cts. fine only and are the first instance of a gold coin of less than standard fineness in England. The "Crown of the Rose," mentioned in the proclamation of the 22nd August, is not known and was probably never struck, otherwise its name would have occurred in the proclamation of the 5th of November, which declares "Crowns of the Sun," which were of exactly the same value, inconvenient pieces. A double sovereign, apparently of this period, is in the British Museum, but it is believed to be unique, and is probably only a pattern. No ryals or angelets of this period are known, nor any half George nobles, and it is very possible that none were ever struck. Although the weight, fineness, and type of the old denominations of coins remained exactly the same after 1526 as before, yet we are enabled by two principal circumstances to distinguish with some certainty between the coins of the two periods. First, the mint-marks on the gold coins are much the same as those on the silver; and as the silver coins were in 1526 both reduced in weight and altered in type, there is no difficulty in distinguishing between the earlier and later mint-marks of that series. And secondly, some of the crowns, half-crowns, and George nobles have the initial besides that of the king, of Queens Katherine, Anne, and Jane, and the mint-marks which occur upon those pieces are thereby fixed to the dates of those queens.

The king's marriage with Katherine, who was the widow of his brother Arthur, was celebrated in 1509, and was formally decreed by Cranmer to be void in 1533, shortly *after* the king had publicly avowed his marriage with Anne Boleyn, which had taken place in November, 1532. Queen Anne was beheaded on the 19th of May, 1536, and on the next day the king married Jane Seymour. Jane gave birth to Edward VI on Oct. 12th, 1537, and died two days afterwards. In Jan. 1540 the king married, and in July he divorced, Anne of Cleves; on the 8th of August in the same year he married Katherine Howard, who was attainted and beheaded in January, 1541-2; and on the 12th July, 1543, he married Katherine Parr, Lady Latimer.

In 1540 Henry assumed the title of King of Ireland, which was conferred upon him by an Irish statute of that year; but it was not ratified by the English Parliament till 1543, and does not seem to have been adopted on the English coins until that year.

DOUBLE SOVEREIGN. *Pattern.* Exactly like that of the first issue, but MM obv. lis, rev. pheon. Four saltires after Ibat. Wt. 470·1 grs. *Unique?* This was bought by the British Museum for £100. The same mint-marks occur together on a groat of the second coinage, but the pheon also occurs on a groat of the first coinage, and it is therefore probable this piece was struck not long after 1526.

SOVEREIGNS. *Value* 22*s or* 22*s* 6*d. Weight* 240 *grs. Standard fineness.* Type same as before. 1. MM lis. Like (54) but saltire-stops as on the first double sovereign. *MB.* 2. MM lis, rev. arrow. Same as (54) but reading TRANSIENS, with no crosses in the spandrils on the reverse. *MB.* 3. Same, but a single ornamented tressure, without lions or lis, on the reverse, as on the double sovereign. Two saltires before Ihesus, one after Ibat. Rud. v. 2. *MB.* 4. MM sun's rays from beneath a cloud. Same as No. 2, but with small crosses in the spandrils. *MB. All rare.*

ANGELS. *Value* 7*s* 4*d or* 7*s* 6*d. Weight* 80 *grs. Standard fineness.* Type same as before. 1. MM pheon. HENRIC ×× VIII × DI × GRA × REX ×× AGL × Z × F ×× Rev. PER × CRVCE × TVA × SALVA × NOS × XPE × RED. (57) *MB.* 2. MM lis. As 1 but FRA, REDET, one saltire between words on obv., two on rev. *MB.* 3. MM sun's rays from beneath a cloud. HENRIC ×× VIII ×× D ×× G ×× R ×× AGL × Z ×× FRA ×× Rev. as last but REDE. *MB.*

GEORGE NOBLE. *Value* 6*s* 8*d. Weight* $71\frac{1}{9}$ *grs. Standard fineness.* Obv. ship as on the reverse of the angels, but a double rose instead of a shield above it, under the cross; h to the left of the cross, K, for Queen Katherine of Aragon, to the right. Rev. St. George on horseback, piercing the dragon through the mouth with a very long spear, the butt end of which marks the end of the legend. The horse's hind feet also pass through the inner circle and divide the legend. The MM is always a rose. 1. HENRIC × DI × G × R × AGL × Z × FRANC × DNS × HIBERNI. Rev. TALI ⁑ DICA ⁑ SIGNO ⁑ MES ⁑ FLVCTVARI ⁑ NEQVIT. Saltire before the MM on rev. (58) *MB.* 2. HENRIC × D × G × R × AGLIE × Z × FRA × DNS ⁑ HIBERIE. Rev. TALI ⁑ DICATA ⁑ SIG ⁑ MES ⁑ FLVCTVARI ⁑ NEQT. *MB.* 3. HENRIC ⁑ D × G R × AGL × Z × FRANC × DNS × HIBERI. Rev. as 1 but SIG° for signo, saltire before Tali. *MB.* Or HIBER, two saltires between the words, rev. as 2. *EVANS.* 4. As 3, but HIBER, DICATT SIG°, NEQT; two saltires between each ? word. Rud. v. 3. In this plate an R is substituted for K in the field of the obverse. These coins, which are very rare, must have been struck between 1526 when they were first authorized, and 1533 when Queen Katherine of Aragon was divorced; or else in 1541-1542, during the short reign of Queen Katherine Howard. The former, however, is far the more probable, as the rose was an early MM, and it is not likely that the striking of these coins should have been deferred for fifteen years after they were first authorized. Mr. Bergne has pointed out in *Num. Chr.*, N. S., v. 296, that the legend on these nobles is taken from a hymn by Prudentius, written in the latter half of the fourth century, entitled "Hymnus ante somnum," in which we are recommended to make the sign of the cross upon our forehead and our heart when we go to bed, because "tali dicata signo mens fluctuare nescit." The hymn is preserved in a manuscript called the "Liber Benedictionalis," in the Monastery of St. Gall, and is quoted in No. 84 of *The Archæological Journal.*

CROWNS. *Value* 5s. *Weight* 57$\frac{21}{57}$ *grs.* 22 *cts. fine.* Obv. double rose crowned, a letter crowned on each side of it. Rev. Shield of arms crowned. The crowns have a single ornamented arch surmounted by globe and cross. 1. MM rose; h to left, K to right, in the field. HENRIC × VIII × RVTILANS × ROSA ⁑ SIE ⁑ SPIA. Rev. DEI ⁑ G × R × AGLIE × Z × FRANC × DNS × HIBERNI. *MB.*

2. Same, but HIBERNIE, saltire between every word, two after Dei, Aglie, Franc, and Dns. Rud. v. 11. 3. Same as 1, but SINE, AGL, HIBERNIE. One saltire after Henric, R, Dns, and Hibernie, two between the other words. *MB.* 4. Same as 1, but SINE, HIBERIE, saltire before obv. MM, after Henric and VIII, and each side of Z, two between the other words. *MB.* 5. Same as last, but HIBERNIE, saltire before obv. MM and between every word, two after Dei and R. The Ns on this coin are of the Roman, not, as on the former ones, of the old English shape. *MB.* 6. Same as 1, but SINE SPINA, HIBERNIE, one saltire after Rosa and Sine and between each word on obv., two after Rutilans and between each word on rev., Roman Ns. *MB.* 7. MM lis. H and K crowned at sides of shield on rev. as well as of rose on obv. Legends as 1 but HIBERNIE. One saltire after Rosa, Sie, Z, and Franc, two between the other words. English Ns. *MB.* 8. Same as last, but SINE ⁑ SPINA, Rev. DEI ⁑ GRA ⁑ R ⁑ AGL ⁑ Z ⁑ FRANCE ⁑ DNS ⁑ HIBERIE. English Ns on obv., Roman on rev., two saltires between each word. *MB.* 9. Same as 7, but SINE SPINA, one saltire between words on obv., two on rev. Roman Ns on obv., except in king's name, English on rev. *MB.* 10. MM arrow. These all have the English N. Same as 7, but HIBERNI, one saltire after Henric, Franc, and Hiberni, two between the other words. *MB.* 11. MM arrow. H and A, for Anne Boleyn, crowned, at sides of rose on obv. and shield on rev., legends as 1 but SINE, HIBERNIE. Saltire between every word, two after Rutilans, Rosa, Dei, and Hibernie. (59) *MB.* See Rud. v. 12, obv. only. The MM here given is a pheon, but this is probably a mistake, as the pheon MM does not seem to have been used as late as Queen Anne's time. 12. MM arrow, h and K crowned at sides of rose on obv., h and I, for Jane Seymour, crowned at sides of shield on rev., legends as 1 but SPI, HIBERNIE, saltire between every word, two after Dei. This has an obverse of the time of

Queen Katherine, before 1533, joined to a reverse of Queen Jane, 1536-7. *MB.* 13. Same as last but I instead of K at side of rose on obv., legends as 1 but HIBERNIE, saltire between each word. Rud. v. 10. *MB.* 14. Legends transposed, the king's name being on the shield side, as on the half-crowns, instead of on the rose side as on the other crowns. MM arrow. H and R (for Rex) crowned at sides of shield on obv. and of rose on rev. Legends HENRIC. D. G. RVTILANS. ROSA. SINE SP Rev. .DEI. GRA. AGL. FRA. Z. HIB. REX. *EVANS.* This coin must have been struck in 1543, after the English Parliament had had ratified the title of King of Ireland, although Henry's marriage with Katherine Parr on the 12th of July in that year had then already taken place, and therefore her initial might have been placed upon the coin.

HALF CROWNS. *Value 2s 6d. Weight* $28\frac{13}{19}$ *grs. 22 cts. fine.* Obv. like the reverse of the crowns. Rev. like the obverse of the crowns, but the letters at each side of the rose are not crowned. 1. MM rose on obv. only. HENRIC ×× 8 ×× DI ×× G ×× R ×× AGL ×× Z ×× FRA. Rev. RVTILANS ×× ROSA ×× SINE ×× SPINA × h and K at sides of rose. *MB.* 2. Same, but MM both sides. *MB.* 3. As 2, but reading HENRIC × 8 × DI × GRA × REX ×× AGL × Z ×× F. *THORBURN.* 4. MM lis, rev. rose. Same as 1 but h and K at sides of shield as well as of rose, only one saltire between words on obv. *MB.* 5. Same but FRAC, SPIA, two saltires after Z. *MB.* 6. MM lis. Legends as 1, h and K at sides of rose. One saltire after Henric, none after R or Fra, two after every other word. Rud. v. 8. 7. MM arrow, on both sides. Same as 1, but h and I at sides of rose and of shield, FRANC, two saltires after Z, only one between the other words on obv. (60) *MB.* 8. Same as last, but obv. legend HENRIC × 8 × D × GRA × REX ×× AGL × Z × FR. *MB.*

THIRD COINAGE, 1543. In this year a new indenture was made with the master of the mint, by which the fineness of the coins was reduced to 23 carats fine gold and 1 carat alloy. A lb. troy of this metal was to be coined into £28. 16*s* by tale. The new sovereigns were to be current for 20*s*, half-sovereigns (now first substituted for ryals) for 10*s*, angels for 8*s*, angelets for 4*s*, and quarter angels (now first coined) for 2*s*. The coinage of pieces of other denominations seems to have been stopped.

In 1544 the standard of fineness was still further debased, and the weight of the coins was lowered, making the sovereign weigh 192 grs., and the other coins in proportion. But unfortunately, while it is difficult to tell the fineness of the metal of a coin without assaying it, and consequently we cannot separate the coins of the two years by this test, the weight was so inaccurately adjusted during these last years of Henry VIII and during the reign of Edward VI that it, too, is but a very uncertain guide to the classification of the coins. The mode of arrangement we have adopted, therefore, is to assign to this third coinage all those pieces, whatever their weight, which have a lis for their mint-mark, as that is the only mint-mark used on the angel, angelet, and quarter angel, which pieces were not coined after 1543; and to give to the coinages of 1544 and 1545 those pieces which have the same mint-marks as the crown and half-crown, which were coined in those years but not in the preceding one.

SOVEREIGNS. *Value* 20*s*. *Weight* 200 *grs*. *Fineness* 23 *carats*. 1. Obv. like the former sovereigns, but the king's figure is different; he wears a short beard and a ruff, and the chain round the field is somewhat different. A rose instead of the portcullis is under the king's feet, and there are no lis on the inner circle. MM lis. HENRIC × 8 × DI × GRA × ANGLIE ×× FRANCIE × ET × HIBE × REX × Saltire before MM. Rev. Shield of arms crowned, supported by lion and dragon, the former crowned, tablet below inscribed HR in monogram. MM lis. IHESVS × AVTEM × TRANCIENS × PER × MEDIVM × ILLORV × IBAT. Rud. vi. 1. *MB*. Wt. 190·4 grs. 2. Type of obv. different; the king wears a long beard, the back of the throne is curved, there is a bird with expanded wings instead of a cross above the arms of the throne, and no chain round the field. Otherwise as last. MM lis. HENRIC 8 DI GRA ANGL FRANCIE Z HIBERN REX. Rev. IHS AVTEM TRANSIENS PER MEDIVM ILLORVM IBAT. Trefoil after each word on obv., two between words on rev., one after Ibat. (61) *MB.* Wt. 188·4 grs. 3. Same but AGL, HIBER. Rev. IHS. AVTEM TRANCIENS PER MEDIV ILLORV IBAT. Two trefoils after 8 and the last four words on obv., one after the others; two after first three words on rev., one after the last three. *MB.* Wt. 189·2 grs. 4. Similar, but the king has his head on one side, and the rose under his feet is smaller and does not divide the legend. MM WS in monogram, with two cinquefoils on obv., one on rev., and cinquefoil between every word. HENRIC 8 DEI GRA AGL FRAN Z HIB REX. Rev. IHS AVTEM TRANSIENS PERMEDIVM ILLOR IBAT. *MB.* Wt. 199·5 grs. This coin was no doubt struck at Bristol, as the MM, which consists of the initials of Sir William Sharington, master of the mint there, occurs on the silver coins of that place only. It is assigned to this rather than to the fourth or fifth coinages on account of its weight, which so far exceeds 192 grs., the authorized weight of the later sovereigns. *All rare.*

HALF-SOVEREIGNS. These all appear from their mint-marks to belong to the later coinages, although there are some that weigh more than 96 grs., the proper weight of those coinages.

ANGELS. *Value* 8*s.* *Weight* 80 *grs.* *Fineness* 23 *cts.* Type as before. MM lis. HENRIC × 8 × D × G × AGL × FRA × Z × HIB × REX × Rev. PER × CRVCE × TVA × SALVA × NOS × XPE × REDE × Annulet to left of angel's head and on side of ship. Rud. vi. 6. *MB.* Or reading PEER, RED, and with two saltires after Rex, Peer, and Nos. (62) *MB.* These are attributed to this coinage, instead of the previous one, because they have the title of

King of Ireland, which does not seem to have been assumed in England till it was granted by the English Parliament in 1543. The weight is the same as in the former coinages, and angels do not appear to have been coined in 1544 or 1545, when the weight was reduced.

ANGELETS. *Value* 4*s*. *Weight* 40 *grs*. *Fineness* 23 *cts*. Type as the angels. MM lis. HENRIC × 8 × D × G × AGL × FR × Z × HIB × REX. Rev. O ° CRVX ° AVE ° SPES ° VNICA° Annulet on side of ship. Rud. vi. 7. *MB*. 39·6 grs.

QUARTER ANGELS. *Value* 2*s*. *Weight* 20 *grs*. *Fineness* 23 *cts*. Type as the angels. 1. MM lis. HENRICVS × VIII × DEI × GRA × AGLIE. Rev. FRANCIE ⁑ ET ⁑ HIBERNIE × REX. Rud. vi. 9. *MB*. Wt. 19·8 grs. 2. Same but DI, a single saltire after every word. (63) *MB*. Wt. 18·7 grs. 3. MM lis, legend on both sides as obv. of 1, but DI; h and rose at sides of cross on rev. omitted, but small R at right of cross, saltire after every? word except the last on rev. Rud. vi. 8. The figure of the angel on the last two of these is slightly different from that on the first. *All very rare*.

FOURTH COINAGE, 1544. FIFTH COINAGE, 1545. Another indenture, of 1544, further reduced the standard to 22 cts. fine and 2 cts. alloy, and a lb. troy of this metal was to be coined into £30 by tale. The coins specified in this indenture are sovereigns, half-sovereigns, crowns, and half-crowns. In 1545 the metal was still further debased to to 20 cts. fine and 4 cts. alloy, the lowest state of degradation which it has ever reached in England. No other difference was, as far as we know, made in the coins in this latter year, and we are therefore unable to separate them from those of 1544. We have already pointed out that the weight of the coins of these two years was so inaccurately adjusted that it forms no guide for distinguishing them from those of the third coinage, and that we assign to these years the crowns and half-crowns, which denominations were not struck in 1543, and such sovereigns and half-sovereigns as seem by their mint-marks to be contemporaneous with them.

SOVEREIGNS. *Value* 20*s*. *Weight* 192 *grs*. *Fineness* 22 *or* 20 *cts*. 1. Like No. 2 of the third coinage but MM annulet enclosing pellet, rev. lis. AGL, HIBER. Rev. IHS AVTEM TRANCIENS PERMEDIV ILLORV IBAT. One trefoil after Di, Gra, and Francie, and the last three words on rev., two after the other words on obv., and the first three on rev. *MB*. 2. Type as the last. MM S. HENRIC 8 DI GRA AGL FRANCIE Z HIBERN REX. Rev. IHS AVTEM TRANSIENS PERMEDIVM ILLOR IBAT. Trefoil between every word and after Ibat, two after 8, Agl, Z, Autem, Transiens, and Medium. Rud. vi. 10. *MB*. Wt. 193·7, or 189·8 grs. 3. Type as the last, struck at Bristol. MM WS in monogram, on obv. only. FRANCI Z HIBER, ILLOR. Trefoil after Henric, Di, and Gra, none after Agl, two between all the other words, two quatrefoils after Rex. *THORBURN*. Wt. 184½ grs.

HALF SOVEREIGNS. *Value* 10*s*. *Weight* 96 *grs*. *Fineness* 22 *or* 20 *cts*. 1. Type like No. 2 sovereign of the third coinage. MM annulet enclosing pellet. HENRIC 8 DI GRA AGL FRANCIE Z HIBERNIE REX. Rev. IHS AVTEM TRANCIENS PER MEDIVM ILLORVM IBA. The stops on both sides are only dots. *MB*. 94·3 grs. See Rud. vi. 11, which reads TRANSIENS. 2. Same, but HIBERN, TRANSIENS, IBAT. *MB*. 94·6 grs.; or HIBERNI. *MB*. 94·7 grs. 3. MM as 1. HENRIC 8 D G AGL FRANCI Z HIB REX. Rev. IHS AVTEM TRANSIE PERMEDI ILLOR IBA. Saltire stops on obv., trefoil on rev. *MB*. 4. MM as 1. HENRIC 8 D G AGL FRANCI Z HIB REX. Rev. IHS AVTE TRANSI PERMEDI ILLOR IBAT. Trefoil after each word on obv. and after Aute and Transi, two after 8, Agl, Ihs, and Illor. *MB*. 97 grs. 5. Similar to last but

TRANSIENS, 96 grs., or FRANCIE, TRANSIENS, MEDIV, 97 grs. *Num. Chron.*, N. S., xii. 187. 6. As 4, but FRANCIE, TRANSIENS; trefoil-shaped stops. *MB*. 7. As last, with annulet on inner circle on obv. under Ǝ in Rex, and on rev. under B in Ibat. *MB*. 8. As 4, but FRANCIE, TRANSIE PER MEDIVM ILLORV. Trefoil between each word, two after Medium and Illoru. Annulet on inner circle on obv. under X in Rex, and on rev. under I in Ibat. (64) *MB*. 9. As 4, but FRANCIE, ILLO. Trefoils between words on both sides, two after Henric, 8, Agl, Hib, and Illo. Annulet on inner circle on rev. under T in ibat. *MB*. 10. As 4, but MM S, FRANCIE, TRANSIE, trefoil between every word, two after Rex, one after Ibat. *MB*. 94·4 grs. 11. Same, but MEDIV. Trefoil between every word, two after 8, Agl, Francie, and Hib, one after Rex. Ǝ below shield. *MB*. 12. As 10, but FRANCI, TRANSIENS, PERMEDIV. Trefoil after every word and before Ihs, three after Agl, two after Transiens and Mediu. Ǝ under shield. *MB*. 13. As 10, but TRASIENS, Ǝ under shield, trefoil after every word on obv. and after Aute, two after 8, Agl, Francie, Hib, Trasiens, and Medi. *MB*. 95 grs. 14. MM as 10, legends as 4 but TRANSIENS, Ǝ under shield, saltire between every word on obv., two after Henric, 8, Agl, and Rex; trefoil between every word on rev. *MB*. Or TRANSIE PERMEDIV, saltire between every word on obv., two after 8, saltire after Ihs, trefoil after Transie, Mediu and Illor. *THORBURN*. 15. MM as 10, legends as 4 but TRANSIENS, Ǝ under shield, saltire after rev. MM, and after words on each side, two before Henric and after 8, Agl, Rex, Transiens and Illor. *MB*. 16. As 10, but the king has no sceptre, Ǝ under shield, FRANCI, TRANSIENS. Trefoil before obv. MM and after each word on obv., two before franci, saltire between each word on rev. *MB*. 94½ grs. 17. Type as 1, MM obv. S rev. Ǝ ?, Ǝ under shield, legends as 4 but FRANCIE, TRANSIENS, saltire after 8, D, G, Z, Aute, Transiens, and Ibat. *Num.*

Chron., N. S., xii. 188. 93¼ grs. 18. Type as 1, MM Є, Є under shield, legends as last but HIBERN. Small mascle after Z, two between the other words on obv. Stops on rev. doubtful. *MB.* 94½ grs. 19. Same, but IBA, mascles for stops on rev. *MB.* 20. Type as 1, MM WS in monogram on obv. only, legends as 17, trefoil after every word, two after 8, Francie, and Z. No letter under shield. *MB.* This, from its MM, was struck at Bristol. See p. 94.

The above coins present but little difficulty except from the variations in their weights; but there is another series of half-sovereigns which must evidently, from their general resemblance and their mint-marks, have immediately succeeded these, but which, together with the name of Henry VIII, bear the portrait of a decidedly youthful king, the same portrait indeed as appears on the half-sovereign of Edward VI, Rud. vii. 3. The mint-marks on these coins, as well as some on the previous series, are the same as on the crowns and half-crowns bearing the name of Henry VIII. It seems very strange that a young face should be substituted for an old one on the latest coins of Henry VIII, and Mr. Evans has therefore suggested that the coins which bear this young face must have been struck under Edward VI, notwithstanding that his father's name was still used. This supposition appears the more probable when we consider the unlikelihood of so great a variety of mint-marks, no less than six altogether, having been used on the same denomination of coin during the two years that elapsed between the issuing of the coinage of 1544 and the king's death; and, moreover, upon the contrary supposition, there must have been almost a cessation of coinage for a time after the accession of Edward VI, as all the early coins bearing the name of that monarch are extremely rare. Such an appropriation, however, would necessitate also the removal to Edward VI of the crowns and half-crowns bearing the same mint-marks as these half-sovereigns, and also of the corresponding silver coins; and in the absence of any explanation of the reasons which could have caused the retention of Henry's name on the coins after there had been time to engrave a portrait of Edward, we do not think that the evidence is sufficient to justify us in making such a change. We will therefore proceed to describe these coins as we find them, as belonging to the coinages of the last two years of Henry VIII.

21. King's face young, beardless, small ruff, fur collar to robe, rose under feet not dividing the legend. Throne very different to the former ones, back round, not chequered, a winged figure standing on the arms of the throne, the legs like those of a chair, not column-shaped. Otherwise like the last half-sovereigns. No MM on obv., S ? on rev. No letter under the shield on rev. HENRIC 8 D G AGL FRAN Z HIB REX. Rev. IHS AVTE TRANSIEN PER MEDI ILLOR IBAT. Diamond-shaped stops between the words on obv., none on rev. *Num. Chron.*, N. S., xii. 188. 91½ grs., or TRANSIE, diamond-shaped stops on both sides, the rev. MM probably intended for an E. *THORBURN*. 22. Type as the last, MM on both sides E, E under the shield, legends as last, but FRANC, AVTEM TRANSIENS. Diamond-shaped stop before Henric and Ihs, and after Henric, Franc, and Z, and each word on rev., two after the other words on obv. *MB.* 92·2 grs. 23. Same, but DEI GRA, FRA. Rud. vi. 2. 85½ grs. Or with the E under the shield reversed, *Num. Chron.*, N. S., xii. 188, 96 grs. 24. As 21, with no MM on obv., E on rev., E under the shield, FRA, TRANSIE, IBA. Diamond-shaped stop between each word on obv., except after Z, three after 8, one ? between each word on rev. *MB.* 96·4 grs. 25. Type as 21, no MM on obv., E ? on rev., HENRIC 8 D G ANGL FRANC Z HIBER REX. Rev. IHS AVTEM TRANSIENS PER MEDIVM ILLOR IBAT. E under the shield. Small pierced cross after Angl, Z, Hiber, and Rex, and after the F in Franc, small saltire between the other words and after Ibat. *MB.* 99 grs. 26. Same as

23 but no MM, K under shield. Rud. vi. 12, obv. only. *Num. Chron.*, N. S., xii. 188. 87½ to 93½ grs. 27. Type as 21. MM arrow. HENRIC 8 D G ANGL FRANC E HIBER REX. Mascle before Henric and after each word except E and Hiber, two after Angl. Rev. legend as 25, small cross after Autem and Ibat. *Ib.* 93 to 97 grs. 28. Obv. as last. Rev. MM as last, IHS AVTE TRANSIE PER MEDI ILLOR IBAT, no stops. *Ib.* 93½ grs. 29. Type and MM as 27. HENRIC 8 D G AGL FRAN Z HIB REX. Rev. legend as last. Mascle after every word, two after 8, three after Rex. (65) *MB.* 94·2 grs. The reverse of this coin has been double struck. Or reading FRANC, AVTEM TRANSIENS, mascle after every word except Per, two after Agl and Rex. *THORBURN.* 30. Type and MM as 27, HENRIC 8 DEI GRA AGL FRA Z HIB REX. Rev. as 28, but AVTEM TRANSIENS. Diamonds between the words. *Num. Chron.*, N.S., xii. 189. 91 grs. 31. Type as 21, MM grappling iron. Obv. legend as last. Rev. IHS AVTE TRANSIEN PER MEDIV ILLO IBAT. Dot after each word except Per. Grappling iron below shield on rev. *Ib.* 96½ grs. 32. Same, but MM on obv. only. HENRIC. 8 : D. G. AGL. FRA. Z. HIB. REX; Rev. IHS. AVTE TRANSIE. PER. MEDI. ILLOR. IBA. *MB.* 33. Type as 21. MM martlet. Legends as last but AVTEM TRANSIENS, IBAT. Dot between each word and after Ibat, two after 8. *MB.* 34. Same but FRANCI, small annulet after 8, D, and G. *Num. Chron.*, N. S., xii. 188. 95¾ grs. 35. As 33, but DEI GRA, AVT, MEDIV ILLO. *Ib.* 93 grs. 36. Type as 21. MM lis. HENRIC. 8 : D. G : AGL. FRANCIE : Z : HIB : REX : Rev. IHS. AVTEM : TRANSIENS : PERMEDI ILLO. IBAT *MB.*

CROWNS. *Value* 5*s.* *Weight* 48 *grs.* *Fineness* 22 *or* 20 *cts.* Type as those of the second coinage, with h and R crowned on each side of the rose on obv. and of the shield on rev. 1. MM annulet enclosing pellet. HENRIC 8

ROSA SINE SPINE. Rev. DEI GRA AGL FRA ET HIB REX. Trefoil before Henric and after Fra, none after Hib, two after every other word. *MB.* 2. MM martlet. HENRIC 8 RVTLANS ROSA SIN SP. Rev. DEI GRA AGL FRA Z HIB REX. *MB.* Wt. 47·2 grs. 3. Obv. MM pierced trefoil? HENRIC 8 ROSA SINE SPINE ⁑ Ornamented cross and four saltires after Rosa and Sine. Rev. MM WS in monogram. D. G. ANGLIE FRA. Z. HIB. REX × Ornamented cross and two saltires after Anglie. *MB.* Wt. 47·8 grs. 4. MM WS in monogram on rev. only, legends as the last, quatrefoil after MM and after Sine, Spine, and Anglie, lis after Rosa, trefoil after Henric, Fra Z, and Hib. Rud. vi. 5. 5. MM obv. cinquefoil, rev. WS in monogram, legends as 3 but HENRICVS. Quatrefoil after Rosa and after rev. MM, pierced cross after Sine and Anglie, slipped trefoil each side of Z, small annulet before Henricus. (66) *MB.* Wt. 48·1 grs. 6. MM's as last. HENRIC VIII ROSA SINE SPINA. Quatrefoil after VIII. Rev. D. G. ANGL. FRANC. Z. HIB. REX, quatrefoil after Angl and Rex. *THORBURN.* Wt. 47 grs. This is the only coin of the last years of the reign which has VIII instead of 8. The WS shows that the last four of these coins were struck at Bristol. See *ante*, p. 94.

HALF - CROWNS. *Value* 2*s* 6*d.* *Weight* 24 *grs. Fineness* 22 *or* 20 *cts.* Type as those of the second coinage, with H and R at the sides both of the shield and of the rose, but on two coins the king's name is on the rose side instead of the shield side. The stops are generally mere dots between the words. 1. MM annulet enclosing pellet, king's name on shield side. HENRIC 8 D G AGL FR Z HB REX. Rev. RVTILANS ⁑ ROSA ⁑ SINE ⁑ SPINA. (67) *MB.* 2. Same, but HIB, omitting REX; SPI; mascles instead of saltires on both sides; the Ns are of the Roman shape. *MB.* 3. MM Є, followed by a small quatrefoil. King's name on the rose side. HENRIC 8 ROSA SINE SPI. Rev. DEI GRA ANG FRA Z HIB REX. Stops doubtful.

MB. 4. Same, but SPIN, AGL. *MB.* 5. MM E on obv. only. As 1, but AG FRA Z HIB, SP. No saltires. The Ns on this and the two next coins are of the Roman, not the English, shape. *MB.* 6. MM E on rev. only?, legends as 1 but SPI, no saltires. Rud. vi. 4. 7. MM arrow, legends as 1 but AG FR Z HIB, SP. The stops between the words are small mascles. *EVANS.* 8. Same, but HI. *MB.* 9. MM arrow. H. D. G. RVTILANS. ROSA SINE SP. Rev. RVTILANS. ROSA : SINE SP The stops are small mascles. Rud. v. 13. Pembroke collection. 10. MM WS in monogram on rev. only. As 1, but ANG FR Z HIB. Two saltires after Rutilans only. Rud. vi. 3. *MB.* 11. Same, but SPI, two saltires between each word on rev. *MB.* The two last were struck at Bristol by Sir Wm. Sharington. *All rare.*

Besides the mint at the Tower, at which the great majority of the coins were struck, Henry VIII had a royal mint, separate from the ecclesiastical one, at Canterbury; in or about the year 1543 he re-established one at Bristol, and in 1545 at York; but the patent for the coinage at this latter city was confined to silver coins, and this was very likely the case at Canterbury also. The ecclesiastical mints, which were at Canterbury, York, and Durham, never struck gold coins. Some, however, were struck at Bristol, and are distinguishable by having for their mint-mark WS, the initials of Sir W. Sharington, master of the Bristol mint. A mint also existed at Southwark in the first year of Edward VI, and perhaps in the last years of Henry VIII, but no coins struck here in Henry's reign have yet been distinguished.

TABLE OF MINT MARKS.

	Double Sov.	Sov.	Ryal.	½ Sov.	Angel.	George Noble.	Crown.	Angelet.	½ Crown.	¼ Angel
1ST COINAGE, 1509.										
Lis, rev. cross-crosslet .	+	+								
Portcullis . . .		+	+		+			+		
Castle					+			+		
2ND COINAGE, 1526.										
Pheon					+					
Rose with K in field . .						+	+		+	
Lis, rev. pheon . .	+									
Lis, rev. rose, K in field .									+	
Lis		+			+					
Lis with K in field . .							+		Rud.	
Lis, rev. arrow . .		+								
Arrow with K in field .							+			
,, ,, A ,, .							+			
,, ,, K and I in field .							+			
,, ,, I ,, .							+		+	
,, ,, R ,, .							Evans			
Sun's rays and cloud . .		+			+					

Table of Mint Marks—*continued.*

	Double Sov.	Sov.	Ryal.	½ Sov.	Angel.	George Noble.	Crown.	½ George Noble.	Angelet.	½ Crown.	¼ Angel.
3rd Coinage, 1543.											
Lis		+ +									+
,, with annulet on side of ship					+				+		
WS		+									
4th and 5th Coinages, 1544, 1545.											
Annulet enclosing pellet, rev. lis		+									
Annulet enclosing pellet				+			+			+	
Same with annulet on inner circle on both sides				+							
Same with annulet on inner circle on rev.				+							
S		+		+							
,, with E under shield				+							
,, rev. E:E under shield				*NC*							
E with E under shield on ½ sov.				+						+	
WS on obv. only		Th.		+							

Table of Mint Marks—*continued.*

	Double Sov.	Sov.	Ryal.	½ Sov.	Angel.	George Noble.	Crown.	½ George Noble.	Angelet.	½ Crown.	¼ Angel.
With Young Face on ½ Sovs.											
S ? on rev. only				*NC*							
E on obv. only										+	
E, E under shield				+							
E on rev. only, E under shield on ½ sov.				+						Rud.	
No MM, K under shield				*NC*							
Arrow				+						+	
Grappling iron				+							
Martlet				+			+				
Lis				+							
Trefoil rev. WS,							+				
WS on rev. only							Rud.			+	
Cinquefoil rev. WS							+				

N.C.—*Numismatic Chronicle*, N. S., xii. 188, 189.

Edward VI, 1546 to 1553.

Edward VI came to the throne on the 28th of January, 1546-7, and although he only reigned six and a half years, no fewer than four distinct series of gold coins were issued during his reign. By the indentures of his first year made with the masters of the mints of Southwark, Canterbury, and the Tower, the money was to remain of the same weight and fineness as the last coinage of his father, in his 37th year. The Bristol mint also continued to be worked at this time, but perhaps only silver money was issued from it, for in the conviction of Sir W. Sharington, the master of the mint, in 1548, for having there in the first year of the king counterfeited £12,000 of coins resembling the Testoons (shillings), no mention is made of gold coins. Nor do we know of any gold coins having been issued at this time from the Southwark or Canterbury mints. Sharington's crime was that he coined money for the use of Lord Seymour, the Lord High Admiral. He confessed it, and was pardoned. His counterfeit coins are not known.

No sovereigns of the first coinage are believed to exist.

HALF-SOVEREIGNS. *Value* 10*s*. *Weight* 96 *grs*. *Fineness* 20 *cts*. Type like the latest half-sovereigns of Henry VIII. The king in robes, with crown with a single arch, seated on throne with plain round back which reaches up to his head, the sides of the back fluted, the figure of an angel on each arm of the throne, the king's hands resting on his knees, sceptre in his right hand, orb in his left, rose under his feet. Rev. plain square shield bearing the arms of France and England quarterly, supported by lion and dragon, the former crowned, a crown above the shield with one ornamented arch surmounted by orb and cross. Under the shield a tablet which is inscribed HR, showing that the reverse dies for these coins were made under Henry VIII.
1. MM E. EDWARD. 6 D G AG FRAN Z HIB REX. Rev. IHS AVTEM TRANSIENS PERMEDI ILLOR IBAT. E under shield. Mascle after every word except

Ag, two after Edward, three after Rex. (68) *MB.* Wt. 95.9 grs. 2. Same but AVTE TRANSIE. Є under shield. No mascle after Ihs or Ibat. *MB.* 3. As No. 1 but rev. legend as 2, no letter under shield, mascle before rev. MM and after Per. *MB.* 4. MM arrow. Large cross above king's crown. Legends as 2. Mascle after Edward and every word on rev., two after every other word on obv. *MB.* Wt. 86·3 grs. See Rud. vii. 3, which, however, has the tablet inscribed ER, and reads MED for Medi.

CROWN. *Value* 5*s.* *Weight* 48 *grs.* *Fineness* 20 *cts.* Type like those of Henry VIII. Obv. rose crowned, between E and R each crowned. Rev. shield with arms, crowned, between letters crowned. 1. MM obv. arrow, rev. annulet enclosing pellet. RVTILANS ROSA SINE SPINE. Rev. DEI GRA AGL FRA Z HIB REX. h and R, each crowned, on each side of the shield. Two mascles after each word on obv., seven after spine. (69) *MB.* Wt. 46 grs. The obverse and reverse are transposed in the plate. 2. Obv. from the same die as the last. Rev. MM arrow. EDWARD 6 D G AG FR Z HIB REX. E and R, each crowned, on each side of the shield. Mascle after Rex, two after every other word. Wt. 48 grs. These two coins are believed to be unique. Both belonged to Capt. Murchison, and are described by him in *Num. Chron.*, xx. 187. The former is in bad condition, and it is not quite as clear on the coin as it is represented in the plate whether the distinguishing letter at the side of the rose on the obverse is an E or an h, while it is clear that that on the reverse is an h, and that the reverse die therefore was engraved under Henry VIII; but Capt. Murchison expressly states that the obverses of the two coins are from the same die, and when they appeared at his sale in 1864 it is evident that no doubt was entertained of their both belonging to Edward VI, as the former was bought for £50 for the British Museum, and the latter (which we have not seen) fetched as much as £83.

HALF-CROWNS. *Value* 2*s* 6*d*. *Weight* 24 *grs*. *Fineness* 20 *cts*. Type like the crowns, but the crown over the rose on obv. is much smaller, and the letters E and R which are on each side of the rose on obv. and of the shield on rev. are not crowned. MM arrow. RVTILANS ROSA SINE SPINE. Rev. EDWARD 6 D G AG FR Z HI REX. Rud. vii. 13. *MB*. Wt. 22 grs. *Ext. rare.*

SECOND COINAGE. On the 24th Jan., 1548, it was declared by proclamation that the king had caused new coins of gold and silver to be made at the same values as the last issue. In this proclamation no mention is made of an improvement in the standard, and it may therefore refer only to a new issue of coins identical with those already in circulation. Several patterns for coins of various types were however made in and about this year. (See Rud. vii. 7, 11, 12, 14; viii. 3; *Num. Chron.* xx. 188.) And by an indenture of the year 1549 the fineness of the coins was somewhat improved by being restored to that established in 1544, though at the same time they were considerably reduced in weight. The lb. of gold of 22 cts. fine and 2 cts. alloy was now to be coined into £34 by tale, into sovereigns at 20*s* a piece, and crowns at 5*s*, with their halves. In the same year the French Crowns of the Sun, which had been made current by Henry VIII at 4*s* 6*d*, were on the 1st Aug. raised to 7*s*, and on the 1st Dec. reduced to 6*s* 4*d*. The pieces which remain to us of this coinage are as follows:—

TREBLE SOVEREIGN. *Value* £3. *Weight* $508\frac{4}{17}$ *grs*. *Fineness* 22 *cts*. SOUTHWARK. Type like the last half-sovereigns, except that the king has no robes, and holds a sword instead of a sceptre in his right hand. The back of the throne is chequered, and there is no rose under the king's feet. There are scroll ornaments round the tablet under the shield on the reverse, which is inscribed ER. MM on both sides y, for Sir John Yorke, master of the mint at Southwark. Legends EDWARD VI DEI

GRA AGL FRAN ET HIBER REX. Rev. IHS AVTEM TRANSIENS PERMEDI ILLOR IBAT. Rud. vii. 1. *MB.* Wt. 505 grs. It is probable that this is only a pattern, as there is no reason to suppose that coins of this denomination were made current in this reign.

SOVEREIGN. *Value* £1. *Weight* $169\frac{7}{17}$ *grs. Fineness* 22 *cts.* LONDON. Same as the £3 piece but MM arrow, which seems to be the mark of Sir Martin Bowes, master of the mint in the Tower of London from the 18th year of Henry VIII, and in the first year of Edward VI. It does not clearly appear when he ceased to hold that office, but it was probably about the third year of Edward VI, when we find some other persons named as Commissioners for performing its duties. The arrow appears to have been adopted by him in reference to his own name. Legends as £3 piece but HIB, MEDIVM. *MB.* Wt. 168·2 grs. Or with no MM on obv., FRANCI ET HIB, PER MEDIV ILLORV. (70) *MB.* Wt. 167½ grs.

SOUTHWARK. Same as the £3 piece in all respects. *MB.* Wt. 171·3 grs. Or with the back of the throne raised higher than the king's head, EDWARD VI D G AGL FRAN ET HIB REX, cinquefoil after Rex. Otherwise as the £3 piece. Rud. vii. 2. *MB.* Wt. 169 grs.

HALF-SOVEREIGN. *Value* 10*s.* *Weight* $84\frac{12}{17}$ *grs. Fineness* 22 *cts.* LONDON. 1. Obv. Bust in profile to right, uncrowned, young face, very short hair, plain armour. MM arrow. SCVTVM FIDEI PROTEGET EVM. Rose after each word. Rev. Oval shield crowned and garnished, between E R. MM arrow. EDWARD VI D G AGL FRA Z HIB REX. Diamond-shaped stops between the words. *MB.* Wt. 83·2 grs. 2. Same, but MM the figure 6. *MB.* (71) This MM has sometimes been called a bow. 3. Same as 1, but the king's head crowned and the legends transposed. *MB.* Wt. 82·8 grs. 4. Same as 3, but the king's crown is larger, cinquefoils rather than roses after each word on rev., one before Scutum. *MB.* Wt., though in fair preservation, only 76·7 grs. 5. As 3, but MM swan, perhaps in reference to the armorial bearings of Sir M. Bowes, slight drapery over armour on breast, cinquefoils rather than roses between the words on rev., none after Eum. *MB.* Wt. 82·9 grs. 6. As 3, but MM grappling iron, slight drapery as on the last coin, rose after each word on both sides. *MB.* Wt. 79·7 grs. It does not appear what this MM refers to, but it occurs also on one of the latest half-sovereigns of Henry VIII with the young portrait. 7. Same as 3, but with MM martlet on both sides, and dots between the words. *EVANS.* Wt. 83 grs.

SOUTHWARK. Same as London No. 1 but MM Y, for Sir John Yorke. *MB.* Wt. 81 grs. Or with no rose after Eum, Rud. vii. 8. *MB.* Wt. 81·2 grs. Or with head crowned, as London No. 3, with rose before Scutum and after every word on rev. *MB.* Rud. vii. 4, where the rose after Eum is omitted.

CROWNS. *Value* 5*s.* *Weight* 42$\frac{6}{17}$ *grs.* *Fineness* 22 *cts.* LONDON. With uncrowned head, same as No. 1 half-sovereign of this coinage, but MM arrow on obv. only, FR for Fra, diamond-shaped stops on both sides, no roses. *MB.* Wt. 39·7 grs. Or with crowned head, same as No. 3 half-sovereign of this coinage, rose after Scutum and Fidei only. (72) *MB.* Wt. 41½ grs.

SOUTHWARK. With uncrowned head, same as the London crown but MM Y. Rud. vii. 9. Or reading FRA. *MB.* Wt. 41½ grs. With crowned head, same as No. 3 half-sovereign of this coinage, but MM Y, PROTEG for Proteget, diamond-shaped stops both sides, no roses. Rud. vii. 5. *MB.* Wt. 40·8 grs. Or with MM Y on obv. only, omitting ER, and reading PROTEGET. *THORBURN.* Or with rev. MM y, legend SCVTV FIDEI PROTEGET EVM. Rose after Scutu. *MB.* Wt. 41·9 grs.

HALF-CROWNS. *Value* 2*s* 6*d.* *Weight* 21$\frac{3}{17}$ *grs.* *Fineness* 22 *cts.* LONDON. Bust with uncrowned head, as No. 1 half-sovereign of this coinage, MM arrow, SCVTVM

FIDEI PROTEGET EVM. Rev. as same but omitting ER at sides of shield, no MM, EDWAR VI D G AGL FR Z H R. Diamond-shaped stops on both sides. Rud. vii. 10. *MB*. Wt. 20·3 grs. With crowned head, MM arrow, EDWARD VI D G AG FR Z HI REX. Rev. as last but SCVTVM FIDEI PROTEGET EVM. Stops as last. *MB*. Wt. 20·7 grs., or reading PROTE. Rud. vii. 6. Or with MM grappling iron, obv. legend SCVTVM FIDEI PROTEG EVM. Rev. EDWARD VI D G AG FR Z H REX. *MB*. Wt. 20·7 grs.

SOUTHWARK. With uncrowned head, same as London but MM Y; PROTEGE, AG, RE. *MB*. Wt. 20·1 grs. Or with crowned head, MM Y, EDWARD VI D G A F Z H REX. Rev. SCVTVM FIDEI PROTE EVM. Very large letters, diamond-shaped stops. (73) *MB*. Wt. 21½ grs., or reading HI, and PROTEG : EV : *THORBURN*.

THIRD COINAGE. In the year 1550 the old standard of gold, namely 23 cts. 3½ grs. fine gold to ½ gr. alloy, which had always been used from the first coinage of Edward III down to the year 1544, was restored, by commission directed to Sir Edmund Peckham, Sir John Yorke, and others. The pound weight of this gold was to be coined into £28. 16*s* by tale, and the coins to be struck were sovereigns of the value of 24*s* each, and angels at 8*s* each, with their respective halves. It would seem, however, that this restoration of the old standard and weight of the coins, notwithstanding the increase in their nominal value, was a greater strain than the Treasury could well bear, and extremely few coins of this description were struck, or at all events have come down to us. The mint-mark upon all of them is a bird's head. The first commissioner of the mint at this time was Sir Edmund Peckham, Knt., who was the High Treasurer of the mint from the reign of Henry VIII to that of Elizabeth; and as the crest of the Peckhams of Nyton in Sussex is an ostrich, it is probable that Sir E. Peckham may have belonged to the same family, and that the mint-mark on these coins may be derived from his crest

DOUBLE SOVEREIGN. *Value* 48*s*. *Weight* 480 *grs*. *Standard fineness*. Obv. king seated, holding sceptre and globe, in robes, with crown with a single arch, back of the throne chequered, with jewelled sides. At each side of the throne is a column supporting an ornamental cross, as on Henry VIII's sovereigns. The legs and seat of the throne are hidden by the king's robes. Under his feet is a portcullis, and round the field, within the inner circle, is a tressure with a trefoil at each angle and a dot in each arch. MM ostrich head. EDWARD × VI × D ×× G ×× ANGLIE FRANCIE ×× Z ×× HIBERN ×× REX× Rev. shield with arms as usual upon a large double rose, within a double tressure of ten arches, two small crosses in each spandril, all within an inner circle. MM ostrich head. IHESV × AVTEM ×× TRANSIENS ×× PER ×× MEDIVM ×× ILLORVM ×× IBAT × *MB*. 475 grs. Or reading HIBERNIE. Rud. viii. 1. 504 grs. It does not appear that coins of this denomination were issued for general circulation, and the difference between the weights of these two coins makes it probable that they were both intended only for patterns.

SOVEREIGN. *Value* 24*s*. *Weight* 240 *grs*. *Standard fineness*. Exactly the same as the double sovereign reading HIBERNIE, with two saltires after Rex and Ibat. (74) Rud. viii. 2. *MB*. 237·3 grs.

HALF-SOVEREIGNS of this coinage are not known.

ANGEL. *Value* 8*s*. *Weight* 80 *grs*. *Standard fineness*. Type similar to the angels of Henry VIII. MM on both sides ostrich head. EDWARD × VI ×× D ×× G ×× AGL ×× FRA ×× Z × HIB ×× REX ×. Rev. PER ×× CRVCE × TVAM ×× SALVA ×× NOS ×× XPE × RED ××. Є to left of cross, rose to right. (75) Rud. viii. 4. *MB*. Wt. 81·4 grs. Or FR ×, REDE ××. *EVANS*. One sold in 1865 is said to have MM sun on both sides, but this is probably a mistake. It brought £32. *Num. Chron.*, N. S., v. 320.

ANGELET. *Value* 4*s*. *Weight* 40 *grs*. *Standard fineness*. Same as the angel, but reading A F Z HI REX. Rev. PER CRV TVA SALVA NOS XPE. Rud. viii. 5. *Ext. rare*.

FOURTH COINAGE. This was issued by virtue of an indenture of the year 1552, by which coins of two different standards of fineness were to be struck, namely, sovereigns, angels, and angelets, of the old standard, and sovereigns, half-sovereigns, crowns, and half-crowns, of the metal which is called crown gold, as having been first used for the crowns and half-crowns when they were introduced in 1526, namely, 22 cts. fine, and 2 cts. alloy. The coins of the old standard were to be made of the same weight as before, but their nominal value was raised, as sovereigns were to be current for 30*s*, angels for 10*s*, and half-angels for 5*s*. If, however, any coins of this standard were made by virtue of this indenture, they must have been of the same type as those of the last coinage, and have borne the same mint-mark, and are, therefore, undistinguishable from them. A pound weight of crown gold was to be made into thirty-three sovereigns at 20*s* a piece, or 132 crowns, with their respective halves. The coins of this metal were the following :—

SOVEREIGN. *Value* 20*s*. *Weight* $174\frac{6}{11}$ *grs*. *Fineness* 22 *cts*. Obv. Three-quarter length of king in profile to right, crowned, in figured armour, sword in right hand, orb in left. The crown has two arches, and is surmounted by a cross. Rev. same as sovereign of second coinage.

LONDON. MM ton, from the last syllable of the name of Throgmorton, master of the mint in the Tower. EDWARD VI D G AGL FRA Z HIBER REX. Rev. IHS AVTE TRANCI PER MEDIV ILLOR IBAT. Rud. viii. 6. *MB*. Or IHS AVTEM TRANSIE PERMEDI ILLORV IBAT. *MB*.

SOUTHWARK. MM y for Sir John Yorke. Same as London but FRAN Z HIB. Rev. IHS AVTEM TRANCI PERMEDI ILLOR IBAT. (76) *MB*.

HALF-SOVEREIGN. *Value* 10*s*. *Weight* $87\frac{3}{11}$ *grs*. *Fineness* 22 *cts*. Obv. type as sovereign. Rev. square shield crowned between E R.

LONDON. MM ton. EDWARD VI D G AGL FRA

Z HIB REX. Rev. IHS AVTEM TRANSIE PER MEDI ILLO IBAT. Diamond-shaped stops on each side. Interior of crown on rev. frosted. *MB.* Or ILLOR. *EVANS.* Or HIBER, TRANCI, ILLOR. Rud. viii. 7. *MB.* Or with the crown not frosted, FRANCI, HIB, TRANSIENS, ILLOR. *MB.*

SOUTHWARK. MM y. Same as the first of London, but rev. crown not frosted, IHS AVTE TRANCI PERMED ILLO IBA. *MB.*

CROWN. *Value* 5*s.* *Weight* $43\frac{7}{11}$ *grs.* *Fineness* 22 *cts.* Same as the London half-sovereign, MM ton, with the crown not frosted, but reading FRA, and rev. legend SCVTVM FIDEI PROTEGET EVM. (77) Rud. viii. 8. *MB.*

HALF-CROWN. *Value* 2*s* 6*d.* *Weight* $21\frac{9}{11}$ *grs.* *Fineness* 22 *cts.* Same as crown, but legends EDWARD VI D G A FR Z HIB REX. Rev. SCVTVM FIDEI PROTEG EVM. Rud. viii. 9. *MB.*

Edward VI's gold coins are all rare. Only two crowns of the first coinage are known, and the half-crown is extremely rare. A sovereign of the third coinage, "presumed to be the finest known," was sold at Captain Murchison's sale, in 1864, for £90; but Mr. Forster's, in 1868, only realized £21. 5*s.* Angels have sold for from £21. 10*s* to £41. 10*s*; and a half-crown of the last coinage, at Captain Murchison's sale, brought £12. 5*s.*

The only mints which appear to have been used for gold coins in this reign are those of the Tower and of Southwark, the coins of the latter place being distinguishable by bearing the MM Y or y, the initial of the master of the mint in that place, Sir John Yorke.

TABLE OF MINT MARKS.

	3 Sovs.	2 Sovs.	Sov.	½ Sov.	Angel.	Crown.	Angelet.	½ Crown.
1st Coinage, 1547.								
E, E under shield				+				
" Ɛ under shield				+				
E				+				
Arrow, rev. annulet enclosing pellet . .						+		
Arrow				+		*NC*		+
2nd Coinage, 1549.			•					
Arrow			+			+		+
,, roses in legend				+		+		
6, roses in legend				+				
Swan, cinquefoils in legend . . .				+				
Grappling iron								+
,, roses in legend . . .				+				
Martlet				Evans				
y •	+		+					
—, cinquefoil on obv.			+					
Y						+		+
—, roses in legend				+				
—, rev. y, rose in legend						+		

NC.—The authority for this is Capt. Murchison in *Num. Chr.* xx. 187.

TABLE OF MINT MARKS—*continued.*

	3 Sovs.	2 Sovs.	Sov.	½ Sov.	Angel.	Crown.	Angelet.	½ Crown.
3RD COINAGE, 1550.								
Ostrich head		+	+		+		Rud.	
4TH COINAGE, 1552.								
Ton			+	+		+		+
y.			+	+				

Mary, 1553 to 1558.

Queen Mary succeeded to the throne on the 6th of July, 1553, and although she debased the silver coins, she completed the restoration of the standard of the gold coins, which her brother had so nearly accomplished, by abolishing the coins of "crown gold," which had been made under the indenture of 1552. By a proclamation of the 20th August, 1553, and an indenture of the same date made with Thomas Egerton, Thomas Stanley, and others, it was ordered that the gold coins to be thenceforth made were to be the sovereign, which was to be current for 30*s*; the half-sovereign, to be called the royal of gold, and to be current for 15*s*; the angel at 10*s*; and the half-angel at 5*s*. All to be of fine gold, *i.e.*, of the old standard, 23 cts. 3½ grs. fine gold to ½ gr. alloy. By a proclamation of the 4th of March, 1553-4, the following foreign gold coins were made current throughout the kingdom, and were ordered to be paid and received, on pain of imprisonment, at the rates fixed, namely, the French crown of the sun at 6*s* 4*d*; the crown of the Emperor's coin at the same rate; the double ducat of Spain, with two faces, at 13*s* 4*d*; the single ducat at 6*s* 8*d*; provided in all cases they were of just standard, weight, and fineness. And to these were added by a proclamation of May 4th, 1554, three Portuguese coins—the single crusade, with the long cross, at 6*s* 8*d*; the same with the short cross, at the same rate; and the pistolett at 6*s* 2*d*. The following are the descriptions of the coins struck by virtue of the indenture of 1553. They are all rare.

SOVEREIGNS. *Value* 30*s*. *Weight* 240 *grs*. *Standard fineness*. Obv. exactly like the sovereigns of the third coinage of Edward VI, but with the queen's figure substituted for the king's, and with no MM. Rev. Shield with arms as usual upon a large double rose, within the inner circle. 1. ⁘MARIA⁘⁘D⁘G⁘ANG°FRA Z⁘HIB⁘REGINA⁘

M:D:LIII. Rev. A : DNO FACTV ° EST : ISTV ° Z : EST : MIRA ° IN : OCVL : NRIS ° A pomegranate, the badge of the house of Aragon from which the queen's mother was descended, is placed after Maria and Dno. Rud. ix. 1. *MB.* 2. Same, but with two annulets after Nris. *MB.* 3. Same as 1, but a half-rose instead of pomegranate after Maria and Dno, dots instead of annulets on rev., one dot after Dno, none after In, two after Nris. *MB.* 4. Same as last, but legends : MARIA : : D.G. ANG. FRA. Z : HIBERNIE : REGINA : Rev. A : DNO. FACTV. EST : ISTV. Z : EST : MIRA. IN OCVL : NRIS : (78) *MB.* 5. Similar to 1, but date MDLIIII. *RASHLEIGH. Unique?*

RYAL. *Value* 15*s.* *Weight* 120 *grs.* *Standard fineness.* Obv. Queen standing in a ship, full face, crowned; her right hand holds a sword, her left supports a shield bearing the arms of France and England. Above her head is the top-castle, below which is a yard-arm and sail. Two ropes from the mast to the stern, four to the prow, which is on the queen's right. At the prow is a flag marked M, and there is a rose on the side of the ship, which is ornamented by dots and one annulet. Legend as first sovereign. Pomegranate between two annulets after Maria, annulet after every other word except G, and after M and D. Rev. like the ryals of Edward IV and Henry VIII, within a double tressure of eight arches is a cross, the centre concealed by a rose upon a sun, the extremities corniced and ending in a lis between two cartouches; a lion, and a crown above him, in each quarter; the whole within an inner circle. A : DNO ° FACTV ° EST : ISTVD ° Z ° EST ° MIRABI ° IN : OCVL ° NRI ° Rud. ix. 2, where NRIS is erroneously substituted for NRI. (79) *MB.* *Ext. rare.* A fine specimen was sold for £63 at Capt. Murchison's sale in 1864; and Mr. Cuff's brought £80 in 1854. Collectors must beware of forgeries of this coin.

ANGELS. *Value* 10*s.* *Weight* 80 *grs.* *Standard fineness.* Type like those of Henry VIII and Edward VI, with M to left, rose to right of cross on rev. 1. MARIA ⁘ ⁘ D ° G ° ANG ° FRA ° Z ⁘ HIB ° REGIN ° Rev. A ° DNO ° FACTV ° EST ⁘ ISTVD Z ° EST ⁘ MIRABI ° Z° This last Z is an abbreviation for etcetera. Pomegranate after Maria and after Istud. Rud. ix. 3, where the stops are not accurately marked. *MB.* 2. Same, but REGI for Regin, annulet before Maria, only one after it. *THORBURN.* 3. As 2, with annulet also before A, only one after the first Est, two before the second Est, one at end of rev. legend. *MB.* 4. As 1, but dots instead of annulets, one dot each side of each pomegranate, REGINA, one dot before A and after each word on rev. *MB.* 5. As 1, but the legend on the obverse is entirely in Roman letters, and reads REGI. Half-rose? after Maria, dot after every other word on obv. Rev. Pomegranate between two dots after Istud, dot before A and after every word. *EVANS.* On all her other coins most of the letters are old English. *Rare.*

HALF-ANGELS. *Value* 5*s.* *Weight* 40 *grs.* *Standard fineness.* Type as the angels. MARIA D ° G ° A ° FR ° Z ° HIB ° REGI. Rev. A ° DNO ° FACTV ° EST °° ISTVD ⁘ Z ⁘ (for etcetera). Pomegranate after Maria and Est. (80) *MB.* Rud. ix. 4, where the stops are slightly different. *Very rare.* Capt. Murchison's sold for £51, but Mr. Cuff's went for £5. 5*s.*

The queen was married to Philip of Spain on the 25th of July, 1554, and as he was given the title of King of England, the legends of the coins had to be altered. This was done by virtue of a Proclamation of the 26th of December following, but the coins with the altered legend are rare. Philip is said to have brought with him to England an enormous quantity of coined gold and silver as well as of bullion, and it may be that these foreign coins, having a legal currency by virtue of the proclamations of the March and May previous, made it unnecessary to undertake any large coinage of English gold. The only gold coins known of Philip and Mary are angels and half-angels.

ANGELS. Similar in all respects to the previous ones, but with P and M, instead of M and rose, to left and right of cross on reverse, and having a lis for MM both on obv. and rev. The legends are, 1. PHILIP. Z. MARIA. D. G. REX. Z. REGIN. Rev. A. DNO. FACTVM. EST. ISTVD. Z. EST. MIRABI. *MB.* 2. Legend same, but REGINA, MIRABILE. Two dots between every word on obv., one after Regina, before and after A, and after Dno and Z; two after Factum, Est, Istud, and Est. (81) Rud. ix. 5. *MB.* 3. Same as 1, but REGINA. A, MIRAB. Two dots after Z, Maria, Factum, Istud, Z, Est. None after Mirab. *THORBURN.* 4. Same as last, but REGINA : AN., MIRABILE. Dot between all the words and after An, two after Z, Maria, Z, Regina, Factum, Est, and Istud. *MB. Rare.*

HALF-ANGEL. Exactly like the angels. PHILIP. Z. MARIA. D. G. REX. Z. REGI, Rev. A. DNO. FACTVM. EST. ISTVD. Z. EST. MIR (82) Rud. ix. 6. *MB. Rare.*

Money for the use of King Philip's foreign dominions seems also to have been coined at the Tower during this reign. See Strype's "Annals," vol. i. p. 27.

TABLE OF MINT MARKS.

	Sov.	Ryal.	Angel.	½ Angel.	
MARY.					
Pomegranate in legends .	+		+	+	
,, in obv. legend .					
Half-rose in legends . .	+				
Half-rose on obv. pomegranate on rev. . . .			Evans		
PHILIP AND MARY.					
Lis			+	+	

ELIZABETH, 1558 TO 1602.

Elizabeth succeeded to the throne on the 17th Nov. 1558. She was in the habit afterwards of boasting that she had restored the coinage to the proper standard; but the boast was true only as regarded the silver coins. The old standard, 23 cts. 3½ grs. fine gold to ½ gr. alloy, had been the only one used for the gold coins during Mary's reign; but Elizabeth, by her first proclamation, dated Dec. 31st, 1558, re-introduced a baser currency by ordering a gold coinage similar in all respects to that of 1552, namely sovereigns, angels, and angelets of the old standard at 30*s*, 10*s*, and 5*s*, respectively, and sovereigns, half-sovereigns, crowns, and half-crowns of "crown" gold, viz., 22 cts. fine, at 20*s*, 10*s*, 5*s*, and 2*s* 6*d* respectively, and all of the same weight as in 1552.

In the indenture of the 8th Nov., 1560, ryals of the old standard at 15*s* each were added to the list, and half-crowns were not mentioned, though they nevertheless continued to be coined; and on the 4th of March, 1561-2, the nominal value of all the current coins, both of gold and silver, was reduced. Of those of fine gold, the sovereign was now to be current for 20*s*, the ryal for 10*s*, the angel for 6*s* 8*d*, and the angelet for 3*s* 4*d*; and of crown gold, the sovereign for 13*s* 4*d*, the half-sovereign for 6*s* 8*d*, the crown for 3*s* 4*d*, and the half-crown for 1*s* 8*d*. By the indenture, however, of the 19th April, 1572, made with John Lonison, only three gold coins were to be made, namely, angels, angelets, and quarter angels, of the old standard and the same weight as before, and these were to be current at their old values of 10*s*, 5*s*, and 2*s* 6*d* respectively.

On the 19th Dec., 1578, a commission was made out, authorizing Lonison slightly to debase the coins, making the gold 23 cts. $3\frac{1}{4}$ grs. fine instead of 23 cts. $3\frac{1}{2}$ grs.; and a pound weight of gold, which had hitherto been coined into £36 by tale, was now to be coined into £36. 1*s* $10\frac{1}{2}$*d*, so that the angel would now weigh $79\frac{61}{77}$ grs. instead of 80 grs. In 1582-3, however, by an indenture with Richard Martin, the old standard and weight were restored, and the coinage was to be as ordered in 1572, and in 1583-4 half-sovereigns and sovereigns, under the name of nobles of 15*s* a-piece, and double nobles of 30*s* a-piece, were again ordered to be coined. In 1592 or 1593 another commission was granted to Martyn (now Sir Richard, and spelling his name with a y) to recommence the coinage of "crown" gold as ordered at the beginning of the reign.

On the 29th of July, 1601, the weight of the money both of gold and silver was somewhat reduced, a commission being granted to Sir R. Martyn and his son for making 73 instead of 72 angels out of a pound weight of gold of the old standard, and $33\frac{1}{2}$ instead of 33 sovereigns out of a pound of crown gold, and the other coins in proportion, all retaining the same nominal value as they had had before.

The following is a description of the coins which were struck by virtue of these several indentures and commissions. We have enumerated only the coins we actually know to exist, but the list might no doubt be made more complete.

SOVEREIGNS. 1558 to 1561. *Value* 30*s*. *Weight* 240 *grs*. *Standard fineness*. Type as before; obv., queen seated on throne, crowned and robed, holding sceptre and globe, back of the throne chequered, jewelled sides, column at each side supporting ornamented cross, portcullis under queen's feet. The tressure round the field is divided by the back of the throne. Rev. square shield bearing arms of France and England quarterly on a large double rose within a double tressure of ten arches, all within the inner circle. 1. MM lis. ELIZABETH : D : G. ANG. : FRA. Z : HIB : REGINA : Rev. A : DNO. FACTV. EST : ISTV. Z : EST : MIRABI. IN : OCV. NRI *MB.* 2. MM cross-crosslet. ELIZABETH : D. G. ANG. FRA. ET HIBE. REGINA : . Rev. A : DNO. FACTV. EST. ISTVD : ET. EST. MIRAB. IN : OCVLIS. NRIS. On this coin, but not on the previous one, a chain hangs down on each side of the portcullis under the queen's feet. (83) *MB.*

Between 1561 when the value of the sovereign of fine gold was reduced to 20*s*, and 1572 when the mint ceased to be authorized to make sovereigns at all, none but those of "crown gold," afterwards described, seem to have been struck.

1584 to 1601. *Value, weight and fineness as in* 1558. Type as before, except that the tressure on the obverse is not divided by the back of the throne, but only by the queen's head. There is a chain from each side of the portcullis, but not exactly like that on the coin with MM cross-crosslet. MM : A : ELIZABETH : D. G. ANG. FRA. ET : HIB. REGINA Rev. MM . A. A. DNO. FACTV. EST. ISTVD. ET. EST. MIRAB. IN. OCVLIS. NRS *MB.* MM scallop ; as last, without the dot on each side of the reverse MM ; *MB.* Or having the sides of the back of the throne ornamented with lis instead of jewels, annulets instead of dots within the chequers on the back, one dot after each word on obv., and first four and last on rev. ; *MB.* Or reading NRIS, sides of back of throne ornamented with annulets, dots within the chequers, one dot after obv. MM and after each word on both sides. *MB.* MM crescent ;

like A but reading OCVL, sides of back of throne ornamented with annulets, one dot each side of obv. MM and between each word. *MB.* The MM on rev. is struck over a scallop. MM ton; like A but reading OCVL, dot after each word except Ang and Istud. *MB.* Rud. ix. 8.

We know of none struck after 1600.

SOVEREIGNS. 1561 *to* 1572. *Value* 13*s* 4*d.* *Weight* 174$\frac{6}{11}$ *grs.* *Fineness* 22 *cts.* The coinage of sovereigns of crown gold was authorized in 1558, but none appear to have been actually struck before 1561-2, when their value was reduced from 20*s* to 13*s* 4*d.* They are of a type very different from that of the coins of fine gold, having on the obverse the queen's bust to left, crowned, with ruff and ermine mantle, within an inner circle formed of a single line and touched only by the breast of the bust. Rev. Shield, slightly garnished, crowned, bearing arms of France and England, between the letters E R, within an inner circle which is pierced by the top of the crown. MM rose. Legends ELIZABETH : D. G. ANG. FRAN. ET : HIB. REGINA. Rev. IHS. AVTEM : TR.ANS. PER : MEDIV. ILLOR. IBAT. Rud. x. 11. *Very rare.*

1592 *to* 1601. *Value* 20*s.* *Weight* 174$\frac{6}{11}$ *grs.* *Fineness* 22 *cts.* In 1572 the coinage of crown gold was stopped, but it was restored in 1592. The sovereigns subsequently coined are like the former ones in general type, but the queen's bust is much larger and reaches down to the inner circle, which is pierced above by her crown. There is no ermine mantle, but the dress is richly ornamented; the hair flows down over both shoulders, the crown on both sides has high pointed arches, and the E and R on the reverse are smaller than on the earlier coins. The inner circle on both sides is beaded instead of being a mere line. Legends ELIZABETH ⁞ D ° G ° ANG ° FRA ° ET ⁞ HIB ° REGINA ° Rev. SCVTVM ⁞ FIDEI ⁞ PROTEGET ⁞ EAM ° MM obv. lion and ton, rev. ton. (84) *MB.* The lion MM belongs to the years 1566 and 1567, the ton to 1592-5; how they come to be united on this coin is difficult to understand. MM ton; dot after each word on obv., two after Et, rev. as last. *MB.* MM woolpack, annulet after each word. *MB.* See Rud. x. 3, which reads Hi. MM obv. woolpack, rev. key; dot after each word on obv., two after Elizabeth, D, and Et, annulet after each word on rev. *MB.* MM key, same, but two dots after Elizabeth, Et, and Hib, one after every other word on both sides. *MB.* MM anchor, as last, but ornaments on dress a little different. *MB.* MM O (signifying the date 1600), dot after every word, dress not so elaborately ornamented. *MB.*

1601-2. *Value* 20*s*. *Weight* $171\frac{63}{67}$ *grs.* *Fineness* 22 *cts.* Type and legends as before, dress as on the coin with MM O, dot after each word. MM 1: (for 1601), *MB.* Rud. x. 10. MM 2: (for 1602), *MB.* The sovereigns of crown gold, though less elaborate in design, are better executed than those of the old standard, are much neater in appearance, and have a graining outside the legend to the edge of the coin, in order to show at once if the coin has been clipped. Their edges, however, are not milled, and their mint-marks are those of the hammered money, to which series all the sovereigns of this reign belong.

RYALS. 1560 *to* 1572, *and* 1584 *to* 1601. *Value* 15*s or* 10*s*. *Weight* 120 *grs.* *Standard fineness.* These, which were in fact the half-sovereigns of the old standard, were first ordered in 1560, were reduced to the value of 10*s* in 1561-2, were ordered not to be struck in 1572, but were restored at 15*s* each in 1584. The only specimens we have seen, however, seem to have been struck about the year 1584. Their type is like that of previous ryals. Obv. queen standing in a ship, three-quarters to left, crowned, sceptre in right hand, globe in left, wearing a ruff. The ship has a very high quarter-deck, from which rises a mast with furled sail on yard-arm and three ropes. Mast behind queen, yard-arm over her head, two ropes to it from prow, three from stern, flag at prow bearing letter Œ. Rose on side of ship, which is adorned, on each side of the rose, with a lion between two lis. Rev. as Mary's ryal, with a trefoil in each spandril of the tressure. 1. MM on rev. only .A. Legends ELIZABET. ANGL. MA. D. G. P C. A. L. REGINA. Rev. IHS. AVT. TRANSIENS. PER. MEDIV. ILLORVM. IBAT. N (85) *MB.* 2. Similar with only two ropes to the mast on the quarter-deck, three from prow to yard-arm, ELIZAB. D. G. ANG. FR. Z. M. PR. C' A. L' REGINA. Rev. IHS. AVT. TRANSIENS. PER. MEDIV. ILLORVM. IBAT *MB.* Rud. x. 1. 3. Type as 1, but obv. legend ELIZAB. D. G. ANG. FR. ET. HIB REGINA. Rev. legend as 2. *MB.* See Rud. ix. 7. 4. As last, but MM scallop? *MB.* 5. One said to have MM crescent, "very fine," was sold at the Whitbourn sale in 1869 for £22, and one with the same MM from the Jackson collection in 1872, for £9. 7*s* 6*d*. *Num. Chr.*, N. S., ix. 289; xii. 220. *All very rare.*

The legends on the obverses of the two first of these coins have not been explained. The N at the end of the reverse legend of No 1 may be compared with the NE at the end of the reverse legend on Henry VII's sovereign (46), but we cannot explain its meaning. It may possibly be a mint-mark here, but it does not appear as such on any other coin.

HALF-SOVEREIGNS. 1558 *to* 1572. *Value* 10*s or* 6*s* 8*d*. *Weight* $87\frac{3}{11}$ *grs.* *Fineness* 22 *cts.* *Not milled.* These are in type like the first sovereigns of "crown" gold, except that the queen is dressed in armour instead of an ermine mantle, and that the bust extends nearly down to the inner circle, which is beaded. The reverse is also similar, but the shield is plain, the crown placed higher in the coin, and the inner circle beaded. MM cross-crosslet. ELIZABETH : D. G. ANG. FRA. ET. HI. REGINA Rev. SCVTVM. FIDEI. PROTEGET : EAM Rud. x. 2. *MB.* MM rose, same but only one dot after Elizabeth, two after each word on rev. (86) *MB.* MM portcullis, as cross-

crosslet but FR, two dots after Elizabeth and Et and between words on rev. *MB.* MM coronet, as last, but SCVTV'. *MB.* Or FR., SCVTVM. *EVANS.*

1561 *to* 1572. *Value* 6*s* 8*d.* *Weight and fineness as before. Milled.* In 1561, about the same time that the nominal value of the coins was reduced, a new process of coining, by means of the mill and screw, was introduced into England from France, apparently by a Frenchman called Eloye Mestrell. The old process had been to place the blank piece of metal upon a die firmly fixed below, and to place another die above it, and then to raise the impressions upon it by striking the upper die with a hammer. The improvement consisted in attaching the upper die to a screw, so as to bring it down on the metal below at once with greater force and greater accuracy, and at the same time the edges of many of the coins so struck were marked with straight lines or "milled," probably by means of including the blanks in a collar so marked, slightly wider than themselves, to the size of which they would expand on being struck with the upper die, and which might be opened to take them out. The new process was used for a time concurrently with the old, but it was not approved of by the officers of the mint, and was but little used after 1572, until it was re-introduced in the reign of Charles II.

The milled half-sovereigns are of similar type to the hammered ones, but the queen's bust is larger, and her armour much more richly ornamented, and there is no inner circle on either side. MM star. ELIZABETH. D. G. ANG. FR. ET. HIB. REGINA Rev. SCVTVM. FIDEI. PROTEGET. EAM. Dot before rev. MM, edge plain. *MB.* Or with armour slightly different, reading FRA. *MB.* Or with armour very slightly different again, reading FRA, and having a slight graining on the edge, and the queen's crown frosted. (87) *MB.* Or with different bust, face and crown smaller, crown on both obv. and rev. has high pointed arches, more of bust shown, much richer dress, shield on reverse larger, coin large, workmanship altogether much better, edge grained; legends as before, with FRA. *EVANS.* MM lis, like the first with MM star, but armour rather different, FRA, no dot after Eam or before rev. MM, edge milled, coin smaller. *MB.* Rud. x. 7. *Rare.*

1592 *to* 1601. *Value* 10*s.* *Weight and fineness as before. Not milled.* Type similar to the first with MM star, but dress different, beaded inner circle on both sides. MM ton. .ELIZABETH. D. G. ANG. FRA. ET. HI. REGINA. Rev. .SCVTVM. FIDEI. PROTEGET. EAM. *MB.*

With much larger bust, greater profusion of hair, crowns on both sides have high double arches and pierce inner circle. Rich armour. Shield on rev. smaller. Workmanship good. MM ton. ELIZAB. D. G. ANG. FRA. ET: HIB. REGINA Rev. SCVTVM: FIDEI: PROTEGET: EAM. *MB.* Or reading REGIN·, one dot after each word on rev. (88) *MB.* Or with bust rather smaller, shield on rev. rather larger, crown over it more like that on the half-sovereigns with MM cross-crosslet, and legends same. MM woolpack. Dot after each word. *MB.* Rud. x. 4. MM key, ELIZAB, HIB. *MB.*

1601-2. *Value* 10*s.* *Weight* $85\frac{65}{67}$ *grs.* *Fineness* 22 *cts.* Type and legends as the last, dot after each word. MM 1: *MB.*

ANGELS. 1558 *to* 1578. *Value* 10*s or* 6*s* 8*d.* *Weight* 80 *grs.* *Standard fineness.* Type as usual, the ship on the reverse is sailing to the right, and has two ropes from the prow, three from the stern. E and rose at sides of cross. MM lis. ELIZABETH: D. G. ANG. FRA. Z. HIB. REG. Rev. A: DNO. FACTVM. EST. ISTVD. Z. EST. MIRABI. Thin plain inner circle on both sides. *EVANS.* MM lis, ELIZABETH: D. G: ANG. FRA. Z. HIB. REGI. Rev. A. DNO. FACTVM. EST. ISTVD. Z. EST. MIRABI. Beaded inner circle on obv., thin plain one on rev. *MB.* On all the rest of the angels the inner circle on both sides is beaded. MM cross-crosslet. ELIZABETH. D. G.

ANG. FRA. ET. HIB. REGINA. Rev. A. DNO. FACTVM. EST. ISTVD: ET EST. MIRABI. *MB.* Rud. ix. 9 reads FR, and the stops on rev. are different. MM coronet; obv. as last, but reading FR and with three dots after Regina. Rev. as last, with one dot after Dno, two after every other word. *MB.* MM ermine. ELIZABETH: D. G. ANG. FR. ET: HI. REGINA Rev. A: DNO: FACTVM: EST: ISTVD: ET: EST: MIRABI. Ship sailing to left instead of right. (89) *MB.* Or reading HIB. *MB.* MM acorn, same, reading HI, but with no stops before Istud. *MB.* This specimen is countermarked, but with what arms is not clear. MM cinquefoil, same as ermine, reading HI, only one dot after Dno. *MB.*

1578 *to* 1582. *Value* 10*s.* *Weight* $79\frac{61}{77}$ *grs.* *Fineness* 23 *cts.* $3\frac{1}{4}$ *grs.* Type as before, ship is always sailing to the right. MM plain cross, legends as ermine with HI. *MB.* Or with only one dot after Factum, Est, Et, and Est. *MB.* MM sword, legends as ermine with HI. *MB.* MM bell, same. *MB.* This last may have been struck either before or after the restoration of the old standard, as the bell MM was used from 1582 to 1584.

1582 *to* 1601. *Value* 10*s.* *Weight* 80 *grs.* *Standard fineness.* Type as before, ship sailing to right. MM A. ELIZABETH: D. G. ANG. FR. ET: HI. REGINA. Rev. A: DNO: FACTVM: EST: ISTVD: ET: EST: MIRABI. *MB.* MM scallop, same, but only one dot after A. *MB.* MM crescent, same as the last. *MB.* MM hand, as A, with only one dot after A. *MB.* MM ton, as A, with no dot after Regina, nor before Istud, and reading, by a blunder, MIRARI for Mirabile; with no dot after it. *MB.* MM key, as A, with only one dot after each word on obv., and after A on rev., and the ship has no bowsprit. *MB.* MM O, as A, but no stops after the last four words on obv., HIB for HI, no stops before Istud, the ship on the reverse is smaller than usual. *MB.*

We do not know of any angels struck after the reduction of weight in 1601.

ANGELETS. These correspond in value, weight, and fineness, with the angels, and are of exactly the same type, except that there is only one rope to the mast from the prow, and two from the stern, and that the ship is always sailing to the right.

1558 *to* 1578. *Value* 5*s or* 3*s* 4*d*. *Weight* 40 *grs. Standard fineness.* MM cinquefoil. ELIZABETH: D: G: ANG: FR: ET HI REGINA Rev. A. DNO. FACTVM. EST: ISTVD ET. EST MIRA: *EVANS*.

1578 *to* 1582. *Value* 5*s*. *Weight* $39\frac{69}{77}$ *grs. Fineness* 23 *cts.* $3\frac{1}{4}$ *grs.* MM plain cross. ELIZABETH: D: G: ANG : FR: ET: HI : REGINA Rev. A: DNO: FACTVM: EST: ISTVD: ET : EST: MIRA (90) *MB*. MM sword. ELIZABETH: D. G. ANG. FR. ET. HI. REGINA Rev. as cross. *MB*. MM bell, as sword. *MB*.

1582 *to* 1601. *Value* 5*s*. *Weight* 40 *grs. Standard fineness.* MM scallop. ELIZAB D. G. ANG FR. ET HIB REGI Rev. A DNO FACTVM EST ISTVD ET EST MIRA Rud ix. 10. MM crescent, as sword. *MB*. MM hand. ELIZABETH D G ANG FR ET HIB REGINA, no stops. Rev. A. DNO FACTV. EST. ISTVD. ET. EST. MIRAB. *MB*.

We do not know of any later angelets than these. The hand MM was superseded by the ton in 1592.

CROWNS. 1558 *to* 1572. *Value* 5*s or* 3*s* 4*d*. *Weight* $43\frac{7}{11}$ *grs. Fineness* 22 *cts. Not milled.* Type like the earliest half-sovereigns of "crown" gold, p. 126. MM. cross-crosslet. ELIZABETH : D. G. ANG. FR. ET. HI. REGINA Rev. SCVTVM : FIDEI : PROTEGET : EAM *MB*. Or HIB. *EVANS*. MM lion, same but bust smaller, HI., PRTEGET: *MB*. MM coronet, like the first but AN, two dots after Et. *MB*.

1561 *to* 1572. *Value* 3*s* 4*d*. *Weight* $43\frac{7}{11}$ *grs. Fineness* 22 *cts. Milled.* Type as the hammered crowns, but bust and shield both larger, dress richer, crown over shield somewhat different, no inner circle. MM star, ELIZA-

BETH. D. G. ANG. FRA. ET. HIB. REGINA Rev. SCVTVM. FIDEI. PROTEGET. EAM. Edge plain. Rud. x. 8. *MB.* MM lis, type like the hammered crowns, but crown on rev. rather smaller, plain inner circle on rev. only. Legends as last but Z. HIB. REGI, dot before rev. MM. Edge plain. (91) *MB.* Or with edge grained, exactly like the milled half-sovereign MM lis, but reading FIDIEI. *MB.* These milled crowns are rare, and have been sold for from £10 to £15. 15*s* each.

1592 *to* 1601. *Value* 5*s*. *Weight* $43\frac{7}{11}$ *grs.* *Fineness* 22 *cts.* Type like the corresponding half-sovereigns, p. 128, with an inner circle which is pierced by the crown. MM ton. ELIZAB. D. G. ANG. FRA. ET. HIB. REGI. Rev. SCVTVM : FIDEI : PROTEGET : EAM *MB.* MM woolpack, same, but with only one dot between words on rev. and reading EA for Eam. *MB.* Or REG for Regi. Rud. x. 5. Or FR. for Fra, with MM at end instead of beginning of obv. legend. *THORBURN.* MM. O, as last but FR. ET. HI : REGINA, dot after Ea. *MB.*

1601-2. *Value* 5*s*. *Weight* $42\frac{66}{67}$ *grs.* *Fineness* 22 *cts.* Like the first with MM woolpack. MM 2 : (92) *MB.*

HALF-CROWNS. 1558 *to* 1572. *Value* 2*s* 6*d* *or* 1*s* 8*d*. *Weight* $21\frac{9}{11}$ *grs.* *Fineness* 22 *cts.* *Not milled.* Type like the corresponding half-sovereigns. Legends ELIZABETH : D. G. AN. FR. ET : HI. REGINA Rev. SCVTVM : FIDEI : PROTEGET : EAM MM cross-crosslet. *THORBURN.* MM lion. *MB.* MM coronet. *MB.* MM castle, same but reading ANG. *EVANS.*

1561 *to* 1572. *Value* 1*s* 8*d*. *Weight* $21\frac{9}{11}$ *grs.* *Fineness* 22 *cts.* *Milled.* Type like the corresponding half-sovereigns, p. 127. Legends as the last half-crowns but ANG. FRA. ET. HIB., one dot between each word. MM star. *MB.* MM lis. *MB.* Rud. x. 9. These coins, though struck by the mill, have the edges plain. *Rare.*

1592 *to* 1601. *Value* 2*s* 6*d*. *Weight* $21\frac{9}{11}$ *grs.* *Fineness* 22 *cts.* Type as corresponding half-sovereigns. Legends

ELIZAB. D. G. ANG. FR. ET. HIB. REGI. Rev. SCVTVM : FIDEI : PROTEGET : EAM. MM ton. *MB.* Or with MM ton on rev. only, two dots after Et. *MB.* MM woolpack, as last. *MB.* Rud. x. 6, which reads HI, PROTEGE. MM O, as ton, but ET. HI :, only one dot after each word on rev. (93) *MB.*

1601-2. *Value* 2*s* 6*d.* *Weight* $21\frac{33}{67}$ *grs.* *Fineness* 22 *cts.* Type and legends like the first with MM ton, one dot between words on rev. MM 2 : *MB.* Or with EA for EAM. *THORBURN.*

QUARTER ANGELS. These correspond in every respect with the angelets. They are not mentioned in the indentures for the coinage before 1572, but a few exist with the rose MM, the date of which is 1565. If these are not patterns, it proves that quarter angels, like half-crowns, were coined under the indenture of 1560 although not mentioned therein. The legends on all are ELIZABETH D G ANG FRANCIE. Rev. ET HIBERNIE REGINA FIDEI.

1558 *to* 1578. *Value* 2*s* 6*d or* 1*s* 8*d.* *Weight* 20 *grs.* *Standard fineness.* MM rose. *EVANS.* *THORBURN.* MM acorn, two dots after Elizabeth, Ang, Regina, and Fidei, one after Et and Hibernie. Rud. ix. 11. *MB.* MM cinquefoil, two dots after Elizabeth and Ang and every word on rev. *MB.*

1578 *to* 1582. *Value* 2*s* 6*d.* *Weight* $19\frac{73}{77}$ *grs.* *Fineness* 23 *cts.* $3\frac{1}{4}$ *grs.* MM plain cross, two dots between words on obv., one after each word on rev. *MB.* MM bell, same. *MB.*

1582 *to* 1601. *Value* 2*s* 6*d.* *Weight* 20 *grs.* *Standard fineness.* MM A, as cross. *MB.* MM crescent. *EVANS.* MM ton, two dots after Elizabeth, one after Ang and between words on rev. (94) *MB.*

We do not know of any later quarter angels.

Besides the English coins above described, a considerable number of foreign coins had a legal currency in the kingdom during this reign. Those made current by Queen Mary have been already enumerated. On the 9th October, 1560, the current value of the French and Imperial crowns was reduced from 6*s* 4*d* to 6*s*, and that of the Portuguese Pistoletts from 6*s* 2*d* to 5*s* 10*d*, at which latter value four other coins, namely two of Spain, one of Venice, and one of Florence, were made current under the same name of Pistoletts; but on the 15th November, 1561, the legal currency of all foreign coins except the French crown and the Flemish or Burgundian crown was abolished by proclamation, and on the 4th March the value of these last was reduced to 4*s* each, at which rate they were continued during the rest of the reign.

In the following list of mint-marks the dates are those which occur in conjunction with the same mint-mark on the sixpences, and other dated silver coins. The mint-marks 0, 1, and 2, of which the first has generally been called an annulet or circle, obviously refer to the date of the year, 1600, 1601, and 1602, in which they were used.

Not Milled.

	Date.	Sov. fine gold.	Sov. crwn gld.	Ryal.	½ Sov.	Angel.	Angelet.	Crown.	½ Crown.	¼ Angel.
Martlet . . .										
Fleur-de-lys . .		+				+				
Cross-crosslet . .		+			+	+		+	Thorbrn.	
Pheon . . .	1561-5									
Rose . . .	1565		Rud.		+					Evans
Portcullis . . .	1566				+					
Lion . . .	1566-7							+	+	
Coronet . . .	1567-70				+	+		+	+	
Castle . . .	1569-71								Evans	
Ermine . . .	1571-3					+				
Acorn . . .	1573-4					+				+
Cinquefoil . . .	1573-7					+	Evans			+
Cross . . .	1577-81					+	+			+
Sword . . .	1582					+	+			
Bell . . .	1582-4					+	+			+
A	1582-4	+		+		+				+
Scallop . . .	1584-6	+		+		+	Rud.			
Crescent . . .	1587-9	+		*Nm. Chr.*		+	+			Evans
Hand . . .	1590-2					+	+			
Lion (1566-7) and ton .			+							
Ton . . .	1592-5	+	+		+	+		+	+	+
Woolpack . . .	1594-6		+		+			+	+	
Key . . .	1595-8		+		+	+				
Anchor . . .	1597-1600		+							
0.	1600		+			+		+	+	
1.	1601-2		+		+					
2.	1602		+					+	+	

MILLED.

	½ Sov.	Crown.	½ Crown.
Star, 1561-6	+	+	+
Fleur-de-lis, 1567-70 . . .	+	+	+
Mullet pierced, 1570 . . .			
Castle, 1571			
Mullet, 1574-5			

JAMES I, 1603 TO 1625.

The union of the two crowns by the accession of James VI of Scotland to the throne of England, on the 24th of March, 1602-3, is commemorated in various ways upon his money. His first coinage was struck by virtue of an indenture made with Sir R. Martyn, and dated the 21st of May, 1603, and was similar to that of the last two years of Elizabeth, except that the Scotch title was inserted in the legend, and that the shield, which had hitherto borne the arms of France in the first and fourth quarters, and those of England in the second and third, now bore, 1 and 4, France and England quarterly; 2, Scotland; 3, Ireland; and this arrangement was continued throughout the reign. This first coinage consisted of sovereigns, half-sovereigns, crowns, and half-crowns, all of which have for MM the Scotch thistle. They are made of "crown" gold, and are all rare.

On the 20th of October 1604, a proclamation was issued ordering the title of King of Great Britain, France and Ireland to be used on the coins, and on the 11th of November an indenture for a new coinage was made with Sir R. Martyn and his son. Crown gold was to be exclusively employed, and a pound weight of it was to be made into £37. 4*s* by tale. The pieces to be coined were, the Unite, at 20*s*; the double crown, at 10*s*; the Britain crown, at 5*s*; the Thistle crown, at 4*s*, and the half-crown, at 2*s* 6*d*; and they were made current on the 16th of the same month. The union of the kingdoms is referred to both in the names and in the legends of these coins. The

Unite reads "Faciam eos in gentem unam," from Ezek. xxxvii. 22. The Britain crown has "Henricus rosas regna Jacobus," "Henry united the roses, but James unites the kingdoms;" and the Thistle crown, which is of a denomination never coined before or since, "Tueatur unita Deus," "May God protect the united (kingdoms)."

To these coins were added next year, by an indenture of July 16th, 1605, some others of the old standard, namely Rose Rialls at 30*s*, Spur Rialls at 15*s*, and Angels at 10*s*. A pound of gold of the old standard was to be made into £40. 10*s* by tale.

By a proclamation of Nov. 23rd, 1611, the nominal value of all the gold coins was raised 2*s* in the £, so that the Unite was to pass for 22*s*, and the Rose Riall for 33*s*, and the others in proportion. The indenture, however, made in accordance with this proclamation on May 18th, 1612, made a slight increase in the weights of the coins, ordering a pound of crown gold to be made into £40. 18*s* 4*d*, and a pound of the old standard into £44. Not many coins were struck by virtue of this indenture, but the only half-angels made during the reign were now struck, though they are not mentioned in the indenture.

The values fixed for the coins in 1611 being found to be very inconvenient, a proclamation for a fourth coinage was issued on July 31st, 1619. The value of the coins now to be made was reduced to that which had been fixed in 1604 and 1605, and the denominations were to be the same, omitting Thistle crowns and Half-crowns; and the weight was reduced proportionally—that is to say, both weight and value were reduced by one-eleventh. As the new pieces were to be current simultaneously with the old ones to which they so nearly approached in weight and value, they were all made very different in type, so as to be easily distinguished. Those made of crown gold have the king's head wreathed with laurel instead of being crowned, and were hence named by the people Laurels, and half or quarter Laurels. The Laurels were also called Broad Pieces. In 1623 the weight was again reduced, and the pound of crown gold was made into £41 by tale, and the pound of the old standard into £44. 10*s*. Sir R. Martyn, master of the mint, died in 1617, and was succeeded by Thomas Lord Knyvet and Edmund Doubleday, and they, in or before 1623, by Randal Cranfield, who was removed for misconduct in 1625.

Besides the above, the Scottish six-pound piece of gold was on April 8th, 1603, made current in England for 10*s* sterling. The French Crown of the Sun also continued to be current in this country. No legal value had been fixed for it since 1561, when it was ordered to be taken for 4*s*, but in 1610 it is said to have passed for 7*s* 3*d*.

The following is a description of the types of the various English coins above mentioned.

ROSE RYALS. 1605 *to* 1612. *Value* 30*s or* 33*s*. *Weight* 213⅓ *grs. Old Standard.* These are similar in type to Queen Elizabeth's sovereigns, but with some alterations. Obv. king seated on throne, crowned and robed, holding sceptre and globe, portcullis under his feet. The throne has a high narrow back, reaching above the king's head nearly to the edge of the coin, the arms terminating in a column supporting a small ornament. Tressure of 19 arches round field within inner circle, each arch terminating in a trefoil. Both tressure and inner circle are interrupted by the portcullis and the back of the throne. Legend IACOBVS. D. G. MAG. BRIT. FRAN. ET. HIBER. REX. Dot each side of MM. Rev. upon a large double rose within a double tressure of ten arches is a square shield, bearing in the first and fourth quarter the arms of England and France, in the second Scotland, and in the third Ireland. Legend .A. DNO. FACTVM. EST. ISTVD. ET. EST. MIRAB. IN. OCVLIS. NRIS. MM rose. Rud. xii. 1. *MB*. Scallop, same. *MB*. Coronet, same, but omitting the dot after Brit. *MB*. Mullet, as coronet. *MB*.

1612 *to* 1619. *Value* 33*s*. *Weight* 216 *grs*. *Old Standard*. Exactly like that with MM coronet, except that they read OCV for Oculis. MM's tower, trefoil. (95) *MB*. The trefoil seems to be struck over a tower. These do not now weigh more than the earlier ones, but the proper difference between them is so small, that perhaps it can hardly be expected to be now perceptible.

1619 *to* 1625. *Value* 30*s*. *Weight* $196\frac{4}{11}$ or $194\frac{14}{89}$ *grs*. *Old Standard*. These have quite a different type. Obv. king seated on throne, crowned and robed, wearing a ruff and the collar of the Garter, sceptre and globe in his hands, his feet resting on portcullis. The throne has a broad square flowered back which reaches nearly as high as the king's crown, its sides jewelled, curved arms, field chequered and ornamented with roses and lis, within a beaded inner circle which is divided by the portcullis and the back of the throne. Rev. shield shaped like the last but much larger, upon cross fleury within two beaded circles, the inner one of which is cut by the ends of the cross. Between the two circles, in each quarter of the cross, is a lion between a lis and a rose. Above the shield XXX, to indicate the value. Legends IACOBVS D: G: MA BRI: FR: ET HIB: REX. Rev. A DNO: FACTVM EST ISTVD ET EST MIRAB: IN OC: NRIS. MM's spur rowel (96) rose, thistle (Rud. xii. 5), lis, trefoil. *MB*. That with MM lis differs in having : after NRIS (as has the plate of Rud. xii. 5), and that with MM trefoil reads HI: and MIRA: and has no dot after NRIS, and the back of the throne is quite plain instead of being flowered.

SOVEREIGN, 1603-4. *Value* 20*s*. *Weight* $171\frac{63}{67}$ *grs*. *Fineness* 22 *cts*. Obv. king in profile to right, half length, crowned, in armour, sceptre in right hand, orb in left; the crown and top of sceptre pierce the beaded inner circle. Rev. square shield garnished, crowned, between I and R. The arms are arranged as on the Ryals. Legends .IACOBVS.

D. G. ANG. SCO. FRAN. ET. HIB. REX. Rev. .EXVRGAT. DEVS. DISSIPENTVR. INIMICI. MM thistle. *MB.* Rud. xi. 1. Another with the same MM has the king's figure larger and the armour more ornamented, and the face is perhaps rather older. (97) *MB.* The legend on the reverse is taken from Ps. lxviii. 1.

UNITE. 1604 *to* 1612. *Value* 20*s or* 22*s. Weight* 154$\frac{26}{31}$ *grs. Fineness* 22 *cts.* Type like the sovereign. MM lis, figure as on the second sovereign, legends .IACOBVS. D. G. MAG. BRIT. FRAN. ET. HIB. REX. Rev. .FACIAM. EOS. IN. GENTEM. VNAM. Dot before the MM both on obv. and rev. *MB.* A similar coin, with MM thistle and a different figure of the king, is Scotch and not English. The Thistle mint-mark was superseded by the lis in England on the 22nd of May, 1604, and it was not till the 20th of Oct. 1604 that the title of King of Great Britain was ordered to be used on the coins. Some silver crowns and half-crowns do indeed seem to have been struck after this with the old mint-mark; but the Unite in question is further distinguished from English coins by the substitution of & for ET in the legend, and by the ornamentation of the crown both on obv. and rev., which is decorated, like the Scotch coins, with a lis between two crosses, instead of, like the English ones, with a cross between two lis. A shilling and other silver Scotch coins similar to this are noticed in Hawkins's "Silver Coins of England," second ed., p. 306. MM rose, like lis. Rud. xi. 5. *MB.* MM scallop, like lis but armour much plainer, falling collar with lace edge. *MB.* MM grapes. *MONTAGU.* MM coronet, same as scallop but HI. for Hib. *MB.* MM key, like coronet but no dot before or after obv. legend. *MB.* MM bell, like scallop but FRA. ET. HI., no dot after Rex. *MB.* MM mullet, like scallop but FRA., no dot after Rex or Unam or before Faciam. *MB.*

1612 *to* 1619. *Value* 22*s. Weight* 154$\frac{418}{491}$ *grs. Fineness* 22 *cts.* MM tower, type like MM scallop, but reading

BRI. FRA. ET. HI. *MB.* MM trefoil. *MONTAGU.* MM cinquefoil, face and collar different, and reading .IACOBVS. D. G. MA. BRI. FRA. ET. HI. REX. Rev. .FACIAM : EOS : IN : GENTEM : VNAM (98) *MB.* MM ton, face slightly different, armour nearly as on MM scallop, legends as cinquefoil but one dot after each word on rev. *MB.* MM book. *MONTAGU.* MM crescent, same as ton. *MB.* MM cross, same as ton but face slightly different. *MB.*

UNITE or LAUREL. 1619 *to* 1625. *Value* 20*s.* *Weight* $140\frac{380}{491}$ or $140\frac{20}{41}$ *grs.* *Fineness* 22 *cts.* These have a type quite different from that of the former Unites, and are the first English coins since the conquest on which the king's head is represented wreathed with laurel. From this circumstance the people soon gave them the name of Laurels. MM spur rowel. Obv. Bust in profile to left, not crowned, laureate, scarf fastened in a bow on left shoulder, nearly concealing the armour. The figures XX, indicating the value, behind the head. The whole within an inner circle. Rev. Plain square shield on cross fleury, crown above it concealing top of cross. The harp in the shield is ornamented by a bird's or griffin's head. IACOBVS D : G : MAG : BRIT : FRAN : ET HIBERN : REX Rev. FACIAM EOS IN GENTEM VNAM *MB.* Or reading BRI : FRAN : ET : HIB :, with : after Eos. Rud. xi. 9. MM rose, face different and very plain, bust smaller, more of armour showing. .IACOBVS D: G: MAG : BRI : FRA : ET HIB : REX. Otherwise like the first. *MB.* MM thistle, like the last but bust a little larger, harp has not got griffin's head, no dot before or after obv. legend. *MB.* Rud. xi. 10, which has : after Eos. MM lis, similar but bust not identical. *MB.* Or reading FRAN : *EVANS.* MM lis, same but bust smaller than before, face different and looking rather bloated. (99) *MB.* MM trefoil, bust broader, face not so bloated, .IACOBVS. D. G. MA. BRI. FRAN. ET. HIBE. REX. *MB.* Or with two dots between each word on obv., none before Iacobus, HIB instead of Hibe. *MB.*

SPUR RYAL. 1605 *to* 1612. *Value* 15*s or* 16*s* 6*d*. *Weight* 106$\frac{2}{3}$ *grs. Old Standard.* Obv. King standing in ship, crowned, sword in right hand, large shield bearing the arms, arranged as on the Rose Ryals, on his left arm. Mast on each side of the king, none visible behind him, but three ropes from above his head to each end of the ship. The ship has a beak and is sailing to left, flag marked I at prow, two rows of port-holes. Rose on side of ship. Beaded inner circle. Rev. like former ryals, rose on sun concealing centre of a cross, each limb of which ends in a lis between two cartouches, a lion with a crown above him in each angle, all within a double tressure of eight arches, having a trefoil in each spandril. .IACOBVS. D. G. MAG. BRIT. FRAN. ET. HIB. REX. Rev. .A. DNO. FACTVM. EST. ISTVD. ET. EST. MIRABILE. MM rose. Rud. xii. 2. *MB.* Scallop, *MB.* Star or mullet, *Cuff's sale catalogue.*

1612 *to* 1619. *Value* 16*s* 6*d*. *Weight* 108 *grs. Old Standard.* Exactly like the others. MM tower, (100) *MB.* Trefoil, *Num. Chron.*, N. S., ii. 232. Cinquefoil, *ib.* iv. 229. Book, *MB.*

1619 *to* 1625. *Value* 15*s*. *Weight* 98$\frac{2}{11}$ or 97$\frac{7}{89}$ *grs. Old Standard.* Obv. lion crowned standing on his hind legs, holding in his right fore-paw a sceptre, his left supporting in front of him a shield bearing the royal arms. To left of shield X, to right V, indicating the value of the coin. The lion's crown extends to the top of the coin, dividing the circle, which is beaded, and the legend. Rev. Rose on sun concealing centre of a cross, each limb of which terminates in a lis, with a crown above it; a lion with a crown above him in each angle; all within a double tressure of eight arches, having a pellet in each spandril. IACOBVS D : G : MAG : BRIT : FRA : ET HI : REX Rev. A DNO : FACTVM EST ISTVD ET EST MIRABI : MM spur rowel, with a dot on each side of it on the obverse. *MB.* Rud. xii. 6. MM rose, same. *MB.* MM trefoil, no such dot, and reading BRI : FR : and MIRABILE. (101) *MB.* Spur ryals are all rare; fine specimens of those before 1619 have sold for from £8 to £13, and those of the later dates for from £9 to £17.

HALF-SOVEREIGN. 1603-4. *Value* 10*s*. *Weight* $85\frac{65}{67}$ *grs*. *Fineness* 22 *cts*. Obv. small bust in profile to right, crowned, in armour, within inner circle. Rev. Plain square shield crowned between I and R, the crown dividing inner circle and legend. MM thistle. .IACOBVS. D. G. .ANGL. SCO. FRAN. ET. HIBER. REX. Rev. .EXVRGAT. DEVS. DISSIPENTVR. INIMICI. (102) Rud. xi. 2. *MB*.

DOUBLE CROWN, or HALF UNITE. 1604 *to* 1612. *Value* 10*s or* 11*s*. *Weight* $77\frac{13}{31}$ *grs*. *Fineness* 22 *cts*. Type like the half-sovereign, but the bust is not the same, the king wears a falling collar with lace edge, and his armour is more ornamented. .IACOBVS. D. G. MAG. BRIT. FRAN. ET. HIB. REX. Rev. .HENRICVS. ROSAS. REGNA. IACOBVS. (Henry united the roses, James unites the kingdoms.) MM lis. *MB*. MM rose, same. *MB*. Rud. xi. 6. MM scallop, face somewhat different and different armour. (103) *MB*. MM coronet, same. *MB*.

1612 *to* 1619. *Value* 11*s*. *Weight* $77\frac{209}{491}$ *grs*. *Fineness* 22 *cts*. Like the last but face and armour different, hair longer, I and R on rev. much smaller; and reading MA. BRI. FRA. MM ton. *EVANS*. MM cross, MA BRI FRAN. *MB*.

DOUBLE CROWN or HALF-LAUREL. 1619 *to* 1625. *Value* 10*s*. *Weight* $70\frac{190}{491}$ or $70\frac{10}{41}$ *grs*. *Fineness* 22 *cts*. Type like the corresponding laurels. The harp on all of them has got the griffin's head. Figure X behind bust. .IACOBVS D : G : MAG : BRI : FRA : ET HI : REX. Rev. HENRICVS ROSAS REGNA IACOBVS MM spur rowel. *MB*. MM rose, bust similar to that on corresponding laurel, legends as last, but HIB :, no dot before or after obv. legend, the MM on rev. is placed after Regna. (104) *MB*. Another specimen has a slightly different bust. *MB*. MM lis, same, with same bust as one of those with MM rose. *MB*. Or reading IACOB' for Jacobus on both sides. *MB*. Or like the last, with HENRIC, and a dot after Rex. *MB*. Or IACOBVS D: G : MAG : BR : FRA : ET HI : REX Rev. HENRIC ROSAS REGNA IACOB *MB*. MM trefoil, bust like those with MM lis. Obv. legend like spur rowel, but no dot before or after it. Rev. HENRIC. ROSAS REGNA IACOB. The MM on rev. is placed after Regna. *MB*. Or IACO. *EVANS*. Rud. xi. 11 reads FR : ET. HIB :.

ANGEL. 1605 *to* 1612. *Value* 10*s* *or* 11*s*. *Weight* 71$\frac{1}{9}$ *grs*. *Old Standard*. Obv. St. Michael and the dragon, as on previous angels. Rev. Ship as on previous angels, but with no cross above the shield in front of the mast, on which is a top-castle. Two ropes from mast to each end of ship, which is sailing to right. Arms on shield arranged as on ryals. I to left, rose to right of mast. .IACOBVS. D. G. MAG. BRIT. FRA. ET. HI. REX. Rev. .A. DNO. FACTVM. EST. ISTVD: MM rose. *MB*. Scallop. *MB*. Coronet, Rud. xii. 3. *MB*. On these three the ship has a bowsprit. MM mullet, same, but with no bowsprit. (105) *MB*. The A in FRA is omitted in the plate.

1612 *to* 1619. *Value* 11*s*. *Weight* 72 *grs*. *Old Standard*. MM tower, like mullet, but MA. BRI. FR., one dot after Istud. *MB*. MM trefoil, like mullet, but only one dot after Istud. *MB*. MM cinquefoil, like tower. *EVANS*. MM ton, like tower, but FRA. *MB*. MM crescent, like tower, but no dot after Istud. *MB*.

1619 *to* 1625. *Value* 10*s*. *Weight* 65$\frac{5}{11}$ or 64$\frac{64}{89}$ *grs*. *Old Standard*. Type of obv. as before, but with the figure X, indicating the value, under the angel's left wing. Rev. Very different ship, sailing to left, side ornamented with lions and lis alternately, a row of port-holes below them; lis on poop, three masts, one large sail set embroidered with the royal arms, above it a pennon with two streamers, embroidered with a lion. A small lion holding a sword stands on the ship's beak, and a small lion crowned on the stern. IACOBVS D: G: MAG: BRIT: FRA: ET HI: REX. Rev. A DNO: FACTVM. EST. ISTVD: Scroll ornament after A. MM spur rowel. This MM is placed on both sides of the mast on rev. *MB.* MM rose, similar, but reading BRI: and HIB: Rev. A DOMINO FACTVM EST ISTVD. No ornament after A, no MM to left of mast on rev., ship slightly different. *MB.* Rud. xii. 7. MM thistle, *Cuff's Sale Catalogue.* MM lis, *EVANS.* MM trefoil, legends as rose, but dot before A and after every word on rev., none after Rex. Ship almost the same as the last. (106) *MB.*

HALF-ANGEL. 1612 *to* 1619. *Value* 5*s* 6*d.* *Weight* 36 *grs.* *Old Standard.* Type like the angels. .IACOBVS D. G. MA. BRI. FRA. ET. HI. REX. Rev. .A. DNO. FACTVM. EST. ISTVD. MM tower. *EVANS.* MM cinquefoil. (107) *MB.* MM cross, same, but IACOBVS. D. G. MA. BR. FR. ET. H : REX, no dot before A on rev. *MB.* Rud. xii. 4. One in Mr. Cuff's collection was catalogued as having MM mullet, and if so it would have belonged to the second coinage, and have been struck in 1611-12. Half-angels are not mentioned in any of the indentures or proclamations, and it is only by their mint-marks that we know when they were struck.

CROWN. 1603-4. *Value* 5*s.* *Weight* $42\frac{66}{67}$ *grs.* *Fineness* 22 *cts.* Obv. like half-sovereign, and rev. similar, but the shield descends through the inner circle nearly to the bottom of the coin, I and R are above it on each side of the crown. MM thistle .IACOBVS. D. G. ANG. SCO. FRA. ET. HIB. REX. Rev. .TVEATVR. VNITA. DEVS. (108). *MB.* Rud. xi. 3.

BRITAIN CROWN. 1604 *to* 1612. *Value* 5*s or* 5*s* 6*d.* *Weight* $38\frac{22}{31}$ *grs.* *Fineness* 22 *cts.* Like the former crown, but the shield on rev. does not descend through the inner circle, and the crown above it is much smaller. . IACOBVS . D. G. MAG. BRIT. FRA. ET. HIB. REX. Rev. .HENRICVS. ROSAS. REGNA. IACOBVS. MM lis. *MB.*

Rose, Rud. xi. 7. *MB.* Scallop. *MB.* Or with a different and larger bust, armour rather plainer, no dot before or after obv. legend, MM mullet. *MB.*

1612 *to* 1619. *Value* 5s 6*d.* *Weight* $38\frac{350}{491}$ *grs.* *Fineness* 22 *cts.* Type as before but bust different again, beard more projecting, armour different, MA. BRI. FRA. ET. HI., no dot at end of legends. MM ton. (109) *MB.*

CROWN or QUARTER LAUREL. 1619 *to* 1625. *Value* 5*s.* *Weight* $35\frac{95}{491}$ or $35\frac{5}{41}$ *grs.* *Fineness* 22 *cts.* Type like the corresponding laurels, but V behind head. The harp on the first three has not the griffin's head, on those with MM trefoil it has. The MM on the reverse is placed after the word Regna, except on the coin with MM lis. IACOBVS. D : G : MAG : BRI : FR : ET HIB : REX Rev. HENRICVS ROSAS REGNA IACOBVS MM rose. *MB.* MM thistle, same but FRA : ET HI : *MB.* MM lis, as last but IACOB' on obv. instead of Jacobus, the MM on rev. placed at the beginning of the legend. *MB.* MM trefoil, bust slightly different, obv. legend as rose but HI : Rev. HENRIC ROSAS REGNA IACOB, the harp has a griffin's head. (110) *MB.* Or same as last with no inner circle on rev. *MB.* Or as last but one, but reading FRA : Rud. xi. 12.

THISTLE CROWN. 1604 *to* 1612. *Value* 4*s or* 4*s* $4\frac{3}{4}$*d.* *Weight* $30\frac{30}{31}$ *grs.* *Fineness* 22 *cts.* Obv. rose on stalk with two leaves, crowned, between I and R. The crown divides the legend. Rev. Thistle on stalk with two leaves, crowned, between I and R; the crown divides the legend. .IA. D. G. MAG. BR. F. ET. H. REX. TVEATVR. VNITA. DEVS. MM lis. (111) *MB.* Rose, Rud. xi. 13. Scallop, *MB.* Bell, *MB.* Mullet, *MB.* Those with the last two mint-marks differ in having no stop before or after obv. legend. These coins do not seem to have been struck after 1611, when the addition to their value made them extremely inconvenient for reckoning.

HALF-CROWN. 1603-4. *Value* 2*s* 6*d*. *Weight* 21$\frac{33}{67}$ *grs*. *Fineness* 22 *cts*. Like the earliest crown, but the crown over the shield on rev. is larger in proportion, though the globe and cross on its top alone divide the legend. IACOBVS. D. G. AN. SC. FR. ET. HI. REX Rev.. TVEATVR VNITA. DEVS MM thistle. Rud. xi. 4.

1604 *to* 1612. *Value* 2*s* 6*d or* 2*s* 9*d*. *Weight* 19$\frac{11}{31}$ *grs*. *Fineness* 22 *cts*. Same type as before, but bust different. Legends .I. D. G. ROSA. SINE. SPINA. Rev. .TVEATVR. VNITA. DEVS MM lis, *MB*. Rose (112) *MB*. Or with stop after Deus. *MB*. Scallop, Rud. xi. 8. *MB*. Coronet. *EVANS*.

1612 *to* 1619. *Value* 2*s* 9*d*. *Weight* 19$\frac{175}{491}$ *grs*. *Fineness* 22 *cts*. As the last but different and larger head, beard more prominent, no dot after Tueatur. MM cinquefoil. *THORBURN*. Same with dot after Tueatur, none after Deus, two after Spina, MM ton. *MB*. Another with the same MM has the bust different again, different armour, broader collar; the shield on rev. scarcely descends through inner circle and does not divide legend, the crown above it does. Only one dot after Spina, none after Deus. *MB*. One with this reverse was sold at the Pembroke sale, in 1848, as having MM crescent. Gold half-crowns were not coined after 1619.

The following list of mint-marks is copied from Hawkins's "Silver Coins of England," and was copied for that book from Snelling.

Table of Mint Marks.

	Date when ordered to be used.	Rose Ryal.	Sov. Unite or Laurel.	Spur Ryal.	½ Sov. Double Crown or ½ Laurel.	Angel.	Crown.	½ Angel.	Thistle Crown.	½ Crown.
1st Coinage.										
Thistle . .	May 21, 1603		+ +		+		+			Rud.
2nd Coinage.										
Lis . . .	May 22, 1604		+		+		+		+	+
Rose . . .	June 20, 1605	+	+	+	+	+	+		Rud.	+
Escallop . .	July 10, 1606	+	+	+	+	+	+		+	+
Grapes . .	June 30, 1607		Montagu							Evans
Coronet . .	Nov. 11, 1607	+	+		+	+				
Key . . .	May 17, 1609		+							
Bell . . .	May 11, 1610		+						+	
Mullet . .	May 9, 1611	+	+	Cuff		+	+	Cuff	+	
3rd Coinage.										
Tower . .	May 22, 1612	+	+	+		+		Evans		
Trefoil . .	Apr. 28, 1613	+	Montagu	*Nm. Chr.*		+				

Table of Mint Marks—*continued.*

	Date when ordered to be used	Rose Ryal.	Sov. Unite or Laurel.	Spur Ryal.	½ Sov. Double Crown or ½ Laurel.	Angel.	Crown.	½ Angel.	Thistle Crown.	½ Crown.
3RD COINAGE—*continued*										
Cinquefoil . .	Oct. 20, 1613		+	*Nm Chr.*		Evans		+		Thorbrn.
Ton . . .	May 17, 1615		+		Evans	+	+			+ +
Book . . .	Nov. 13, 1616		Montagu	+						
Crescent . .	Aug. 23, 1617		+			+				Pemb.
Plain Cross . .	May 15, 1618		+		+			+		
Saltire Cross . .	June 9, 1619									
4TH COINAGE.										
Spur Rowel . .	Aug. 20, 1619	+	+	+	+	+				
Rose . . .	June 23, 1620	+	+	+	+ +	+	+			
Thistle . .	June 8, 1621	+	+			Cuff	+			
Lis . . .	July 3, 1623	+	+ +		+	Evans	+			
Trefoil . .	June 27, 1624	+	+	+	+	+	+			

Charles I, 1625 to 1648.

Charles I succeeded his father on the 27th of March, 1625, and was proclaimed the following day; and on the 1st of April a commission was directed to the wardens of the mint, Sir Edward Villiers and Sir Wm. Parkhurst, and others, to continue the mint at work according to the last indenture of James I, which had expired upon his death. The dies of the late king were to be used until others should be provided. The coins thus ordered to be made were Unites, Double Crowns, and Britain Crowns, of "crown" gold, and Rose Ryals, Spur Ryals, and Angels of the old standard or "angel" gold, and, excepting that no Ryals were actually coined, and that during the civil war £3 pieces were issued at Oxford, no alteration was afterwards made during the reign either in the denominations of the coins or in the purity of the metal. Considering the straits to which the king was often driven for want of money, and considering that Henry VIII, Elizabeth, and James I, had all either increased the nominal value of the coins or diminished the quantity of gold contained in them, this fact must be considered creditable to Charles I and his advisers. There was indeed a Commission issued on the 14th of August, 1626, which, after stating that the king had resolved to continue his monies, to be coined at his mint, of the same standard as they then were, proceeds to order that the pound of crown gold should be made into £44 by tale (£41 being the amount previously fixed) and the pound of silver into £3. 10*s* 6*d* (instead of £3. 2*s*). The Commission contains no recital of an intention to diminish the weight of the coins, and it is probable that no such intention existed, and that the sums named were inserted by mistake, for on the 4th of September a proclamation was issued that all monies of gold and silver coined since the 1st day of August in any other manner than according to the proclamations which were in force on that day, should be esteemed as bullion and not be current; and a commission of the 7th of September to Villiers and

Parkhurst, and an indenture of the 8th of November with Sir Robert Harley, fixed the same weights as in the last indenture of James I. Angels were not coined after 1634, and ever since that time crown gold has been the only standard used for the coins.

Several mints besides that in the Tower were used during this reign, both before and after the breaking out of the civil war, but those at Bristol and Oxford are the only ones at which gold is known to have been coined. The legends introduced by James I were all discontinued, and instead of them were used "Amor Populi Præsidium Regis," "Florent Concordiâ Regna," and "Cultores sui Deus Protegit;" but during the civil wars "Exurgat Deus dissipentur inimici" (Ps. lxviii. 1) was revived upon the coins struck by the king's party, together with an abbreviation of "Religio Protestans, Leges Angliæ, Libertas Parliamenti," referring to Charles's declaration at Wellington, September 19th, 1642, that he would "preserve the Protestant religion, the known laws of the land, and the just privileges and freedom of Parliament." The type upon which this inscription occurs is hence called the "Declaration" type.

No legal currency was given to any foreign gold coins during this reign, though about the year 1644 several are said to have been commonly current in the southern and western counties.

The types and descriptions of the various coins are as follows:—

UNITES. *Value* 20*s.* *Weight* $140\frac{20}{41}$ *grs.* *Fineness* 22 *cts.* These are of several different types, corresponding to a great extent with those of the silver shillings. The dates of the various mint-marks are given in the table on p. 165.

TOWER MINT. Type 1. King's bust in profile to left, crowned, with ruff, royal mantle, and collar of the garter, XX behind head. Two inner circles, the innermost thin and plain, the outermost beaded. CAROLVS D. G. MAG. BR.

FR. ET HI. REX. Rev. square shield garnished, the crown over it divides the legend. Inner circles as on obv. The harp in the arms has a bird's or griffin's head. FLORENT: CONCORDIA : REGNA : MM lis. (113) *MB*. Rud. xiii. 1 reads BRI, and has a different arrangement of dots. MM cross on step, same, but only one inner circle on obv., no stops on rev. *MONTAGU*.

Type 1*a*. Different bust, crowned, with ruff, armour nearly concealed by scarf fastened on left shoulder, only one inner circle, which is beaded, and is slightly pierced both by crown above and by front of scarf below. The rest of the bust does not touch the inner circle. XX behind head. Rev. square shield very slightly garnished. The harp always has a griffin's head except with the Plume mint-mark. MM cross on step. Legends as type 1, but only one dot after Regna. *THORBURN*. Or BRIT. FRA., dot after Carolus, Et, and Regna, none after other words on rev. *MB*. MM negro's head, legends as type 1, but two dots instead of one on obv., none after Rex or on rev. *MB*. Or reading CAROLVS. D : G : MAG. BRI : FR. ET. HIB. REX., one dot after each word on rev. *MB*. Or BR., no dots on rev. *EVANS*. MM castle, legends and dots as type 1, but dot before Carolus, none after Rex or on rev. *MB*. Or dot before Carolus and after every word except Carolus on obv., none on rev. *MB*. Or reading BRI, dot before Carolus and after every word except HI on obv., one before and after rev. legend, but none between words on rev. *MB*. BRI, no dots except after D and G. *THORBURN*. Or BR, HIB, dot before Carolus and after every word on obv., none on rev. *MB*. MM anchor, BR. FRA. ET HIB., dot after every word on obv. except Et and Rex, none on rev. *MB*. Or with the obv. mint-mark placed under the bust, . . BRI. FRA. ET. H., dot after every word on obv., none on rev. *MB*. Or reading MA. BR. FR ET HI, no stops on rev. *MONTAGU*. MM heart, much neater workmanship, plain inner circle on both sides within beaded one, .CAROLVS. D. G.

MA. BR . . FR. ET. HI. REX., dot after every word on rev. and after rev. mint-mark. *MB.* MM obv. heart, rev. plume. HIB. Plain circle on both sides of beaded inner circle. *EVANS.* MM plume, like the last but one, but: after the abbreviated words on obv., no stops between words on rev., no plain inner circle on rev. *MB.* One with MM plume and with the same bust as the preceding ones has a thick plain inner circle on obv. and reads CAROLVS D : G : MA : BR : FR : ET HI : REX Rev. like the next type, with dot before Florent, after every word, and after mint-mark. *MB.*

Type 2. Obverse nearly the same, but rather more armour visible. CAROLVS. D. G. MAG. BRIT. FR. ET. HIB. REX. Rev. oval shield garnished, crowned, between C and R, dot in field each side of crown. .FLORENT. CONCORDIA. REGNA. Dot after mint-mark. Plain inner circle within beaded one on both sides. MM plume. *MB.* Rud. xiii. 4. Or with dot before Carolus, none before Florent. *MB.* MM large rose, no plain inner circle on rev., no dot before Carolus or Florent. *MB.* Or BRI. FRA., as first of this type but no plain inner circle on obv. *MB.* Or MM small rose on obv., large rose on rev. BR. FR. ET. HI. Rude workmanship. *EVANS.*

Type 3. Bust crowned to left, in armour, face larger, no ruff nor scarf, long hair, lovelock on left shoulder, deep falling collar edged with lace, ribbon of the garter suspended on breast. XX behind head. .CAROLVS. D. G. MAG. BRIT. FRA. ET. HIB. REX. Rev. oval shield garnished, different from the last, crowned, between C and R crowned. Beaded inner circle on both sides interrupted by crown. FLORENT CONCORDIA REGNA, MM harp. *MB.* Rud. xiii. 5 reads BRI. FR. MM portcullis, bust rather smaller, less shoulder visible, BR. FR. ET. HI. No dot before or after obv. legend, one after Florent and Concordia, three after Regna. *MB.* Or HIB, with no stops on rev. *MONTAGU.* MM bell, .CAROLVS. D. G. MA. BR. FR. ET. HIB. REX. Dot before Florent, after every word on rev. and after rev. mint-mark. *MB.* MM crown, as bell but HI, no dots on rev. *MB.* MM ton, as crown, but dot between words on rev. *MB.* MM prostrate anchor, as bell, but no dot before Florent or after Regna. *MB.* Or reading B. FR. ET. HI : : *THORBURN.* MM (P), as bell, but MAG. BRI. FRA. *MB.* This coin is later than most of those next to be described, as the (P) mint-mark is placed by Folkes and Ruding immediately before, and by Pollet, who is probably right, immediately after the (R) mint-mark.

The following are of similar type, but the face is more marked, the armour different, the lace on the collar of a stellate pattern. MM triangle, CAROLVS. D. G. MAG. BRI. FRA. ET. HIB. REX, dot after every word on rev. and after rev. mint-mark. (114) *MB.* MM star, same with dot each side of obv. mint-mark. *MB.* MM triangle within circle, as last. *MB.* Or reading FLORRENT by mistake for Florent. *THORBURN.* MM (R), bust very slightly different, dot before Florent, otherwise as last. *MB.* One with MM eye is mentioned in *Num. Chron.*, i, p. 33. With bust different, hair brushed more forward, collar smaller and lace of a different pattern, armour different, harp in arms much smaller, MM sun, legends as star. *MB.* MM sceptre, same, with legends as triangle. *MB.*

Briot. The coins executed by Nicholas Briot, who was first employed in England in 1628, and was appointed chief engraver in 1633, are smaller and much neater and better executed than the others. 1. Bust similar to type 3 but better executed, with scarf fastened by rosette over left shoulder, ·XX· behind head. CAROLVS. D : G. MAGN. BRITANN. FRAN. ET. HIB. REX. Rev. Square shield garnished, crowned, between C and R crowned, a lozenge beneath each of these letters. .FLORENT. CONCORDIA. REGNA. MM on obv. flower with B (for Briot) under it, on rev. B only. The dots are all lozenge shaped. (115). *MB.* 2. Same but B to left of, instead of under, obv. MM, HIBER for Hib. Rev. C and R placed higher in the field, no lozenge under them, nor before or after legend. *MB.* Rud. xiv. 1 is like this but reads BRITAN and HIB and has lozenge before and after rev. legend. 3. Bust like that on the coins with MM triangle, &c., letters behind head larger. .CAROLVS. D: G. MAG. BRIT. FR. ET. HIB. REX. Rev. similar to the last but one. FLORENT. CONCORDIA. REGNA. MM anchor. Dots all lozenge shaped. *MB.* There is no B on this coin to show that it was executed by Briot, but there is a B on a shilling with the same MM.

Oxford Unites. The mint originally established for coining silver at Aberystwith, and brought from that place to Shrewsbury at the beginning of the civil war, was removed to Oxford and set up there in New Inn Hall on the 3rd of January, 1642 (old style), under the direction of Sir William Parkhurst and Thomas Bushell. The only distinction between the coins struck at Shrewsbury and at Oxford in 1642, seems to be in the form of the plumes in the field of the coins, the plumes on the Shrewsbury coins springing from a large coronet with no bands under it, those on the Oxford ones from a small coronet with bands. We are not aware of the existence of any Shrewsbury gold coins, but the following varieties were struck at Oxford.

1642. Half-length figure in profile to left descending to inner circle, crowned, in armour, plain falling collar, large sword upright in right hand, olive branch in left, XX behind head. CAROLVS: D: G: MAG: BRIT: FRAN: ET: HI: REX. Rev. Inscription in two lines across the field, RELIG: PROT: LEG ANG: LIBER: PAR, a wavy line above, between, and below the two rows of words, three plumes, with bands beneath them, above, 1642 below. Legend EXVRGAT: DEVS: DISSIPENTVR: INIMICI: No MM. (116) *MB.* For the meaning of the inscription see ante, p. 150.

1643. The workmanship in this year is decidedly better than in 1642.

1. Bust descends through inner circle to edge of coin, hair much longer, deep falling lace collar, longer sword in

right hand, longer olive branch in left, badge of the Garter suspended by chain on breast, XX behind head. Legend begins at bottom of coin. .CAROLVS. D: G: M: BR: FR: ET. HI: REX. Rev. type as the last, but the inscription is in three lines and is placed on a scroll connected with the inner circle, so that the legend and inscription read continously. .EXVRGAT: DEVS: DISSIPENTVR: INIMICI RELIG: PROT LEG: ANG LIBER: PAR. No MM. Date 1643 below scroll, three plumes above it. *MB.*

2. Obv. same. Rev. similar but scroll shaped rather differently, no dot before Exurgat, one after each word of legend and before Leg, ANGL: for Ang. *MB.* This is almost identical with a double crown, Rud. xiii. 11, *post*, p. 162.

3. Obv. similar, but the figure does not descend through the inner circle, the crown slightly pierces it above. A good deal of the lace collar is shown behind the hair and over the left shoulder, the olive branch slopes backwards more than on the previous coins. The legend begins at the top of the coin, CAROLVS: D: G: MAG: BRIT: FR: ET: HI: REX. Rev. scroll shaped as on No. 2, EXVRGAT: DEVS: DISIPENTVR (*sic*): INIMICI RELIG: PROT LEG: ANG LIBER: PAR Plumes above, 1643 below. *MB.*

4. Obv. similar to the last, but the figure is smaller and the crown does not pierce the inner circle; no collar visible behind the hair, the badge suspended on the breast is larger and much more prominent. Legend CAROLVS: D: G. MAG: BR: FR: ET: HIBER: REX Rev. similar to the last, EXVRGAT. DEVS. DISSIPENTVR. INIMICI: RELIG: PROT: LEG: ANG: LIBER: PAR *MB.*

5. Obv. from the same die as the last. Rev. scroll of different shape, otherwise as No. 3 but DISSIPENTVR: *MB.*

1644. 1. Similar to 4 but figure different, medal on breast and letters behind head much smaller, olive branch much larger. MM very small plume. CAROLVS. D: G: MAG: BRI: FR: ET. HIB: REX. Rev. like 1643

(1), but date 1644, with OX for Oxford below it. .EXVRGAT DEVS. DISSIPENTVR. INIMICI. RELIG : PROT LEG : .ANG : LIBER : PAR. *MB.* Rud. xiii. 10.

2. Figure similar but placed lower in field, interrupting inner circle but not legend, head and crown larger. MM plume, and legend as last but BR :, HI :, dot before Carolus. Rev. Inscription in three lines across field within inner circle, a straight line above and below it, three plumes between two lozenges above it, $\overset{\cdot 1644 \cdot}{\cdot \mathrm{OX} \cdot}$ below. EXVRGAT. DEVS. DISSIPENTVR .INIMICI : Inscription RELIG. PR. LEG. ANGL LIBER. PA. All the dots are lozenge-shaped, except those between the words of the inscription. *MB.*

1645. Bust almost identical with the first of 1644 but placed rather lower in field, olive branch smaller, MM and legend same but BRIT :, HI :, two dots between every word. Rev. similar but scroll of different shape, date 1645, without OX, below it; no dot before Exurgat, one after it, two after Prot, none after Par. *MB.*

1646. Bust similar, but neater and better executed. No MM. CAROLVS. D : G : MAG : BRI : FRAN : ET. HIB : REX. Rev. usual legend on a band round the field, the ends of which are separated at the top of the coin by the MM plume. Dot between each word. Inscription in three lines on wavy scroll, RELIG : PRO LEG : ANG LIBER : PAR Nothing except the MM above it, $\overset{1646}{\mathrm{OX}}$ below. (117) *MB.*

Bristol Unite. Bust similar to the second Oxford one of 1644, but ruder, collar of different shape, sword very small, crown pierces inner circle, which is not interrupted by the bust. The letters XX behind the head are large. MM BR in monogram. .CAROLVS. D : G : MAG : BR : FR : ET : H : REX. Rev. Inscription on scroll continuous with the legend, but divided from it by the monogram BR; three very small plumes above inscription, 1645 below. EXVRGAT. DEVS. DISSIPENTVR. INIMICI. :REL : PRO LEG : AN. LIB : PA : *MB.* This, as well as some silver coins of dates from 1643 to 1645, is ascribed on account of the mint-mark to Bristol, which was in the king's hands during those years. The workmen for this mint must no doubt have been brought from Oxford. A specimen of this coin was sold for £29 at Capt. Murchison's sale in 1864. *Num. Chr.*, N. S., iv. 229. That in the Museum was bought for £12. Compare the Double Crown (124).

UNCERTAIN UNITES. 1. Small rude bust, copied from the Tower Unite with MM triangle. The type of the whole coin is the same, but the execution much ruder. MM plume. : CAROLVS. D. G. MA. BR. FR. ET. HI. REX : Rev. .FLORENT. CONCORDIA. REGNA. Dot after mint-mark. *MB.* It seems not improbable that this may have been executed at Aberystwith, though we know no record of gold having been coined there. The mint at Aberystwith was worked from 1637 or 1638 to 1642, and the type of some of the silver coins struck there is identical with that of the coins struck at the Tower with the triangle MM, the date of which is 1639. The mint-marks on the Aberystwith silver coins are a Book or a Crown, but all coins struck there were ordered to be marked on both sides with a plume, and this Unite, which has the plume on one side though not on both, may have been struck at Aberystwith during the period of confusion in 1642, while the regular workmen of the mint were removing to Shrewsbury and Oxford. (See Hawkins's "Silver Coins," 2nd ed., pp. 316, 322.)

2. Type like an uncertain shilling, Hks. (530), Rud. E. 11, but no dots on armour, medal on breast much smaller, XX behind head. Shield oval, garniture similar but not identical with that on the shilling, crowned, between C and R crowned. MM on obv. only, uncertain. CAROLVS : D : G. MA : BR. FR : ET HIB. REX. Rev. ° FLORENT ° CONCORDIA ° REGNA ⁰₀ *MB.* The silver coins of this type resemble those which are believed to have been struck at Weymouth, and they as well as this gold coin

were probably therefore produced there, or at least by the same artists.

THREE POUND PIECES. *Value* 60*s.* *Weight* 421$\frac{19}{41}$ *grs.* *Fineness* 22 *cts.* These are all of the type of the Oxford Unites, and were all probably struck in that city. Like the silver pounds, they occur of the dates 1642 to 1644.

1642. 1. Exactly like the Unite of 1642, but plume with bands below it instead of the figures behind the head, and rev. inscription in three lines across the field, .III., indicating the value, and three plumes, above it, 1642 below. MM plume on obv. CAROLVS : D : G : MAG : BRIT : FR : ET : HIB : REX Rev. ·:· EXVRGAT : DEVS : DISSIPENTVR : INIMICI RELIG : PROT LEG : ANG LIBER : PAR *MB.* Rud. xiii. 9 is similar, but reads FRAN : ET : HI : and has only two dots before Exurgat.

2. Similar, but king's figure smaller, not touching inner circle, sword smaller, FRAN : ET : HI : Rev. similar, but the inscription is on a scroll in continuation of the inner circle. LEGI : Only one dot before Exurgat. *MB.*

1643. 1. Same as the last, but inner circle is made part of the scroll; LEG : Date 1643. *MB.* The reverse is identical with that of the first Unite of 1643, except for the .III. above the inscription.

2. Obv. like the first Unite of 1643, but the bust is confined within the inner circle, and has a large scarf flowing out behind it, and plume instead of figures behind the head. The legend begins at the top of the coin, CAROLVS : D : G : MAGN : BRIT : FR : ET : HI : REX MM plume. Rev. almost exactly the same as Unite No. 5, but EXVRGAT : DEVS : ET : DISSIPENTVR : INIMICI : RELIG : PROT : LEGI. : ANGL : LIBER : PAR. *MB.*

3. Like last but without scarf, figure rather smaller, FRAN : ET : HIB : REX .: Only one dot after Carolus and G. Rev. identical with the Unite of 1643, No. 4, except

that it has III above the scroll, and has : after PROT as well as before LEG. *MB.*

4. Obv. from same die as last. Rev. similar, but a rosette each side of III, two after each word in legend and inscription except Par, three after Prot, two before Leg, one before Liber and after Par. OXON in small letters under date, rosette each side of it and each side of date. (118) *MB. Very rare.*

1644. 1. Bust almost the same as Unite of 1643, No. 3, coin considerably smaller and thicker than the former ones. CAROLVS. D : G : MAG : BRI : FRA : ET. HIBER : REX. MM plume. Rev. Scroll of rather different shape from the last, legend and inscription the same, plumes above scroll very small, $^{1644}_{OX}$ below it. Lozenge each side of III and date, after Relig, Leg, Ang, and Liber, and before Leg, two before Exurgat and between words of legend, one between four dots after Inimici. *MB.*

2. Obv. from same die as last. Rev. same but OXON, dots instead of lozenges, one between each word of legend, after Liber, and each side of date and Oxon, two after Relig, Leg, Ang, and Par, and before Leg, five after Inimici. *MB.*

3. As last but coin still smaller and thicker, crown does not pierce inner circle, lozenges instead of dots on obv. Rev. as last, but of rather neater execution, plumes larger, one dot after each word of legend, two after each word of inscription and before Leg, one each side of date and Oxon. *MB.*

ANGEL. *Value* 10*s.* *Weight* 64$\frac{64}{89}$ *grs.* *Old Standard.* Obv. St. Michael and the Dragon, as usual. Spear pierces dragon's mouth and comes out the other side. Two inner circles, the innermost plain, the other beaded. CAROLVS. D. G : MAG : BRI : FR : ET. HI : REX Rev. as James I's latest angels. AMOR. POPVLI. PRÆSIDIVM. REGIS : MM cross on step, placed to left of St. Michael's head and right of mast. (119) *MB.* MM negro's head, X in field by Dragon's head, rev. mint-mark to left of mast, FRA. ET. HIB., only one dot between each word, none at end of legends. *MB.* MM castle, as cross on step but X in field by St. Michael's left wing, rev. mint-mark to left of mast, no dots after Regis. *MB.* MM anchor, same but : after D on obv., no stops on rev. *MB.* MM heart, *bought by Mr. Shepherd at Mr. Cuff's sale.* MM rose, X under St. Michael's right wing, pellet between his legs above the dragon. Only one dot between words on obv., none on rev. *MB.* The mint-mark on this specimen seems to be struck over the preceding MM plume. MM portcullis, as last but BRIT. FRA., dot after Rex and between words on rev. *MB.* MM bell, as last, dot after rev. mint-mark. Rud. xiii. 8. This is erroneously stated to be in the British Museum.

Briot. Like the other angels, but the coin is considerably smaller and the workmanship neater. Type as before but St. Michael's figure is smaller and has both legs straight, X under his left wing. CAROLVS. D : G. MAG. BRITANN. FRAN. ET. HIB. REX. Rev. more rigging visible, the harp on the sail not concealed, as on the other coins, by the foremast, cannons protruding from the port-holes, no flag above sail but one marked with cross at stern, no lion on prow or stern but small B (for Briot) in front of prow, with lozenge above and below. AMOR. POPVLI. PRÆSIDIVM. REGIS. All the stops are lozenge-shaped. *MB.* Rud. Suppl. vi. 25.

DOUBLE CROWN. *Value* 10*s.* *Weight* $70\frac{10}{41}$ *grs.* *Fineness* 22 *cts.* These correspond in type to the Unites. They all have X behind the head, to indicate the value.

Type 1. Like Unites type 1, but shield rather differently garnished. CAROLVS. D. G. MAG. BR. FR. ET. HIB. REX. Rev. CVLTORES SVI DEVS PROTEGIT. MM lis, which on rev. is to right of crown. *MB.* Or with rev. MM to left of crown, : after D, Mag, Br, Fr, and Hib, before Cultores, after each word on rev., and after rev. mint-mark. *MB.* Rud. xiii. 2 reads HI : and has the stops rather different.

Type 1*a*, like Unites type 1*a*, but the crown does not

pierce the inner circle. CAROLVS: D: G: MAG: BRI FRA: ET: HI: REX. Rev. CVLTORES SVI DEVS PROTEGIT MM cross on step. *MB.* MM negro's head, same with no inner circle, BR. FR., one dot before Carolus, after every word, and each side of rev. mint-mark. *MB.* MM castle, as last but no dot before or after Carolus or after Et, two between the other words on obv., one after Rex, none on rev. *MB.* Or reading BRI. FR. ET. HIB., only one dot between each word on obv. *THORBURN.* MM anchor, as cross on step, but no inner circle on obv., BR : FR :, no dots after Carolus, Et, or Rex, one between each word on rev., beaded inner circle on rev. *MB.* Or MA. BR. FR. ET. HIB., faint plain inner circle on rev. *EVANS.* MM heart. These differ slightly by having the front part of the bust descending nearly to the edge of the coin and dividing the legend. The X in the field is larger than before, and there is an inner circle on both sides. Legends as first with MM lis, but MA., HI., no dot after Rex. *MB.* Or with dot after every word on both sides, except Sui; before Cultores, and after rev. mint-mark. (120) *MB.* Or with dot also after Sui, none after Rex or before Cultores. *MB.* MM plume, bust similar but smaller, dividing inner circle but not legend; X smaller. Rev. as before but the harp is smaller and has no head. Inner circle both sides. Legends as first with MM lis but MA., dot after every word and before Cultores, and after rev. mint-mark. *MB.* Or legends as first with MM plume but HI., plain and beaded inner circle on rev. *EVANS.*

Type 2. Like Unites type 2 but no dot each side of crown on rev. MM rose. Legends as first with MM lis, dot after every word on both sides except Carolus, before Carolus and after rev. mint-mark. (121) *MB.*

Type 3. Like Unites type 3, but bust not the same, confined within inner circle, lace different, more hair, MM rose, that on obv. being much larger than that on rev. and of a different shape. Legends as first with MM lis but

MA., HI., dot after every word except Rex, two before Cultores. *MB.*

With bust like Unites type 3, but confined within inner circle. MM harp. . CAROLVS. D. G. MAG. BRI. FR. ET. HIB. REX. Rev. CVLTORES SVI DEVS PROTEGIT (122) *MB.* MM portcullis, same with dot between each word on rev. *MB.* MM bell, MA. BR. FR. ET. HI. Dot after each word on rev. and after rev. mint-mark. *MB.* Rud. xiii. 6. MM crown, as last but no dot either side of rev. mint-mark. *MB.* MM upright anchor, copied from the last but ruder, legends as MM bell, but no dot before or after obv. legend, dot between each word on rev. and after rev. mint-mark. *MB.* MM prostrate anchor, similar to but not identical with the last, dot before Carolus. *MB.* MM triangle, identical with last, but FRA. ET. HIB., dots on obv. as MM harp. *MB.*

With bust similar but broader, the figures in the shield larger, and letters and crowns on each side of shield larger. MM star. Legends as MM harp but BRI : FRA : ET. HI :, no dot before or after Carolus, one after every word on rev. and after rev. mint-mark. *MB.*

Briot. 1. Exactly like Briot's first Unite, but BRITAN., no lozenge after Rex, rev. legend CVLTORES. SVI. DEVS. PROTEGIT. All the dots are lozenge shaped. *MB.* 2. Same, but lozenge with B under it instead of mint-mark on obv., MAG. BRITAN., lozenge after Rex. *MB.* 3. Obv. exactly like Briot's second Unite, but MAG. BRITAN. FRAN. ET. HIB. REX Rev. same as the last two. *MB.* Rud. xiv. 2.

Oxford Double Crowns. 1642. Coin very broad and thin, bust copied from type 3 but ruder workmanship, within inner circle; ·X· behind head. MM plume. CAROLVS : D : G : MAG : BR. FR : ET : HI : REX Rev. Type like the Oxford Unites, inscription on scroll which is connected with the inner circle, three plumes, with bands under them, above it, 1642 below. EXVRGAT. DEVS.

DISSIPENTVR : INIMICI : RELIG : PROT LEG : ANG LIBER : PAR. (123) *MB.*

1643. Bust much larger, lace and armour different, bust descends to edge of coin, legend begins at bottom, and is the same as on the first Unite of 1643 (p. 154), except that there is no dot before Carolus. Rev. same as second Unite of 1643, with small annulets for stops. There is one before Exurgat and Liber, and after every word. *MB.* Rud. xiii. 11.

1644. A coin similar to the last but reading MAG :, and with the date 1644, OX, is said to have been sold at Miss Currer's sale in 1862, in extremely fine preservation, for £43, and another, very fine, with four pellets and a lozenge after Inimici, at Capt. Murchison's sale in 1864 for £40. *Num. Chr.*, N. S., ii. 232 ; iv. 229.

Bristol Double Crown. Like the Bristol Unite, but bust small, entirely confined within inner circle. MM·BR· in monogram between two plumes. .CAROLVS. D. G. MAG : B : F : ET. HIB : REX. Rev. EXVRGAT. DEVS. DISSIPENTVR. INIMICI. REL : PRO : LEG : ANG : LIB : PAR : Monogram BR. between legend and inscription. Date under scroll, 1645. (124) *MB.*

BRITAIN CROWN. *Value* 5*s.* *Weight* $35\frac{5}{41}$ *grs.* *Fineness* 22 *cts.* These correspond in type to the double crowns, but have V instead of X behind the head.

Type 1. MM lis, exactly like the first double crown with MM on rev. to right of crown, but HI. instead of HIB. *MB.* Rud. xiii. 3 reads BRI. for Br. and omits the reverse mint-mark.

Type 1*a.* MM cross on step, like double crown with same mint-mark. CAROLVS. D. G. MAG. BR. FR. ET. HI. REX Rev. CVLTORES. SVI. DEVS. PROTEG, dot after rev. mint-mark. *MB.* MM negro's head, same, but breast divides legend, MA., PROTEGIT, dot before Carolus, none on rev. *MB.* MM castle, no inner circle, breast does not divide legend, CAROLVS D : G : MA : BR : FR ET.

HI REX Rev. CVLTORES SVI DEVS PROTEG: *MB.* or MAG, *EVANS*, or PROTEGIT, no stops on rev., : after Fr and Hi, none after Et. *MB.* MM heart, like negro's head, but smaller and neater. Dot after every word except Protegit, one before Carolus, Fr, and Cultores, and after rev. mint-mark, two after D, G, Ma, Fr, and Hi. *MB.* MM plume, same, with no dots on rev. *MB.*

Type 3. MM harp, like double crown with same mint-mark, but reading BR. FR. ET. HI., and with no inner circle. *THORBURN.* MM portcullis, like double crown with same mint-mark. CAROLVS. D. G. MA. BR. FR. ET. HI. REX Rev. CVLTORES. SVI. DEVS. PROTEGIT *MB.* MM crown, same with dot before and after obv. legend, none on rev., shield on rev. smaller. *MB.* MM ton, as last, but dots as portcullis. *MB.* Rud. xiii. 7. MM anchor, prostrate on obv., upright on rev., bust slightly different, hair finer, legends as portcullis but no dot after Hi, shield as crown and ton. (125) *MB.* MM triangle, type copied from the last. CAROLVS. D. G. MAG BRI. FR ET HI. REX Rev. CVLTORES. SVI. DEVS. PROTEGIT *MB.* MM star, same as last but D: G: MA BR: FR: ET HI *MB.* On this coin the MM star on the obverse is struck over a triangle. MM triangle in circle, same as triangle but MAG. BR. FR. ET. HIB. *THORBURN.* MM (P) on obv. only, type as MM crown, legends as triangle but FRA. *MB.* MM sun, type as crown, .CAROLVS. D: G: MAG: BRI: FRA: ET. HIB: REX. Rev. as triangle. *MB.*

Briot. Same as his second double crown, but obv. legend CAROLVS. D: G. MAG. BRIT. FR. ET. HIB. REX *MB.*

No gold coins of this small denomination seem to have been struck at any of the provincial mints.

The dates attached to the mint-marks in the following table are those given by Ruding, who copied them from Folkes.

Table of Mint Marks.

	Unite.	£3.	* Angel.	Double Cr.	Brit. Cr.
Type 1.					
Lis, 1625. Bust in ruff and collar of garter; sq. shield . .	+			+	+
Cross on step, 1625, 1626 . . .	Montagu				
Type 1*a*.					
Cross on step, 1625, 1626. Bust in ruff, armour, sq. shield .	+		+	+	+
Negro's head, 1626, 1627 . . .	+		+	+	+
Castle, 1627 . .	+		+	+	+
Anchor, 1628 . .	+		+	+	
Heart, 1629 . .	+		Cuff	+	+
Heart, rev. Plume .	Evans				
Plume, 1630 . .	+			+	+
" " oval sh. .	+				
Type 2.					
Plume, 1630, Bust in ruff, armour, oval sh.	+				
Rose, 1631 . .	+		+	+	
Type 3.					
Rose, 1631, Bust in collar, oval shield .				+	
Harp, 1632 . .	+			+	Thorburn
Portcullis, 1633 .	+		+	+	+
Bell, 1634 . .	+		Rud.	+	
Crown, 1635 . .	+			+	+
Ton, 1636-1638 .	+				+
Upright Anchor, 1638				+	
Prostrate Anchor, 1638	+			+	+
Triangle, 1639 .	+			+	+
Star, 1640 . .	+			+	+
Triangle in circle, 1641	+				Thorburn
(P), 1643 . .	+				+
(R), 1644 . .	+				
Eye, 1645 . .	*NC*				
Sun, 1645 . .	+				+
Sceptre, 1646 . .	+				
Briot.					
Flower and B, rev. B., 1632 . .	+			+	
No MM on obv., rev. B.			+		
B on both sides .				+	+
Anchor, 1638 . .	+				

* The descriptions of type do not apply to the angels.

TABLE OF MINT MARKS—*continued.*

	Unite.	£3.	Angel.	Double Cr.	Brit. Cr.
OXFORD.					
1642, Declaration type	+				
„ MM plume		+		+	
1643, Declaration type	+			+	
„ MM plume		+			
„ Oxon, MM plume		+			
1644 Ox., MM plume .	+	+		*NC*	
„ Oxon, MM plume		+			
1645, MM plume	+				
1646 Ox., MM plume .	+				
BRISTOL.					
1645, BR, declaration type . .	+			+	
UNCERTAIN.					
Plume, bust in collar, oval shield . .	+				
A round object .	+				

COMMONWEALTH, 1648 TO 1660.

On the 6th of February, 1648-9, what then remained of the House of Commons voted that the House of Peers was useless and dangerous and ought to be abolished, and on the 7th that the kingly office was unnecessary, burdensome, and dangerous, and ought to be abolished. The bills carrying out these resolutions were not declared to be statutes till the 17th and 19th of March, but on the 13th the House ordered that money of gold and silver should be coined with its own style and authority, and the type and inscription were settled by a resolution of the 25th of April and an Act of the 17th of July, 1649. This alteration Sir Robert Harley, master of the mint, refused to carry out, and he was accordingly removed, as well as other officers of the mint who refused either to deliver up their patents from the late king or to accept new ones; and Dr. Aaron Guerdain was appointed master of the mint.

The new coins were all of crown gold, and consisted of

pieces of 20*s*, 10*s*, and 5*s*, all bearing the same device, from the appearance of which they got the name of "breeches money." The weight of the Unite was 140½ grs., and the others in proportion. They all have on the obverse a shield bearing St. George's Cross, with a sprig of laurel to the right, and of palm to the left, with the inscription THE COMMONWEALTH OF ENGLAND; and on the reverse two shields, one bearing the cross of St. George, the other the harp, touching at the top, within an inner circle, numerals indicating the value above the shields. Legend GOD WITH VS, and the date above. The mint-mark is always a sun or an anchor, and is placed on the obverse only. Coins with the anchor mint-mark are rare.

UNITES. MM sun, . XX . above shields on rev., dot after every word, before The, and after date. 1649, Rud. xiv. 4. 1650, 1651, 1652, 1653 with no dot after VS or THE (or with dot, *EVANS*), 1654 and 1656 like 1649, 1657; there are two dies of this last date, the principal difference being in the shape of the laurel branch. The dots, &c. are as in 1649. MM anchor, 1660, otherwise as 1649. (126) All in *MB*. except that of 1654, which is in Mr. Evans's collection.

DOUBLE CROWN. MM sun, . X . above shields, otherwise as first Unite. 1649, 1650 (127), 1651 no dot before or after obv. legend, 1652 and 1653 like 1649. MM anchor, 1660, otherwise as 1649. Rud. xiv. 5. All in *MB*.

BRITAIN CROWN. MM sun, . V . above shields, no dot before or after obv. legend, otherwise as first Unite, 1649. 1650 with dots (128), 1651 with no stops on obv. 1652, as 1649, or with no stops on obv. and reading ENGLAN. 1653, as 1651. 1654, dot after every word and before legend on both sides of the coin. MM anchor, no stops on obv., ENGLAN, 1658, Rud. xiv. 6, 1660. All in *MB*. except that of 1654, which is in Mr. Evans's collection.

On the 23rd February, 1656-7, the proposal was made to the House of Commons, which was afterwards carried, to offer to the Protector the title of King; and on the 4th February,

1657-8, the Protector dissolved his last Parliament after a 16 days' Session, because it was not submitting to his authority. The idea of exalting the personal authority of Cromwell was therefore rife in those years; and this may explain the fact that in 1656 and 1658 the officers of the mint struck some 20*s* pieces, as well as some silver coins, with Cromwell's head on one side and a shield crowned on the other side. They were beautifully engraved by Simon, and were made with the mill and screw which were now re-introduced; and upon them the name and title of OLIVAR D. G. R. P. ANG. SCO. ET. HIB &c PRO (Protector of the Republic of England, &c.) takes the place of the name of the Commonwealth; but he appears never to have ventured to put them into circulation, and they therefore do not come within the design of this book as current coins. Those of 1656 did not occur in the trial of the Pix made on the 3rd December, 1657, as they would have done if they had been then current; and there was but little time to put those of 1658 into circulation before the death of the Protector, which took place on the 3rd September in that year. They are not mentioned in the proclamation of 1661, which called in all coins stamped with the name of the Commonwealth.

Table of Mint Marks.

	Unite.	Double Cr.	Brit. Cr.
Sun, 1649	+	+	+
1650	+	+	+
1651	+	+	+
1652	+	+	+
1653	+	+	+
1654	Evans		Evans
1656	+		
1657	++		
Anchor, 1658			+
1660	+	+	+

CHARLES II, 1660 TO 1684.

Charles II upon his restoration made no alteration in the coins, except by restoring the type used by his father, with a laureated bust substituted for a crowned one. The indenture for this coinage was made with Sir Ralph Freeman, on the 20th of July, 1660, and Unites, Double Crowns, and Britain Crowns were made by virtue of it, the dies being engraved by Simon. But it was very soon resolved to establish permanently in the mint the improved process of coining by the mill and screw, a process which had been introduced and abandoned in the reign of Elizabeth, and re-introduced under the Protectorate, though in consequence of the opposition made to it in the mint it was only used for Cromwell's pattern pieces, and not for the public currency. In 1661 it was ordered that the necessary engines should be erected; in 1662 Blondeau was engaged to make the new money, and Roettier to engrave the dies, and it was first coined on the 6th of February, 1662-3, and was made current by a proclamation of March 27th, 1663. Of the new gold money, pieces of 100*s*, 40*s*, 20*s*, and 10*s* were made; but previously to this, on August 26th, 1661, the value of all current gold coins had been raised, the first unites of James I, 1604 to 1619, being raised to 23*s* 6*d*, and all coined since 1619 to 21*s* 4*d*, and the other coins in proportion; and accordingly the new pieces, which were of the same standard as before, had to be made lighter than the old ones, the 20*s* pieces now weighing $131\frac{29}{41}$ grs. The ancient coins made of gold of the old standard were also raised at the same time, the rose ryal of James I to 35*s*, and the angels of James I and Charles I to 11*s* 8*d*. As a great deal of the gold of which the new coins were made had been imported from Guinea by the African Company, the new 20*s* pieces received the name of Guineas, the old ones being distinguished by the name of Broads. In 1670 the weight was still further reduced, it being ordered that a pound of crown gold should now be made into £44. 10*s* by tale, the same sum which Charles I had made out of a pound of the old standard. This made the weight of the guinea $129\frac{39}{89}$ grs., and all subsequent guineas have been of this weight. All the coins were made of crown gold, *i.e.*, 22 cts. fine to 2 cts. alloy, a mixture which has ever since been exclusively used.

HAMMERED MONEY. Of this there are two different coinages, one weighing $140\frac{20}{41}$ grs. to the unite and having no numerals behind the head, the other weighing $131\frac{29}{41}$ grs. to the unite and having the value of the coin indicated by numerals behind the head. Neither has any inner circle. The date of the second coinage is fixed by a warrant of November 28th, 1661, which ordered the values of all new pieces to be stamped upon them. On all these pieces the king's bust is represented in profile to the left, laureate, long hair, neck bare, armour with scarf over it. The reverse has an oval shield garnished, crowned, between C and R. The shield is the same as on Charles I's type 3, but the crown is broader and flatter, and the C and R at the sides are not crowned. The legends on the unites and double crowns are CAROLVS. II. D. G. MAG. BRIT. FRAN. ET. HIB. REX Rev. FLORENT. CONCORDIA. REGNA. The crowns have the obverse legend slightly abbreviated. They all have MM crown on obv. only, and they are the last coins on which any mint-mark appears. Of the first coinage, we have the Unite, Rud. xv. 2, *MB.* One of these has . before and after the reverse legend. The Double Crown, of which one variety has two dots after D and one before and after the reverse legend, *MB.*, and the other has a different scarf over the armour, (129) *MB.*; and the Crown, of which one variety reads FR and has a dot before and after the reverse legend, Rud. xv. 4, *MB.*, and the other reads BR : FR : ET : HI :, and has all the letters smaller, : between each word on obv., rev. as the last. (130) *MB.*

Of the second coinage, with the numerals XX, X, or V, behind the head, the Unite is like the first unite, except that the scarf is the same as that on the second double crown, and that the coin is rather smaller and thicker. Rud. xiv. 9, where, however, the difference in the scarf is scarcely shown. (131) *MB*. The Double Crown has bust and legends like the first unite, but the letters, and the coin itself, are much smaller and neater than in the former coinage, and there is a dot before and after the rev. legend. (132) Rud. xiv. 10. *MB*. The Crown is almost exactly the same as the first crown, reading FR. ET. HIB. Rud. xv. 1. *MB*.

Milled Money.

For the engraving of the dies for this money there was a competition between Simon, who had made those for the hammered money and for Cromwell's milled patterns, and Roettier, a native of Antwerp, who had been presented to the king before the Restoration. Some patterns for gold unites and double crowns (Rud. xiv. 8, xv. 3), as well as for silver coins, were executed by Simon, but those of Roettier were approved and adopted, and Simon was not afterwards employed upon English coins.

The milled coins have the king's bust to the right (instead of like the hammered ones to the left), laureate, long hair, no drapery. The bust descends nearly to the edge of the coin, and divides the legend both above and below. Rev. four shields placed crosswise, crowned, England above, France below, Scotland to right, Ireland to left. In the centre between the shields are four Cs interlinked, from which issue four sceptres, one in each interval between the shields, terminating respectively in an orb, thistle, lis, and harp. The legends on all are CAROLVS. II. DEI. GRATIA, Rev. MAG. BR. FRA. ET. HIB. REX., with the date at the top of the coin. There is no inner circle on either side. Before 1670 the weights were in the proportion of $131\frac{29}{41}$ grs. to the guinea, afterwards $129\frac{39}{89}$ grs. The current value of the guinea throughout the reign was 20*s*, and the metal was crown gold, 22 cts. fine.

Many of the coins have an elephant with, after 1675, a castle on his back, under the bust. These are the coins which were made of the gold imported by the African Company, whose charter gave them the privilege of having coins made of gold or silver imported by them thus marked.

FIVE GUINEAS. These have their edges marked with the words DECVS ET TVTAMEN (the legend being so placed for the purpose of being both "an ornament and a protection" to the coin against being clipped), followed by the date ANNO REGNI VICESIMO, or as the case may be. The reign was calculated as having begun on the day of the death of Charles I.

Type 1. Lovelock in front of shoulder, truncation of bust pointed. 1668, with and without elephant under bust, ANNO REGNI VICESIMO. (133). 1669, with elephant, VICESIMO PRIMO. These are of the weight of $651\frac{22}{41}$ grs. The following weigh only $647\frac{17}{89}$ grs. 1670, VICESIMO SECVNDO. 1672, VICESIMO QVARTO. 1673, VICESIMO QVINTO. 1675, VICESIMO SEPTIMO, all without the elephant. 1675, VICESIMO SEPTIMO with the elephant. 1676, VICESIMO SEPTIMO without the elephant. 1676, VICESIMO OCTAVO with the elephant and castle. 1677, VICESIMO NONO, with and without elephant and castle. 1678, TRICESIMO, with elephant and castle. All these are in *MB*. Rud. xv. 5.

Type 2. *Weight* $647\frac{17}{89}$ *grs*. Bolder work, no lovelock, truncation rounded. 1678, 1679, 1680, 1681, 1682, 1683, without, and 1681 and 1684 with, elephant and castle. The dates on the edges are respectively TRICESIMO, and TRICESIMO PRIMO, SECVNDO, TERTIO, QVARTO, QVINTO, SEXTO. All in *MB*. Rud. xv. 9.

TWO GUINEAS. These are similar to the five guineas, but their edges are milled and have no inscription. Type 1, *weight* $263\frac{14}{41}$ *grs.*, type like the first five guineas; 1664, both with and without an elephant under the bust. *MB*. Rud. xv. 6.

Type 2. *Weight* $258\frac{78}{89}$ *grs.*, type like the second type of the five guineas; 1675, 1676, 1677, 1678, 1679, 1681, 1683, 1684, without, and 1676 and 1684 with elephant and castle under bust. All in *MB.* (134) Rud. xv. 10.

GUINEAS. Similar to the two guineas.

Type 1, *weight* $131\frac{29}{41}$ *grs.*, type like the first type of the five guineas, 1663 with and without the elephant. *MB.*

Type 2, like the former guineas but the head a little broader, and the hair brought more forward on the shoulder, 1664 and 1665 with the elephant, Rud. xv. 7, 1664, 1666, 1667, 1668, and 1670, without. (135) *MB.*

Type 3. *Weight* $129\frac{39}{89}$ *grs.*, type like the second type of the five guineas; every year from 1672 to 1684 inclusive without, and 1675, 1676, 1677, 1682, 1683, with the elephant and castle under the bust. All in *MB.* Rud. xv. 11.

HALF-GUINEAS. Similar to the two guineas.

Type 1 like the first type of the five guineas, 1669, weighing $65\frac{35}{41}$ grs., and 1670 weighing $64\frac{64}{89}$ grs., without the elephant. *MB.* Rud. xv. 8 has an elephant, but the reverse is not given, and it does not appear what the date or the weight is.

Type 2. *Weight* $64\frac{64}{89}$ *grs.*, type like the second type of the five guineas; 1672, 1675, 1676, 1679, 1681, 1683, and 1684 without, and 1676, 1677, 1678, with, elephant and castle under bust, all in *MB.* (136) Rud. xv. 12.

Hammered Money.

		Unite.	Double Cr.	Brit. Cr.
1660-1	MM crown, no numerals .	+	+	+
	,, ,, smaller letters . . .			+
	,, ,, different scarf . . .		+	
1661-2	,, numerals behind the head . .	+	+	+

	5 guas.	2 guas.	1 gua.	½ gua.
1663 Lovelock, truncation pointed			+	
1663 „ „ elephant			+	
1664 „ broad bust on guinea		+	+	
1664 „ „ elephant		+	+	
1665 „ „ broad bust, elephant			+	
1666 „ broad bust			+	
1667 „ broad bust			+	
1668 „ broad bust on guinea	+		+	
1668 „ „ elephant	+			
1669 „ „				+
1669 „ „ elephant	+			
1670 „ „ broad bust on guinea	+		+	+
1672 „ „	+			
1672 No lovelock, truncation rounded			+	+
1673 Lovelock, truncation pointed	+			
1673 No lovelock, truncation rounded			+	
1674 „ „ „			+	
1675 Lovelock, truncation pointed	+			
1675 „ „ elephant	+			
1675 No lovelock, truncation rounded		+	+	+
1675 „ „ elephant and castle			+	
1676 Lovelock, truncation pointed	+			
1676 Lovelock, truncation pointed, elephant and castle	+			
1676 No lovelock, truncation rounded		+	+	+
1676 „ „ elephant and castle		+	+	+
1677 Lovelock, truncation pointed	+			
1677 „ „ elephant and castle	+			
1677 No lovelock, truncation rounded		+	+	
1677 „ „ elephant and castle			+	+
1678 Lovelock, truncation pointed, elephant and castle	+			

MILLED MONEY—*continued.*

	5 guas.	2 guas.	1 gua.	½ gua.
1678 No lovelock, truncation rounded . .	+	+	+	
1678 " " elephant and castle . .				+
1679 " "	+	+	+	+
1680 " "	+		+	
1681 " "	+	+	+	+
1681 " " elephant and castle . .	+			
1682 " "	+		+	
1682 " " elephant and castle . .			+	
1683 " " .	+	+	+	+
1683 " " elephant and castle . .			+	
1684 " "		+	+	+
1684 " " elephant and castle . .	+	+		

JAMES II, 1684 TO 1688.

James succeeded his brother on the 6th of February, 1684-5, and continued the coinage on the principles established in 1670, the metal being crown gold, and the guinea weighing 129$\frac{38}{89}$ grs., and being current at 20*s.* The legends are, obv. IACOBVS. II. DEI. GRATIA, Rev. .MAG. BR. FRA. ET. HIB REX. with the date. The type is the same as that of his brother, except that the bust is turned to the left and the hair is differently arranged, a long lock lying along the side of the neck; and the Cs in the centre of the reverse are omitted. The elephant and castle appears on some of the coins, but not the elephant alone.

FIVE GUINEAS. These are inscribed on the edge DECVS ET TVTAMEN ANNO REGNI, &c. 1686 SECVNDO. On this piece the sceptres are erroneously arranged, the harp and lis having changed places, the harp being placed between the French and Irish, and the lis between the Irish and English shields. There is no elephant. (137) *MB.* The rest have the sceptres correctly arranged. 1687 TERTIO and 1688 QVARTO without, and the same dates with, elephant and castle under bust. All in *MB.* Rud. xv. 13, 17.

TWO GUINEAS. Like the five guineas, except that the edges are milled instead of being inscribed, and that the sceptres are always correctly arranged. 1686 with elephant and castle, Rud. xv. 18. We do not know this coin, and Ruding does not say in what collection it was to be found. 1687, 1688, without elephant and castle. *MB.* Rud. xv. 14.

GUINEAS. Like the two guineas; 1685, 1686, 1687, 1688 without, and the same dates with, the elephant and castle. All in *MB.* (138) Rud. xv. 15, 19.

HALF GUINEAS. Like the two guineas. 1686, 1687, 1688 without, and 1686 with the elephant and castle. All in *MB.* Rud. xv. 16, 20.

	5 guas.	2 guas.	1 gua.	½ gua.
1685			+	
With elephant and castle			+	
1686 Sceptres erroneous on 5 guas . . .	+		+	+
With elephant and castle		Rud.	+	+
1687	+	+	+	+
With elephant and castle	+		+	
1688	+	+	+	+
With elephant and castle	+		+	

William and Mary, 1688 to 1694.

Throughout this reign gold continued to be coined on the principles established in 1670. The type of all the coins is, obv. busts of king and queen to right, necks bare, he laureate; legend GVLIELMVS. ET. MARIA. DEI. GRATIA Rev. square shield, garnished, crowned, bearing the arms of, in first and fourth quarter France and England quarterly, second Scotland, third Ireland; those of Nassau on an escutcheon of pretence; legend MAG. BR. FR. ET. HIB. REX. ET. REGINA. with the date at the top of the coin. There is no inner circle.

FIVE GUINEAS. These have on their edge, like the previous ones, DECVS ET TVTAMEN ANNO REGNI &c. They occur of the dates of 1691 TERTIO, 1692 QVARTO, and 1693 QVINTO, without, and the same dates and 1694 SEXTO with the elephant and castle under the busts, the mark of the African Company (*ante*, p. 172). Rud. xvi. 1, 5. All are in *MB*. except that of 1693 without the elephant.

TWO GUINEAS. Like the five guineas, but edges milled, not inscribed; 1693 and 1694 without, and 1694 with elephant and castle under busts. (139) Rud. xvi. 2. *MB*. Ruding, xvi. 6, gives also 1691 with elephant, but he gives no authority for the coin. On all his representations of the coins of this and the last reign the castle on the elephant's back is omitted.

GUINEAS. Like the two guineas, but the shield on rev. is scarcely garnished; 1689, 1690, 1691, 1692, 1693, 1694 without, and 1689, 1691, 1692, 1693, 1694 with elephant and castle. Rud. xvi. 3, 7. That of 1694 with elephant and castle was exhibited to the Numismatic Society in February, 1881, by Mr. Copp. The others are in *MB*.

HALF-GUINEAS. These are like the guineas, but the busts on that dated 1689 have the hair arranged differently, none being drawn down over either forehead, and the ringlets curling back from the neck. This coin is without the elephant. (140) The others have the busts like those on the guineas, with the ringlets hanging down the side of the neck, and occur of the dates 1690, 1691, 1692, 1694 without, and 1691 and 1692 with the elephant and castle. Rud. xvi. 4, 8. That of 1694 was in Mr. Marshall's collection, the others are in *MB*.

	5 guas.	2 guas.	1 gua.	½ gua.
1689 Ringlets on ½ gua. curling back . . .			+	+
elephant and castle .			+	
1690			+	+
1691	+		+	+
elephant and castle .	+	Rud.	+	+
1692	+		+	+
elephant and castle .	+		+	+
1693	+	+	+	
elephant and castle .	+		+	
1694		+	+	Marshall
elephant and castle .	+	+	Copp	

William III, 1694 to 1701.

Queen Mary died on December 28th, 1694. At this time the silver coins in circulation had become so much deteriorated that they contained on an average scarcely more than half their proper quantity of silver, and, accordingly, the guinea, which was nominally worth 20*s*, was usually given and received for 30*s*. In 1695 a proclamation put an end to the currency of all silver coins "clipped within the ring" from the ensuing 13th of February, and an Act was passed for calling in and recoining all such clipped money, which was carried into effect in the two following years. In consequence of these measures the current value of the guinea fell rapidly. The House of Commons resolved, on the 15th of February, 1695-6, that no guineas should pass in any payments at above the rate of 28*s*, which they reduced on the 28th of the same month to 26*s*. In accordance with the latter resolution an Act was passed to impose a penalty on any person who should, after March 25th, 1696, receive or pay any guineas at a higher rate than 26*s*, or the other gold coins in proportion; provided that nothing in the Act should be construed to compel any person to receive guineas at that rate; and, by another Act of the same session, the penalty is extended to all who, after April 10th, 1696, shall receive or pay them at a higher rate than 22*s* for a guinea. A third Act called in all the hammered silver money and made it no longer current from December 1st, 1696; and in 1698 the House resolved that no one was obliged to take guineas at 22*s*, and their current price fell to 21*s* 6*d*, at which rate they were received by the officers of the revenue.

The bad state of the silver coins having raised gold coins to so high a price, a great quantity of gold bullion was imported by private persons, who got it coined at the Tower and made thereby great profits, since, by an Act of the 18th Charles II, which, though originally temporary, had been constantly renewed, all bullion of gold and silver was there coined, without any charge whatever, for the person who brought it. In 1695 700,411 guineas were so coined for private persons, besides 21,389 for the African Company. While 30*s* could be obtained for a guinea, this occasioned a great drain of silver coins of good weight out of the kingdom, for gold was imported and coined to buy them, and when bought they were melted down, and the bullion exported; so to stop this it was enacted in 1695 that, from March 2nd, 1695, to January 1st, 1696, no guineas should be imported, and the mint should be under no obligation to receive or coin any gold whatever except for the Royal African Company, whose gold, imported in return for goods sent to Africa, was to be coined into half-guineas. This Act, however, was repealed almost as soon as it came into force, and the great recoinage of silver soon reduced the gold coins to their proper proportional value. On

February 5th, 1700-1, a proclamation was issued that the French louis d'or and the Spanish pistole should not go for more than 17*s*, which brought such a vast quantity of them to the mint that £1,400,000 was coined out of them. This abundance in the country of French coin gave rise to a report, mentioned by Burnet, that it was imported by the French ambassador, Count Tallard, for purposes of corruption. See also Smollett, vol. i. p. 419.

No gold was coined during this reign elsewhere than at the Tower, the country mints used during the great recoinage of silver having been employed for that metal only.

William III's coins have on the obverse his bust to right, laureate, long hair, neck bare. GVLIELMVS. III. DEI. GRA. Rev. four shields placed crosswise, each crowned, England above, France below, Scotland to right, Ireland to left, like the coins of Charles II and James II. Between them, in the centre of the coin, is the shield of Nassau, whence issue four sceptres, terminating respectively in orb, thistle, lis, and harp. Legend ·MAG. BR. FRA. ET. HIB. REX. with the date.

FIVE GUINEAS. These have the edge inscribed DECVS ET TVTAMEN ANNO REGNI, &c. The bust has a lovelock brought forward on the shoulder. Dates 1699 VNDECIMO, with and without the elephant and castle (141); 1700 DVODECIMO without; 1701 DECIMO TERTIO without; the work of this last is much finer and bolder than the others. Rud. xvi. 9, 13. *MB.*

TWO GUINEAS. These were only struck in 1701, and are like the five guineas of that year, except that there is no lovelock on the shoulder, and that the edge is milled, not inscribed. (142) Rud. xvi. 10. *MB.* One with the elephant and castle, dated 1699, given in Rud. xvi. 14, is, according to his editor of 1840, "unknown and supposed to be imaginary."

GUINEAS. The following are like the five guineas,

but the lovelock is not brought forward on the shoulder, and the edges are milled; 1695, 1696 without, and 1695 with the elephant and castle. (143) Rud. xvi. 11. The following are similar, but the head is somewhat larger, and berries are introduced in the laurel wreath; the lettering also is somewhat bolder: 1698, 1699, 1700, 1701 without, and 1699, 1700 with the elephant and castle. Rud. xvi. 15. Another of 1701, without the elephant and castle, is like the five guinea of that date, with the lovelock brought forward on the shoulder, and the workmanship bolder. (144) All in *MB.*, except the guineas of 1696 and 1699 without the elephant, which were in Mr. Marshall's collection.

HALF-GUINEAS. Like the guineas of 1698. Dates 1695, 1697, 1698, 1700, 1701 without, and 1696, 1698 with the elephant and castle. (145) Rud. xvi. 12, 16. *MB.*

	5 guas.	2 guas.	1 gua.	½ gua.
1695			+	+
,, With elephant and castle .			+	
1696			Marshal	
,, With elephant and castle .				+
1697				+
1698 Head large, berries in wreath . . .			+	+
,, ,, with elephant and castle .				+
1699 Lovelock on shoulder .	+			
,, ,, elephant and castle . .	+			
Head large, berries in wreath . . .			Marshall	
,, ,, with elephant and castle .		Rud.	+	
1700 Lovelock on shoulder .	+			
Head large, berries in wreath . .			+	+
,, ,, with elephant and castle .			+	
1701 Head large, berries in wreath . . .			+	+
Lovelock on shoulder, fine work . . .	+		+	
Fine work, no lovelock .		+		

Anne, 1701 to 1714.

Anne succeeded her brother-in-law on March 8, 1701-2, and carried on the coinage on the same principles as before. Her coins have her bust turned to the left, hair filleted. She is said to have objected to being represented with bare neck and breast, as her predecessors had been, and accordingly, although there is a pattern guinea of 1702 without drapery, all her current coins have drapery over the shoulders, which is fastened in front by a brooch. The reverse has four shields crosswise crowned, with sceptres between them, like William III's coins. The elephant and castle is placed under the bust on the coins made from the gold of the African Company, and the word VIGO on some coins struck in 1702 and 1703, of gold captured in the town of Vigo, in Gallicia, which was taken from the Spaniards in October, 1702. An alteration in the arms took place after the Union with Scotland on May 1st, 1707, the arms of England and Scotland impaled being then placed in the top and bottom shield, France to the right, Ireland to the left. The Articles of Union provided that the coin should be of the same standard and value throughout the United Kingdom as it was at that time in England; and that a mint should be continued in Scotland under the same rules as the mint in England, and the present officers of the mint continued, subject to such regulations and alterations as Her Majesty, her heirs and successors, or the Parliament of Great Britain, should think fit. The silver coins struck after this time at the Edinburgh mint have E under the bust; but it does not appear that any gold was struck there. The mint there was finally abolished in 1817, and the buildings sold.

FIVE GUINEAS. The first of these have the bust to left, hair filleted, two small curls above fillet on top of head, fillet tied in a bow, of which both ends but only one loop are visible behind the head, lovelock brought over right shoulder, drapery over the shoulders, fastened in front by a brooch. ANNA. DEI. GRATIA. Rev. Four shields placed crosswise, crowned; England above, France below, Scotland to right, Ireland to left. In the centre, between the shields, is a rose, from which issue four sceptres, terminating respectively in an orb, thistle, lis, and harp. MAG BR. FRA ET. HIB REG. with the date. On the edge DECVS ET TVTAMEN ANNO REGNI, &c. These occur of the dates 1703 SECVNDO with VIGO under the bust, Rud. xvi. 17; 1705 QVARTO; 1706 QVINTO. After the Union the obverse remained as before, but on the reverse the top and bottom shields were England and Scotland impaled, with France to right, Ireland to left, and in the centre the star of the Order of the Garter took the place of the rose. BRI. FR. is substituted for BR. FRA. 1706 QVINTO, this date is a mistake, as, though the Act of Union was passed in 1706, it did not come into operation till 1707. 1709 OCTAVO, on this the letters of the legends are larger. The following have the reverse like the last, but the bust is different, flatter work, the hair in front curls over the fillet, there is only one curl above it, and both loops of the bow are seen behind; 1711 DECIMO; 1713 DVODECIMO (146), 1714 DECIMO TERTIO. Rud. xvii. 4, 8. All in *MB*.

TWO GUINEAS. These were only coined after the Union, and are like the five guineas of 1706 after the Union, except that the edges are milled, not inscribed. 1709, 1711, 1713, 1714. Rud. xvii. 9. *MB*. Ruding's xvi. 18 and xvii. 5, dated respectively 1703 with VIGO, and 1705, with shields as before the Union, but the star in the centre of the reverse, are imaginary, and do not exist.

GUINEAS. Before the Union, like the five-guinea pieces of 1705, but edge milled not inscribed, 1702; 1703 with VIGO under the bust (147), Rud. xvi. 19; 1705, Rud. xvii.

2; 1706; 1707. After the Union, like the five-guinea of 1706 after the Union. 1707, 1708, 1710, 1711, 1712, 1713, 1714 without, and 1707, 1708, 1709, with elephant and castle under the bust. Rud. xvii. 3, 6, 10. Rud. xvii. 1, dated 1704, and with an object described as a George in the centre of the reverse, is not known, and if it exists it is probably a pattern. That of 1707 before the Union was in Mr. Marshall's collection. The others are in *MB.*

HALF-GUINEAS. Before the Union, like the guineas before the Union; 1702; 1703 VIGO under the bust, Rud. xvi. 20; 1705. After the Union, like the guineas after the Union, every year from 1707 to 1714 inclusive. (148) Rud. xvii. 7, 14. All in *MB.* except 1712, which was in Mr. Marshall's collection.

	5 guas.	2 guas.	1 gua.	½ gua.
Before the Union.				
1702 Rose in centre of rev. . .			+	+
1703 " " Vigo .	+		+	+
1705 " " . .	+		+	+
1706 " " . .	+		+	
1707 " " . .			Marshall	
After the Union.				
1706 Star in centre of rev. . .	+			
1707 " " . . .			+	+
" " elephant and castle			+	
1708 " " . . .			+	+
" " elephant and castle			+	
1709 " " large letters on 5 guas.	+	+		+
" " elephant and castle			+	
1710 " " . . .			+	+
1711 " " two loops to bow on 5 guas. . . .	+	+	+	+
1712 " " . . .			+	Marshall
1713 " " two loops to bow on 5 guas. . . .	+	+	+	+
1714 " " " .	+	+	+	+

GEORGE I, 1714 TO 1727.

No alteration was made during this reign in the weight or metal of the coins; but the value of gold coin as compared with silver had been steadily going down since the great re-coinage of silver under William III. A guinea, which was coined at the mint at 20*s*, but which in 1695 had passed current for 30*s*, was reduced in 1698 to 21*s* 6*d*, and although it was generally received and paid at this latter rate during the reign of Queen Anne, yet Sir Isaac Newton gave it as his opinion that it was not worth in silver bullion more than 20*s* 8*d*, and in consequence of an address from the House of Commons its current value was on December 22nd, 1717, reduced to 21*s*. The same proclamation ordered that the ancient gold coins of the kingdom which had been current at 23*s* 6*d* (which would be the unites from 1619 to 1661, the weight of which was $140\frac{20}{41}$ grs.) should be received at 23*s* and no more, and those which had been current at 25*s* 6*d* (which would be the two first unites of James I, 1604 to 1619) at 25*s* and no more. The only other alterations in the coins during this reign were the issuing quarter guineas for the first time in 1718, and the changes in the royal arms and titles. The following is a description of the coins.

FIVE GUINEAS. Bust to right, laureate, a loop and one end of the tie appear behind, hair long and curly, one lock drawn forward on the shoulder, no drapery. GEORGIVS. D. G. M. BR. FR. ET. HIB. REX. F. D. Rev. four shields crosswise, each crowned; England and Scotland impaled above, France to right, Ireland below, the shield of the Electorate to the left; in the centre, between the shields, is the star of the Garter, from which issue four sceptres, terminating respectively in an orb, thistle, lis, and harp. BRVN ET. L. DVX S. R. I. A. TH ET. EL. with the date. On the edge DECVS ET TVTAMEN ANNO REGNI, &c. The meaning of the reverse legend is "Brunsvicensis et Lunenburgensis Dux, Sancti Romani Imperii Archi-Thesaurarius et Elector." The F D on the obverse for Fidei Defensor appears now for the first time on the coins, though the title had been used on the great seal ever since it had been granted by the Pope to Henry VIII. The dates of the five-guinea pieces are 1716 SECVNDO; 1717 TERTIO; 1720 SEXTO; 1726 DECIMO TERTIO. The D upon the edge of the coin of 1717, and the Ns on that of 1726, are turned upside down. On those of 1716 and 1717 there is a cross before Decus and after Tutamen. (149) Rud. xvii. 12. All in *MB*.

TWO GUINEAS. Like the five guineas, but the edge milled with oblique lines, not inscribed. 1717, 1720, 1726. Rud. xvii. 13. All in *MB*.

GUINEAS. Bust to right, similar to that on the five guineas, laureate, two ends of the tye but no loop appearing behind, hair long and curly but not brought forward upon the shoulder, no drapery. GEORGIVS. D. G. MAG. BR. FR. ET. HIB. REX. F. D. Rev. like the five guineas but legend BRVN. ET LVN. DVX S. R. I. A. TH. ET. PR. EL. 1714. Edge milled with oblique lines. (150) Rud. xvii. 16. *MB. rare.* The obverse of this is of much better workmanship than the other coins of this reign, and in higher relief. The letters PR mean Prince and appear on no other coins.

The next guineas resemble the five guineas, except that the edge is milled with oblique lines, not inscribed, and that two ends of the tye and no loop appear behind. 1715, there are two different busts of this date, one larger and in rather less relief than the other. (151) (152) *MB*. The rest of this type have a head rather larger than either of those of 1715, and the tye has a loop and only one end. 1716, 1717, 1718, 1719, 1720, 1721; 1721 with elephant and castle below the bust; 1722, 1723. (153) Rud. xvii. 14, 18. *MB*.

The following have a bust similar to the preceding, but the back of the neck is more bare, the hair curls back from the side of the face, and no lock is brought forward upon the shoulder; the tye has two ends and no loop, the face is older, and the relief higher. Dates 1723, 1724, 1725, 1726, 1726 with elephant and castle, 1727. All in *MB*.

There is also a guinea of 1727 with reverse from the same die as the last, and with the same obverse legend, but with a very different bust, which, and especially the neck, is longer than on any of the previous pieces and in much higher relief; the laurel has no berries, and its points extend into and divide the legend, the hair is long and in four ringlets, one of which comes forward on the breast, as in the five guineas. This cannot have been engraved by Croker, who executed the other dies, and it is evidently the work of some young artist, but it is not known who he was. There is nothing to show that pieces from this die were ever in circulation, and it was very likely executed as a pattern by some pupil of Croker's. *MB*.

HALF-GUINEAS. Resembling the guineas of 1715, dates 1717, 1718, 1719, 1722. Rud. xvii. 15. Resembling the guineas of 1724, dates 1725, 1726, 1727. (154) All in *MB*.

QUARTER GUINEAS. These are all dated 1718, and resemble the guineas of 1724. (155) Rud. xvii. 17. *MB*. They were coined, no doubt, to supply the want of small money occasioned by the great scarcity of silver currency which was felt at that time, but as they were the first of their kind, a great number seem to have been laid by as curiosities, and they did not enter into circulation to any very appreciable extent. The amount of them coined was only 210 lb., or £37,380.

	5 guas.	2 guas.	1 gua	½ gua.	¼ gua.
1714 Tye with two ends, PR.EL.			+		
1715 Tye with two ends, lock on shoulder . . .			+		
Similar, but larger head .			+		
1716 Tye with loop and one end, lock on shoulder . .	+		+		
1717 ,, ,, ,,	+	+	+		
Tye with two ends, lock on shoulder . . .				+	
1718 ,, loop and one end, lock on shoulder . .			+		
,, two ends, lock on shoulder . . .				+	
,, two ends, no lock on shoulder, old head .					+
1719 Tye with loop and one end, lock on shoulder . .			+		
,, two ends . .				+	
1720 ,, loop and one end	+	+	+		
1721 ,, ,, ,,			+		
1721 As last, elephant and castle under bust . . .			+		
1722 Tye with loop and one end, lock on shoulder . .			+		
,, two ends, lock on shoulder . . .				+	
1723 Tye with loop and one end, lock on shoulder . .			+		
1723 Tye with two ends, no lock on shoulder, old head .			+		
1724 ,, ,, ,,			+		
1725 ,, ,, ,,			+	+	
1726 Tye with loop and one end, lock on shoulder . .	+	+			
Tye with two ends, no lock on shoulder, old head .			+	+	
As last, elephant and castle under bust . . .			+		
1727 Tye with two ends, no lock on shoulder, old head .			+	+	
Long head, long points to wreath, lock on shoulder			+		

George II, 1727 to 1760.

The coinage of George II was conducted on the same principles as that of his father, and his coins were of the same denominations and value, except that no quarter guineas were made. In 1732-3 all hammered gold coins, hitherto current by the name of broad pieces at the rates of 25*s* and 23*s*, with their halves and quarters, having become much diminished by wear and clipping, were called in and declared to be no longer current, a measure which had been adopted with respect to the hammered silver money by William III. And a practice having been discovered of filing the edges of the milled money and imitating the milling with a file, in 1739 new dies were made for every species of coin, and the graining, which had hitherto been by diagonal strokes, was now on the two-guineas and guineas made with curved lines, so as to be more difficult to imitate with a file. The dies up to this time had been engraved by Croker; those for these new coins were made by Tanner, and the head is older in appearance, and becomes older still after 1745. On all the gold coins of this reign the armorial bearings are emblazoned upon one shield, as on William and Mary's coins, instead of upon separate shields placed crosswise, as they had been on all other milled money and on all the silver coins of this reign. On some of the coins the letters E I C are placed under the king's bust, indicating that they were made for the East India Company, or from gold sent by them to the mint. LIMA, in the same position, occurs on coins dated 1745 and 1746, which, according to Pollet, were made from bullion captured by the Prince Frederick and Duke privateers, but, according to others, from the gold taken by Lord Anson in the great Acapulco galleon, which traded between Manilla, in the Philippine Islands, and Acapulco, in Mexico, exchanging at the latter place the merchandize of Manilla for the ore of Peru. This vessel was captured in June, 1743; but Anson did not arrive with the treasure in England till June, 1744, having previously, during the same voyage, captured a considerable quantity of bullion in a ship bound from Callao, which is the port of Lima, to Valparaiso, and a much larger quantity in the Peruvian town of Paita. On all the bullion so captured the name of Lima, the capital of Peru, might not inappropriately be inscribed.

FIVE GUINEAS. Bust to left, laureate, young head, two ends of the tye appear behind, hair long and curly, no drapery. GEORGIVS. II DEI. GRATIA Rev. Shield garnished, crowned, bearing in the first quarter England and Scotland impaled, second France, third Ireland, fourth Electorate. M. B. F. ET. H. REX. F. D. B. ET. L. D. S. R. I. A. T. ET. E. with the date. For the meaning of this legend see *ante*, p. 186. On the edge DECVS ET TVTAMEN ANNO REGNI, &c. Dates 1729 TERTIO; some with this date have E I C under the bust for East India Company (156). Rud. xviii. 5. 1731 QVARTO; 1738 DVODECIMO; 1741 DECIMO QVARTO. The young head is retained on this coin, though an older one had been substituted for it on the two-guinea pieces in 1739. Rud. xviii. 1. The following have an old head, but resemble the previous coins in other respects, except that a lock of hair is brought forward over each of the king's shoulders, and that a loop as well as ends of the tye appear behind. 1746 DECIMO NONO, with LIMA under the bust, Rud. xviii. 13. 1748 VICESIMO SECUNDO; 1753 VICESIMO SEXTO. Rud. xviii. 9, 17. All in *MB.*

TWO GUINEAS. Type like the five-guinea pieces, but edge milled, not inscribed. Like the earliest five guineas, with young head, edge milled with diagonal straight lines, dates 1735, 1738, 1739. With edge milled with curved lines, and head older, similar to but not so old as that on the later five guineas, 1739, 1740. (157) Rud. xviii. 10. With edge as the last and head older, like that on the later five guineas, 1748, 1753. All in *MB.* Ruding gives also one dated 1727, stated to have been in Dr. Walker's collection, Rud. xviii. 2, and others dated 1729 with EIC under the bust, 1746 with LIMA, and 1747, all of which may be imaginary. Rud. xviii. 6, 14, 18.

GUINEAS. Like the two-guinea pieces. With young head, and edge milled with diagonal straight lines, 1727, of this there are two varieties, one having the shield larger, and being altogether a broader coin than the other; 1729 with EIC under the bust, 1731, 1731 with EIC, 1732 with EIC, 1733, 1734, 1735, 1736, 1737, 1738. With old head and curved milling, 1739, 1739 with EIC, 1740, 1745, 1745 with LIMA, 1746. Similar but older head, the letters on the obverse of these are larger, and are placed nearer the edge in order to show whether the coin has been diminished by clipping. 1747, 1748, 1749, 1750, 1752, 1753, 1755, 1756, 1758, 1759, 1760. (158) Rud. xviii. 11, 15, 19. All in *MB*.

HALF-GUINEAS. Like the two guineas, except that the edges of all of them are milled with diagonal straight lines, being perhaps too narrow for the curved lines. With young head, 1728, 1729, 1729 with EIC, 1731, 1732, 1734, 1736, 1737, 1738, 1739. Rud. xviii. 4, 8. With old head, 1740, 1745, 1745 with LIMA, 1746. (159). With older head, 1753, 1755, 1756, 1758, 1759, 1760. Rud. xviii. 12, 16, 20. All in *MB*.

	5 guas.	2 guas.	1 gua.	½ gua.
1727 Young head		Rud.	+ +	
1728 ,, straight milling* .				+
1729 ,, ,, ,, .	+			+
,, ,, ,, EIC .	+	Rud.	+	+
1731 ,, ,, ,, .	+		+	+
,, ,, ,, EIC .			+	
1732 ,, ,, ,, .				+
,, ,, ,, EIC .			+	
1733 ,, ,, ,, .			+	
1734 ,, ,, ,, .			+	+
1735 ,, ,, ,, .		+	+	
1736 ,, ,, ,, .			+	+
1737 ,, ,, ,, .			+	+
1738 ,, ,, ,, .	+	+	+	+
1739 ,, ,, ,, .		+		+
1739 Old head, curved milling* .		+	+	
,, ,, ,, EIC .			+	
1740 ,, ,, ,, .		+	+	+
1741 Young head	+			
1745 Old head, curved milling* . .			+	+
,, ,, ,, LIMA .			+	+
1746 ,, ,, ,, .			+	+
Older head, curved milling,* LIMA	+	Rud.		
1747 ,, ,, ,, .		Rud.	+	
1748 ,, ,, ,, .	+	+	+	
1749 ,, ,, ,, .			+	
1750 ,, ,, ,, .			+	
1752 ,, ,, ,, .			+	
1753 ,, ,, ,, .	+	+	+	+
1755 ,, ,, ,, .			+	+
1756 ,, ,, ,, .			+	+
1758 ,, ,, ,, .			+	+
1759 ,, ,, ,, .			+	+
1760 ,, ,, ,, .			+	+

* The edges of the five guineas are not milled. Those of the half-guineas are throughout the reign milled with diagonal straight lines.

George III, 1760 to 1820.

The earlier coinages of George III consisted of guineas and half-guineas of the same standard, weight, and value as those of his grandfather, with the addition of one issue, in 1762, of quarter guineas. An indenture made between the king and the Honourable C. S. Cadogan, master of the mint, in 1770, provided for the making of five and two-guinea pieces, guineas, half-guineas, seven shilling pieces, and quarter guineas; but it was declared that the master should not be obliged to coin seven-shilling pieces or quarter guineas except when he should be ordered to do so by the king or the lord high treasurer or the commissioners of the Treasury for the time being. Patterns of five-guinea pieces were made in 1770, 1773, and 1777, and of two-guinea pieces in 1768, 1773, and 1777, but none were ever issued for circulation; the only quarter guineas made during this reign were those issued in 1762, and a pattern in 1764; and although patterns for seven shilling pieces were made in 1775 and 1776, none were issued for circulation till 1797.

In 1774 the gold coins in circulation had become very much diminished in weight by filing and other malpractices, while those issued new from the mint were melted down and exported; and accordingly an Act of that year called in and made no longer current (except for payment of taxes) all gold coins below a weight, which was fixed by proclamation at 128 grs. to the guinea for coins made since Dec. 31st, 1771, and at 126 grs. for earlier coins; and in 1776 all coins weighing less than 128 grs. to the guinea were made no longer current. In 1797, there being very great lack of silver money, a proclamation was issued for giving currency to a new gold coin of the value of 7*s*, which was intended to some extent to supply the deficiency. It was to be of the same standard as the other gold coins, and to weigh 43·146 grs., being almost exactly one-third of a guinea. These pieces continued to be coined down to 1813.

In the year 1800 the kingdoms of Great Britain and Ireland were united, and on the 1st January following, a proclamation was issued that from thenceforth his Majesty's royal style and title should be Georgius Tertius, Dei Gratia Britanniarum Rex, Fidei Defensor; and that the arms of the United Kingdom should be, quarterly, first and fourth England, second Scotland, third Ireland; and on an escutcheon of pretence the arms of his Majesty's dominions in Germany, ensigned with the electoral bonnet, for which in 1817, in consequence of the treaty of Vienna having erected the Electorate of Hanover into a kingdom, was substituted a royal crown. This change, by which the title and arms of France were tacitly abandoned, was immediately carried out upon the coins.

In 1813 was the last coinage of guineas, half-guineas and seven-shilling pieces; in 1816 gold coins were made the sole standard measure of value and legal tender, the silver coins being diminished in weight and made legal tender for 40*s* only; and in 1817 a new coinage was issued of sovereigns and half-sovereigns, the sovereign to weigh 123·27447 grs. and to be current for 20*s*, and the half-sovereign in proportion. No alteration was made in the fineness of the metal, but the type was entirely different from that of the guinea, having St. George and the Dragon on the reverse, and the coins themselves were smaller and thicker. No sovereigns lighter than 122¾ grs. were to be current, nor half-sovereigns lighter than 61¼ grs. Guineas, &c., when not below the weights fixed in 1776, were to remain current money.

The following are the types and dates of the gold coins struck for circulation in England during this long reign.

GUINEAS. *Type* 1. Bust to right, laureate, wreath curved, the tye has two ends, hair long, curling towards the face, no drapery. GEORGIVS. III. DEI GRATIA Rev. shield garnished, crowned, similar to that of George II, and arms arranged in the same way. M. B. F. ET. H. REX. F. D. B. ET. L. D. S. R. I. A. T. ET. E. Date 1761.

(160) Rud. Suppl. pt. 2, pl. iii. 10. *MB.* *Type* 2. Bust to right, laureate, no laurel berries, tye has two ends, hair long and curly, a lock in front of left shoulder, no drapery. Legends and rev. as type 1. 1763, 1764. Both in *MB.* Rud. Suppl. vi. 28. *Type* 3. Similar to the last, but the head larger, the laurel extending upwards within the legend and bearing berries. 1765 to 1773 inclusive. (161) *MB.* On one specimen of 1773 in *MB.* the berries are omitted.

The dies for all the preceding coins were engraved by Yeo; those for the next were by Thomas Pingo. *Type* 4. Large bust to right, laureate, dividing the legend above and below, tye has two ends, hair curls forward on both shoulders and under the bust, concealing the back of the neck. Legends and rev. as before. 1774, 1775, 1776, 1777, 1778, 1779, 1781, 1782, 1783, 1784, 1785, 1786. (162) All in *MB.*

Type 5. In 1787 a new type was adopted, for which the dies were engraved by Lewis Pingo. Smaller bust, not dividing the legend above, to right, laureate, the tye has a loop and two ends, and encloses all the hair behind, curl on right shoulder. Rev. spade-shaped shield, whence the coin has obtained the name of the spade guinea; crowned, not garnished; the crown is small, and differs from the previous ones in having the arches angular. Legends same as type 1, but that on the reverse begins at the bottom of the coin and is not interrupted by the shield or crown. The date is at the bottom of the coin under the shield. All dates occur from 1787 to 1799 inclusive, and all are in the Museum except that of 1796. (163).

Type 6. After 1799 the only guineas issued were those of 1813, the dies for which were by Lewis Pingo, who copied the bust from a model by Marchant. The obverse has a small bust of the king, to right, laureate, the tye has a bow and two long ends, hair short, neck bare, legend GEORGIVS III DEI GRATIA, not interrupted by the king's head. The king's title and arms having been changed in 1801, the reverse is different from the previous ones. The shield is small and angular, bearing 1 and 4 England, 2 Scotland, 3 Ireland, with the arms of the German dominions on an escutcheon of pretence surmounted by the Electoral cap. The shield is inclosed within the garter inscribed HONI SOIT QUI MAL Y PENSE, with a small crown above; legend commencing at top BRITANNIARUM REX FIDEI DEFENSOR. In the field under the shield is the date, 1813. (164) *MB.*

HALF GUINEAS. *Type* 1. Bust to right, laurel wreath with berries, tye has two ends, hair long, descending below the bust, no drapery. Legends and rev. like the first guinea. 1762. (165) *MB.* *Type* 2. Like the second guinea, but the tye encloses one lock of hair. 1763. Rud. Suppl. vi. 29. *MB.* *Type* 3. Like the last, but laurel bearing berries, the tye less bent, and not enclosing any hair, dates 1764, 1765, 1766, 1772, 1773, 1774. (166) All in *MB.* *Type* 4. The later half-guineas of 1774 and those of 1775 (167), 1776, 1777, 1778, 1781, 1784, 1785, 1786, are copied from the guinea of 1774, but those of 1774 and 1775 are of inferior workmanship to the coins of the subsequent years. All in *MB.* *Type* 5. Same as the guinea of 1787. Dates 1787, 1788, 1789, 1790, 1791, 1793, 1794, 1795, 1796, 1797, 1798, 1800. All in *MB.* *Type* 6. Obverse as the last, reverse like the guinea of 1813, but letters smaller. 1801, 1802, 1803. (168) All in *MB.* *Type* 7. Same as the guinea of 1813, but letters on rev. smaller. 1804, 1806, 1808, 1809, 1810, 1811, 1813. All in *MB.* Rud. Suppl. pt. ii., pl. iii. 13.

SEVEN SHILLING PIECES. *Type* 1. Bust to right, laureate, hair short, tye has two loops and two long ends, neck bare. GEORGIVS III DEI GRATIA. Rev. a crown, with angular arches, of the same shape as on the guineas of 1787. Legend beginning at bottom of coin, MAG. BRI. FR. ET. HIB. REX. Date at bottom of coin, under the crown. 1797, 1798, 1799, 1800. All in *MB.* (169) Rud. Suppl. pt. ii. pl. iii. 12. *Type* 2. After the union with Ireland and change of the king's titles. Like the previous ones, but rev. legend + BRITANNIARUM REX FIDEI DEFENSOR beginning at top of coin. Date in field under the crown, 1801, 1802, 1803. (170) All in *MB*. *Type* 3. Obverse like the guineas of 1813, reverse same as last, except that there is a mullet instead of a cross at beginning of legend. 1804, 1806, 1808, 1809, 1810, 1811, 1813. Very few were issued of this last year. Mr. Cuff had one, but there is no specimen in the British Museum, which has all the rest. (171) The dies for all are by L. Pingo, but the bust on type 3 is copied by him from Marchant's model.

QUARTER GUINEAS. These were only issued in 1762, and are of the same type as the guinea of 1763. (172) Rud. Suppl. vi. 30. *MB*.

SOVEREIGNS. *Weight* 123·27447 *grs*. These are much smaller and thicker coins than the guineas. They have on the obverse the king's head to right, laureate, hair short; the tye has a loop and two ends; neck bare. Legend commencing at bottom of coin, GEORGIUS III D : G : BRITANNIAR : REX F : D : Date at bottom of coin under bust, 1817, 1818, 1820. Rev. St. George and the Dragon within the garter, which takes the place of the legend and is inscribed with its usual motto, HONI. SOIT. QUI. MAL. Y. PENSE. On the ground, under the broken shaft of the spear, are the letters BP incuse, the initials of the artist, B. Pistrucci; but they are extremely small, and on many coins hardly visible. (173) Rud. Suppl. pt. ii. pl. xiv. 6. *MB*. This device was originally intended for a gem to be engraved for Lord Spencer, but Sir Joseph Banks having seen and admired it, recommended its adoption on the forthcoming coinage.

HALF SOVEREIGNS. *Weight* 61·63723 *grs*. Bust same as the sovereigns, legend GEORGIUS III DEI GRATIA, beginning at bottom of coin. Date at bottom, under head, 1817, 1818, 1820. Rev. Angular shield, crowned, bearing 1 and 4 England, 2 Scotland, 3 Ireland, the German dominions on an escutcheon of pretence surmounted by a royal crown. Legend beginning at bottom, interrupted by the crown, ·BRITANNIARUM REX FID : DEF : (174). Rud. Suppl. pt. ii. pl. xiv. 7. *MB.*

		gua.	½ gua.	7*s.*	¼ gua.
1761	First bust, by Yeo .	+			
1762	Similar bust . .		+		
	Second bust, by Yeo .				+
1763	,, ,, .	+	+		
1764	,, ,, .	+			
	Third bust, by Yeo .		+		
1765	,, ,, .	+	+		
1766	,, ,, .	+	+		
1767	,, ,, .	+			
1768	,, ,, .	+			
1769	,, ,, .	+			
1770	,, ,, .	+			
1771	,, ,, .	+			
1772	,, ,, .	+	+		
1773	,, ,, .	++	+		
1774	,, ,, .		+		
	Bust by T. Pingo .	+	+		
1775	,, ,, .	+	+		
1776	,, ,, .	+	+		
1777	,, ,, .	+	+		
1778	,, ,, .	+	+		
1779	,, ,, .	+			
1781	,, ,, .	+	+		
1782	,, ,, .	+			
1783	,, ,, .	+			
1784	,, ,, .	+	+		
1785	,, ,, .	+	+		
1786	,, ,, .	+	+		
1787	Bust by L. Pingo .	+	+		
1788	,, ,, .	+	+		
1789	,, ,, .	+	+		
1790	,, ,, .	+	+		
1791	,, ,, .	+	+		
1792	,, ,, .	+			
1793	,, ,, .	+	+		
1794	,, ,, .	+	+		
1795	,, ,, .	+	+		
1796	,, ,, .		+		
1797	,, ,, .	+	+	+	
1798	,, ,, .	+	+	+	
1799	,, ,, .	+		+	
1800	,, ,, .		+	+	
1801	,, after the Union .		+	+	
1802	,, ,, .		+	+	
1803	,, ,, .		+	+	
1804	Bust by Marchant .		+	+	

	gua.	½ gua.	7s.
1806 Bust by Marchant		+	+
1808 ,, ,,		+	+
1809 ,, ,,		+	+
1810 ,, ,,		+	+
1811 ,, ,,		+	+
1813 ,, ,,	+	+	Cuff

	Sov.	½ Sov.
1817 Bust by Pistrucci	+	+
1818 ,, ,,	+	+
1820 ,, ,,	+	+

George IV, 1820 to 1830.

The first gold coins of George IV were sovereigns and half-sovereigns, which were struck by virtue of an Order in Council, dated March 5th, 1821, and were made current by proclamation on May 5th; the sovereign was ordered to have St. George and the Dragon on the reverse, and the half-sovereign the arms in a shield surrounded by the rose, thistle, and shamrock, with the word Anno and the date of the year. These coins were of the same value and weight as those of George III, but the minimum weight for a current coin fixed in 1817 having been found to be too high, a proclamation of February 6th, 1821, ordained that every sovereign weighing not less than 122½ grs., and every half-sovereign weighing not less than 61⅛ grs., should be thenceforth received as current money; and these still remain the least current weights. The half-sovereign of this coinage was, however, soon suppressed, because the type was so like that of the sixpence that the latter was gilt and passed for a half-sovereign; and an Order in Council of September 19th, 1823, directed the coinage of a double sovereign and of a new half-sovereign, the reverse of which, though described in the order in the same way as the first had been, was differently executed to distinguish it from the sixpence.

A new coinage both of gold and silver was ordered on June 14th, 1825. The gold coins mentioned in this order are the £5 piece, £2 piece, sovereign, and half-sovereign, but though patterns were made for the two former pieces, none were actually issued for currency.

The types of the coins are as follows :—

DOUBLE SOVEREIGN. Bust to left, head bare, not laureate, hair short, neck bare, I.B.M., the initials of the engraver Merlin, below the bust. Legend, beginning at bottom and interrupted by the head, GEORGIUS IIII D : G : BRITANNIAR : REX F : D : Rev. St. George and the Dragon. No legend, but 1823 in the exergue, with B.P., the initials of Pistrucci, in small letters ; on the ground, under the broken shaft of the spear, WWP for William Wellesley Pole, the master of the mint. On the edge, DECUS ET TUTAMEN ANNO REGNI IV. (175) Rud. 2 Ʀ. 10. *MB.* The obverse of these coins was by Merlin, who copied the bust from one by Chantrey; the reverse was by Pistrucci. The latter had been ordered to engrave the obverse also, but the king insisted that the bust should be copied from Chantrey's model, which Pistrucci thought it beneath his dignity to do, and Merlin was accordingly employed instead. Some were struck also with the dates 1825, 1826, both of which have on the edge ANNO REGNI SEPTIMO in very slightly raised letters. They are of similar type to the later sovereigns, but were not issued for circulation. *MB.*

SOVEREIGN. The first of these have on the obverse the king's bust to left, laureate, tye has a loop and two ends, hair short, neck bare, BP (for Pistrucci) below the bust. Legend and reverse as the double sovereign; edge milled. 1821, 1822, 1823, 1824, 1825. The later sovereigns have the king's bust to left, not laureate, hair short, neck bare, date under bust. Rev. Square shield, arms as on George III's half-sovereigns, garnished, crowned, crown interrupting legend, which begins at bottom, BRITANNIARUM REX FID : DEF: Dates 1825, 1826, 1827, 1829, 1830. All in *MB.* (176) Rud. 2 R. 13. The earlier sovereigns are by Pistrucci; of the later ones the obverse was engraved by W. Wyon, the bust being copied from a medallion of the size of life by Chantrey; the reverse was by Merlin.

HALF SOVEREIGNS. The first of these have the same obverse as the first sovereigns, but on the reverse a garnished shield crowned, surrounded by roses, thistles, and shamrocks; arms as on George III's half-sovereigns; ANNO to left, 1821 to right of shield, the feet of the letters being towards the edge of the coin. The letters WWP (for William Wellesley Pole, master of the mint) are in the respective centres of three of the shamrock leaves. (177) Rud. 2 R. 11. *MB.* These half-sovereigns being withdrawn in consequence of their resemblance to the sixpences, the next, having the same obverse, have on the reverse a plain square shield, arms as before, colours marked; underneath it a thistle and shamrock issuing from a rose. ANNO to left of shield, date 1823, 1824, or 1825 to right, the feet of the letters being towards the shield. (178) Rud. 2 R. 12. All in *MB.* The later half-sovereigns are exactly like the later sovereigns, and are dated 1826, 1827, 1828. All in *MB.* A mint return shows that 4205 half-sovereigns were coined in 1829, but as none are known with this date they must have been struck with the dies of the previous year.

	2 Sovs.	Sov.	½ Sov.
1821 By Pistrucci; head laureate .		+	+
1822 " " " .		+	
1823 " " " plain shield on ½ sov. . .		+	+
Obv. Chantrey and Merlin, rev. Pistrucci . . .	+		
1824 Pistrucci, head laureate, plain shield on ½ sov. . :		+	+
1825 " " " .		+	+
Obv. Chantrey and Wyon, rev. Merlin . . .	+	+	
1826 " " " .	+	+	+
1827 " " " .		+	+
1828 " " " .			+
1829 " " " .		+	
1830 " " " .		+	

William IV, 1830 to 1837.

William IV succeeded his brother on the 26th of June, and an Order in Council of the 22nd Nov., 1830, directed the coinage of a double sovereign, sovereign, and half-sovereign of gold, and the usual silver and copper coins. These were made current by proclamation on April 13th, 1831, but though proofs were struck of the double sovereign, no coins of that denomination were actually issued for currency. No alteration was afterwards made in the gold coins, excepting that a Treasury order of April 14th, 1835, directed that a half-sovereign should be coined, of the same weight and type as the former ones, but reduced in size; but the only half-sovereigns answering this description are those which are dated 1834.

SOVEREIGN. Bust to right, head and neck bare, WW (for William Wyon) incuse on the truncation of the neck. Legend, beginning at bottom and interrupted by king's head, GULIELMUS IIII D : G : BRITANNIAR : REX F : D :

Rev. Square shield, garnished, crowned, arms as George III's half-sovereigns, colours not marked; under the shield the date, ANNO 1831, 1832, 1833, 1835. (179) *MB.* The obverses were executed by Wyon, after a model by Chantrey; the reverses were by Merlin.

HALF SOVEREIGNS resemble the sovereigns, and occur of the dates 1834, 1835, 1836, 1837. All in *MB.* Those of 1834 are a good deal smaller in diameter than the previous and later ones, though of the same weight. (180) The date 1832, given in Rud. 2 R. 20, is a fanciful one, as no half-sovereigns were struck between 1828 and 1834.

	Sov.	½ Sov.
1831 Obv. by Chantrey and Wyon, rev. by Merlin	+	
1832 ,, ,, ,, .	+	
1833 ,, ,, ,, .	+	
1834 ,, ,, ,, .		+
1835 ,, ,, ,, .	+	+
1836 ,, ,, ,, .		+
1837 ,, ,, ,, .		+

Victoria.

Queen Victoria began her reign upon the death of her uncle on the 20th June, 1837, and, whatever may be the case in other respects, no reign has ever been more Conservative than hers with regard to the type and denomination of the gold coins. An order in Council was issued on the 8th of June, 1838, followed by a proclamation on the 5th of July, ordering the making of £5 pieces, sovereigns, and half-sovereigns, all of the same type, which is described in the order. Two patterns for five-pound pieces were produced, not, however, of this type, but having Una and the Lion on the reverse, in reference it is presumed to the government of the British nation by a queen; but no such coins have ever been issued to the public, and the sovereign and half-sovereign are the only gold coins which have been struck for currency during this reign. A coinage of £5 and £2 pieces is, however, provided for by the Coinage Act, 1870, by which the coinage is at present regulated, and Her Majesty in Council has power to order any other denominations of coins to be coined at the mint, provided that the weight and fineness of such coins shall be proportioned to that of the existing sovereigns and half-sovereigns.

The standard fineness of the coins is the same as that of all coins since the Restoration, namely 22 carats fine gold to 2 carats alloy; and the weight is that which was fixed in 1817, namely 123·27447 grs. to the sovereign. No sovereign weighing less than 122½ grs., and no half-sovereign weighing less than 61⅛ grs., is lawful tender.

Until the year 1871 both obverse and reverse of the gold coins remained unchanged. The portrait of the Queen on the sovereigns is the same as on most of the silver coins, and is thus described by Mr. Hawkins in the "Silver Coins of England:"—"The bust of the Queen is represented turned to the left, the head is bound with a double fillet, and the hair gracefully collected into a knot behind. The likeness of Her Majesty is excellent, and is copied from a model in wax taken from the life by Mr. Wyon, the chief engraver to the mint, by whom the dies are engraved with admirable taste and skill." The legend is VICTORIA DEI GRATIA, with the date below the bust, and WW, the initials of the engraver William Wyon, in relief on the truncation of the neck. On the reverse is a square shield, ungarnished, crowned, bearing the arms of England in the first and fourth quarters, Scotland in the second, and Ireland in the third. The colours are expressed. The arms of Hanover are, of course, omitted, as the right to that kingdom is limited to the male line only, and devolved, after the death of William IV, on his next brother the Duke of Cumberland. A branch of laurel is placed on each side of the shield, and the legend is BRITANNIARUM REGINA FID : DEF : (181).

The half-sovereigns are exactly like the sovereigns, except that the letters W W do not appear on the obverse, and on the reverse the shield is garnished, and the laurel branches are omitted. (183.)

On the reverses of some of the gold coins of 1863, and on all those of the following years, may be observed a very small numeral under the shield. On figure (181) the numeral is 18. These numerals were placed on the dies in order to test how long each particular die lasted, every die having a different numeral, and the series of numerals beginning again at the beginning of each year. Thus every sovereign of the year 1868, with the numeral 18 on it, is made from the same identical die. Of course, as every die was made by the same punches, there is no substantial difference, except the numeral, between one die and another. It was found that a single die could generally produce 100,000 sovereigns before wearing out. These numerals were used on the sovereigns as long as the shield of arms continued to be the type of the reverse, and on the half-sovereigns until

1880 inclusive. They were not found, however, to be of any practical use, and are now discontinued.

On the 14th of January, 1871, an order in Council was issued, authorizing the use of the type of St. George and the Dragon on the reverse of the coins, and the remarkable expedient was adopted of reviving, for the sovereigns, the old reverse dies, engraved by Pistrucci for George IV, with no alteration whatever except of the date in the exergue (182). The obverse remained as on the Queen's former sovereigns, except that, as there was no legend on the reverse, the full title, VICTORIA D:G:BRITANNIAR: REG:F:D: was placed on the obverse. These were struck concurrently with sovereigns bearing the shield on the reverse from 1871 to 1874, and since 1874 no other type but that of St. George and the Dragon has been used on sovereigns struck in England. The half-sovereigns have continued the same throughout the reign.

We have seen that in former reigns the coins of foreign countries were frequently made current in this country at certain specified values by royal proclamation. But the power to do this appears to have been taken away by the Act of the 56th year of George III, c. 68, by which the great recoinage of silver in 1816 was regulated; for that Act declares the gold coin of this realm to be the only legal tender for payments within the United Kingdom of any higher amount than forty shillings, and that its weight and fineness shall be regulated by the indenture at that time in force with the master of the mint. But the immense discoveries of gold in Australia made it very convenient to establish a mint there, and accordingly in 1863 an Act was passed (26 & 27 Vict., c. 74) which, after reciting that Her Majesty had by proclamation established at Sydney a branch of the Royal Mint for making gold coins of the same weight and fineness and of the same denominations as the gold coins issued by Her Majesty's mint in London, enacted that it should "be lawful for Her Majesty by proclamation, issued with the advice of her Privy Council, to declare that, after a date specified in such proclamation, gold coins made at the said branch mint, of designs approved by Her Majesty, at Sydney aforesaid, and being of the same weight and fineness as are required by law with respect to gold coins of the same denominations made at Her Majesty's mint in London, are to be a legal tender for payments within the United Kingdom of Great Britain and Ireland." And in 1866, by the Colonial Branch Mint Act, 1866 (29 & 30 Vict., c. 65), a general power was given to Her Majesty, by proclamation issued in like manner, to declare that gold coins so made at any colonial branch mint which she had established, or might thereafter establish, "are to be a legal tender for payments within any part of Her Majesty's dominions, to be specified in such proclamation, in which gold coins issued from Her Majesty's mint in London shall, at the date of the issue of such proclamation, be a legal tender." The only branch mints established at present are at Sydney and Melbourne, of which the former was opened on the 14th of May, 1855, and the latter on the 12th of June, 1872; and by virtue of the two Acts above mentioned the coins there struck have been made legal tender in this country. Those struck at Sydney were at first of a different type from those struck in this country; the bust of the Queen is different, though similar, and the head is encircled with a laurel wreath. The legend on the obverse is the same as on the sovereigns with St. George and the Dragon, and the date is under the bust, but the reverse is entirely different, having AUSTRALIA across the field, with a crown above it, the words SYDNEY MINT above, and ONE SOVEREIGN or HALF-SOVEREIGN below. Those now issued at Sydney, however, are exactly the same as those struck in London with the arms on the reverse, except that a minute S, for Sydney, is placed under the arms in the position occupied on the English sovereigns by the small numeral to which we have already alluded. The Melbourne sovereigns are the same as the London ones with St. George and the Dragon, but have M, for Melbourne, below the bust. The half-sovereigns of both mints have the arms on the reverse. The dies for all the Australian coins are made in London.

The gold coins of the present reign cannot be said to be rare, although few people, perhaps, are able to obtain quite as many of them as they would like to possess. None of them are dated 1837, and in 1881 and 1882 there was no coinage of English gold at the mint, partly because the buildings and machinery there were being rearranged and altered during those years; but from 1838 to 1880 inclusive sovereigns have been struck every year except in 1840, 1867, 1875, and 1877, and half-sovereigns every year except in 1840, 1862, and 1868; and the mint returns show that the number of sovereigns coined in London during this reign to the end of 1882 is 162,656,796, and the number of half-sovereigns is 54,116,322; besides which, 45,990,500 sovereigns and 2,170,500 half-sovereigns have been issued from the mint at Sydney, and 21,126,600 sovereigns and 393,000 half-sovereigns from that at Melbourne down to the end of the same period. Of these coins a considerable number are believed to find their way into the melting pots of working goldsmiths and jewellers, who obtain by this means gold of a known standard; but the figures nevertheless indicate the enormous extent of a commerce which can require such a circulating medium. It has been pointed out by previous writers that the designs upon the coins are not such as enable an artist to exhibit his taste and skill, and that devices containing allusions to important historical events are never allowed. Such devices were frequently adopted in former times. The coinage of Edward III, for instance, alludes to his claim of sovereignty over the seas; that of James I to the union of the kingdoms; and that of Charles I to the king's declared principles of government; the mint-marks contain constant allusions to contemporary personages; and several military and commercial successes are recorded on the coins from Charles II to George II. In a reign so eventful and so prosperous as the present it would surely not be difficult to find achievements, whether military, or scientific, or social, of which not one party only but the whole nation is proud, and which might well be commemorated on our national coinage. We have no doubt that artists would be found equal to the occasion, and a grand opportunity would thus be utilized of rewarding illustrious services and of developing artistic taste.

FAREWELL.

TABLE

SHOWING the current value of a coin containing 113 grains of pure gold, being equivalent to our modern sovereign, from the first coinage of gold by Henry III to the present time.

			s.	d.
1257 to 1265—	113 grs. of pure gold =		4	2¼
1265—1343	”	”	5	0¼
1343—1344	”	”	6	3¾
1344—1346	”	”	5	5¾
1346—1351	”	”	5	10¾
1351—1412	”	”	6	3¾
1412—1464	”	”	7	0
1464—1465	”	”	8	9
1465—1526	”	”	9	5½
1526	”	”	10	5
1526—1543*	”	”	10	9
1543	”	”	11	9½
1544	”	”	12	10
1545—1549	”	”	14	1½
1549	”	”	14	6½
1550—1552	”	”	11	4¼
1552—1561*	”	”	14	1½
1561—1572*	”	”	9	5
1572—1578	”	”	14	2¼
1578—1582	”	”	14	3¼
1582—1601*	”	”	14	1½
1601—1604	”	”	14	4

* In these instances crown gold and standard gold were being coined simultaneously, and the value of a coin containing 113 grains of pure gold would vary by a penny or two, according to the quantity and value of the alloy mixed with it. The values given in these instances in the table are the values for crown gold, which is the metal of which the present sovereign is made. The coins of standard gold from 1552 to 1561, and from 1582 to 1601, were of the same value as from 1572 to 1578, during which latter period standard gold only was coined.

			s.	d.
1604 to 1611—113 grs. of pure gold =			15	11
1611—1623*	,,	,,	17	6
1623—1661	,,	,,	17	6½
1661—1670	,,	,,	18	8¾
1670—1698	,,	,,	19	0½
1698—1717	,,	,,	20	5¾
1717—1884	,,	,,	20	0

The above table shows the comparative value of gold and silver money in England ever since the former was first coined, and it may be found useful in estimating the real prices paid for articles at various periods of our history. Thus wheat, for instance, is said to have been most extraordinarily dear in 1257, when it was sold at 24*s* a quarter; but the above table shows that it would have taken nearly six coins containing the same amount of gold as our modern sovereign to make up those 24*s*, so that the real price of a quarter of wheat, in our present language, was not 24*s*, but £5. 14*s* 7½*d*. The Statute of Labourers in 1350 fixes the price of a bushel of wheat at 10*d*, and a day's wages for haymaking at 1*d*. But at that time our present sovereign was worth only 5*s* 10¾*d*, so 1*d* at that time was equivalent in metal value to about 3½*d* of our money. Of course it must not be forgotten that metal value is a very different thing from purchasing value; for instance, 10*d* in 1350 would purchase about $\frac{1}{7}$ part of a sovereign, or about 34*d* of our present money; but it would also purchase a bushel of wheat, which, according to the last tithe averages, would now cost about 5*s* 8*d*.

INDEX.

EDWARD III.

Plate 1.

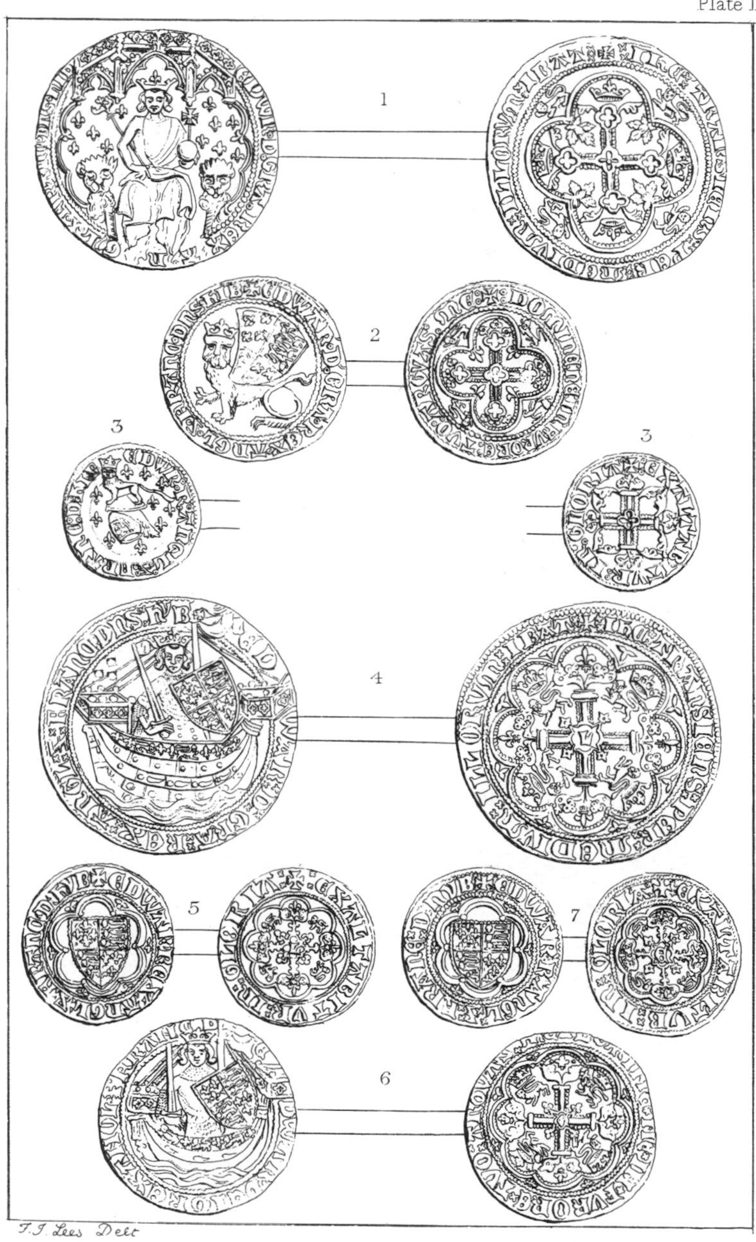

T. J. Lees Delt

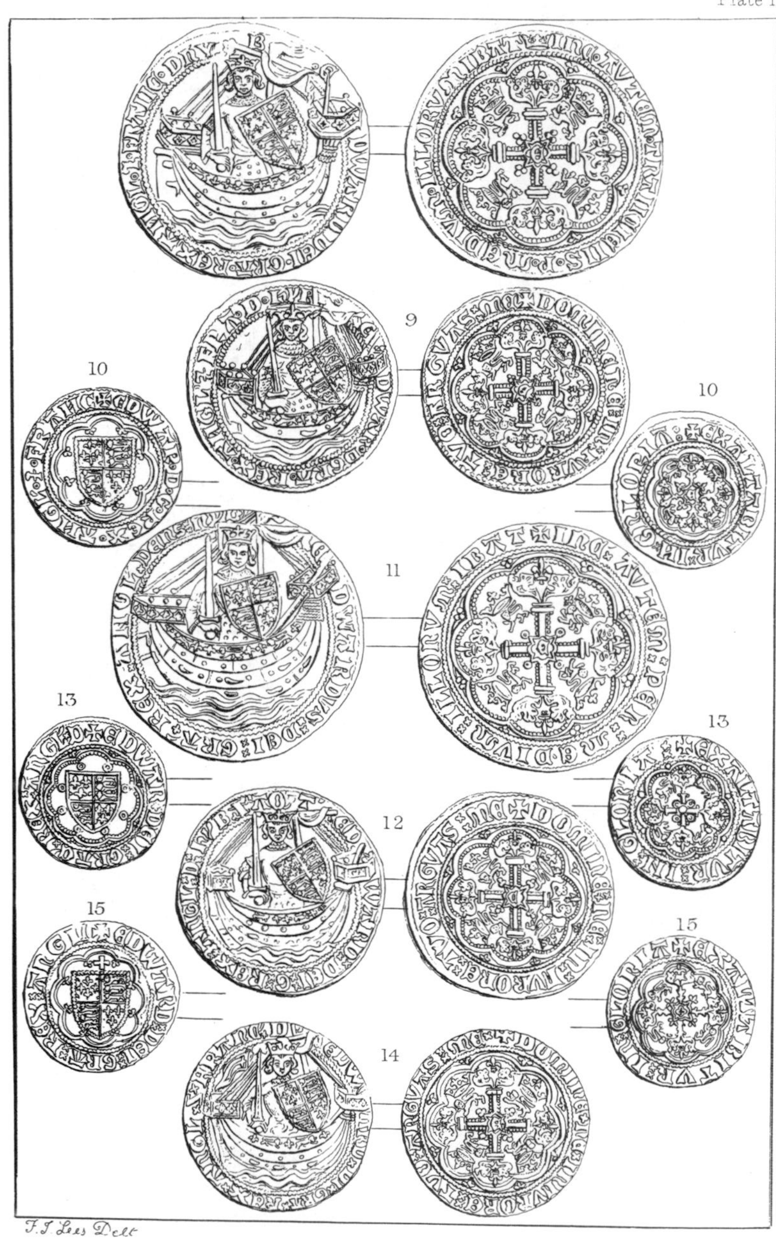

F. J. Lees Delt

RICHARD II.

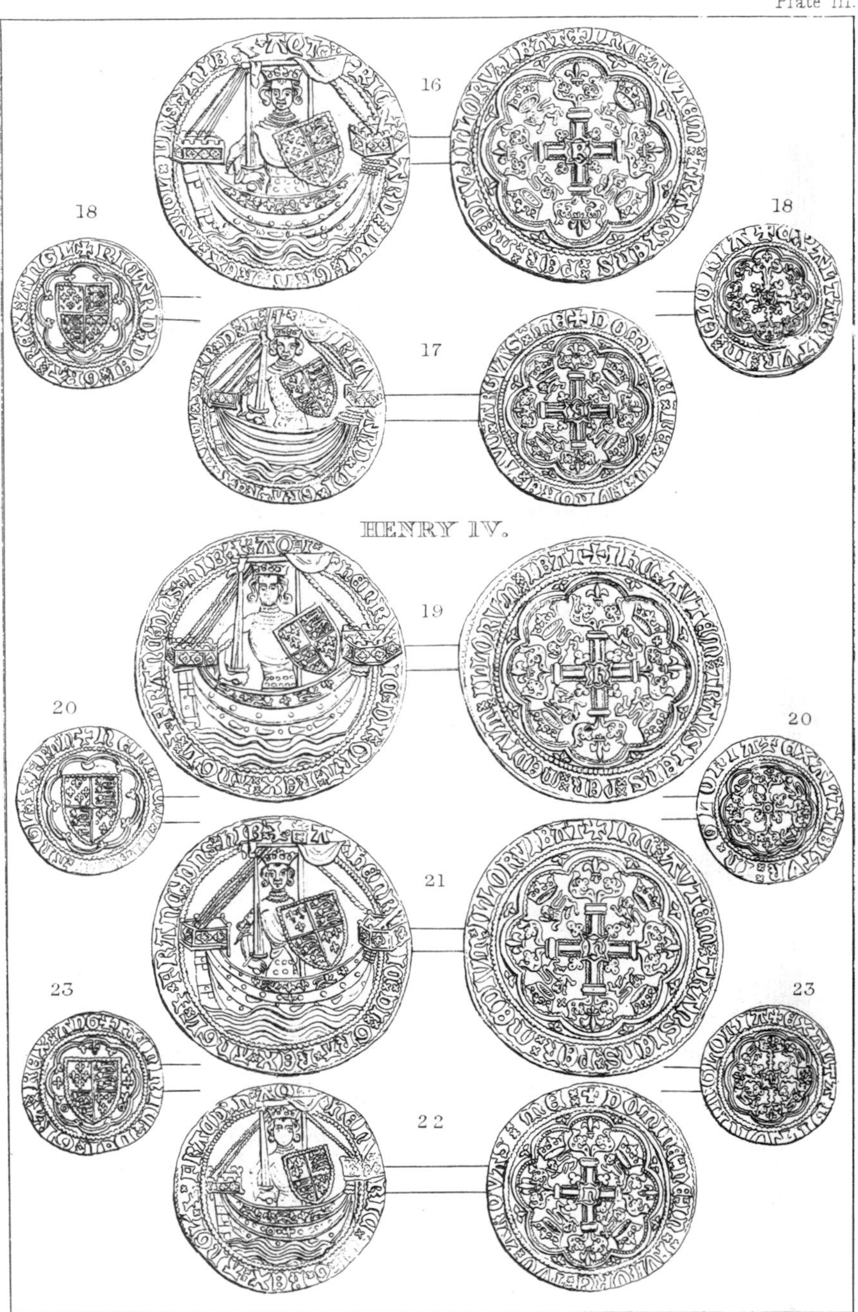

F. J. Lees Delt.

HENRY V.

Plate IV.

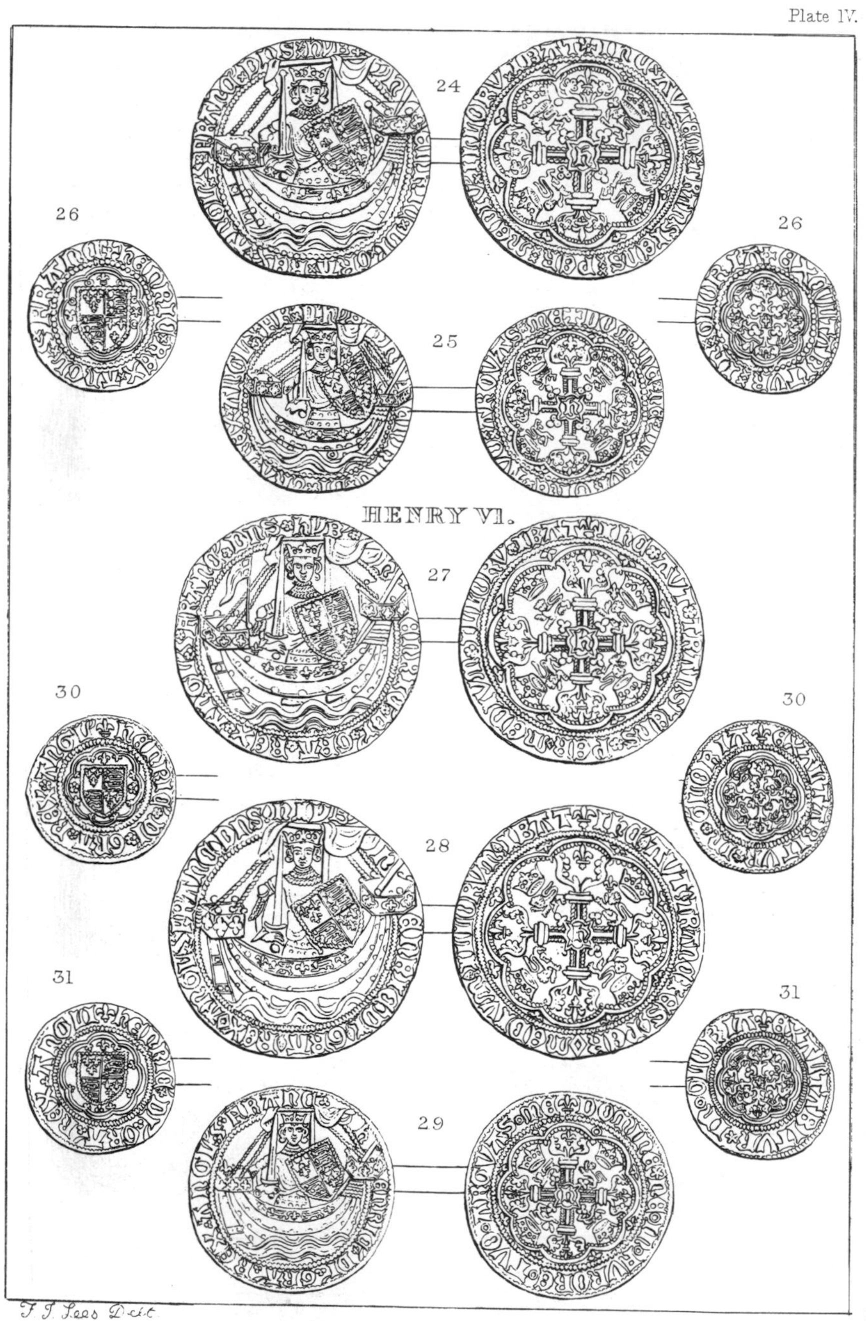

F. J. Lees Delt

HENRY VI.

Plate V.

T. J. Lees Delt.

EDWARD V.

Plate [illegible]

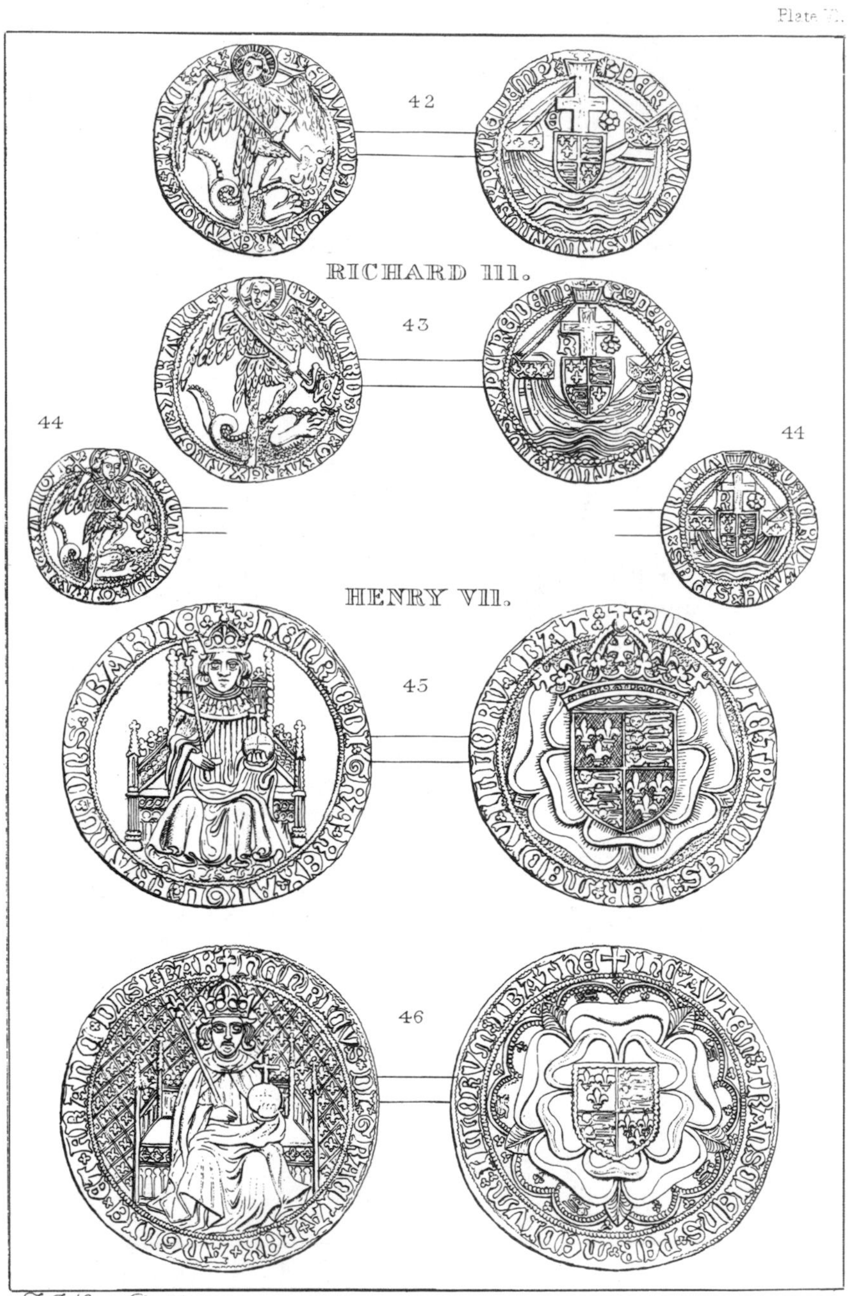

F. T. Lees Delt

HENRY VII.

Plate VII.

F. J. Lees Delt

HENRY VIII.

Plate VIII.

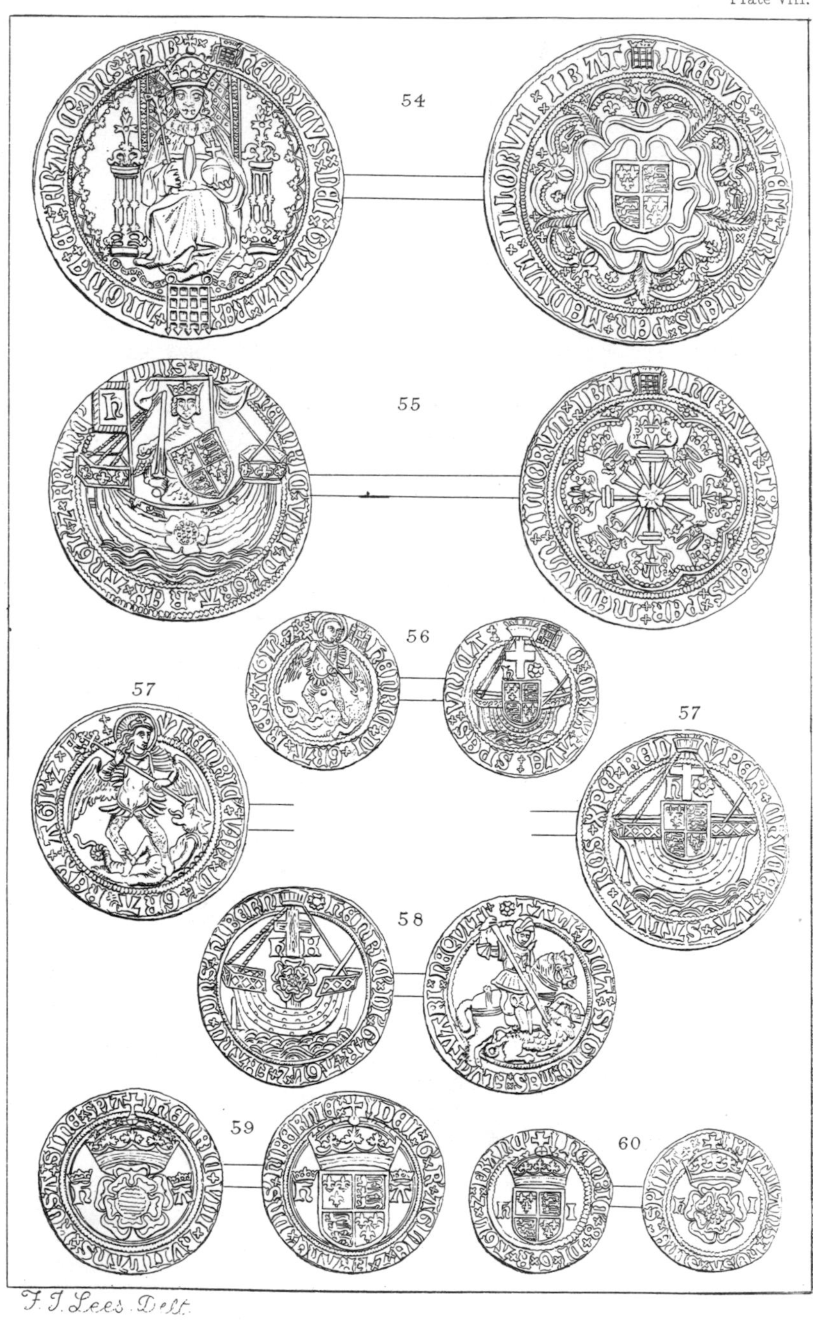

F. J. Lees Delt.

F. J. Lees Delt.

Plate X.

F. T. Lees Delt

EDWARD VI.

Plate X.

ELIZABETH.

Plate XII.

F. J. Lees Delt

ELIZABETH.

Plate XIII.

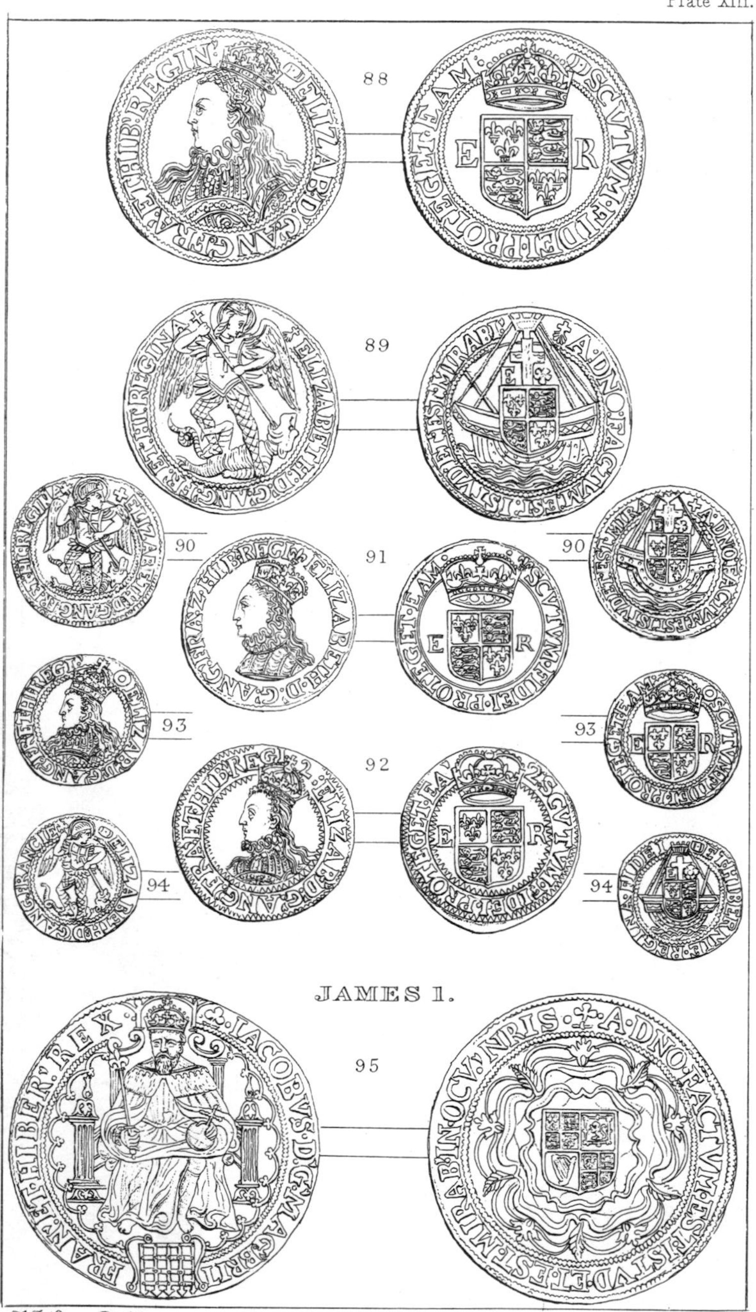

J. J. Lees Delt

Plate XIV.

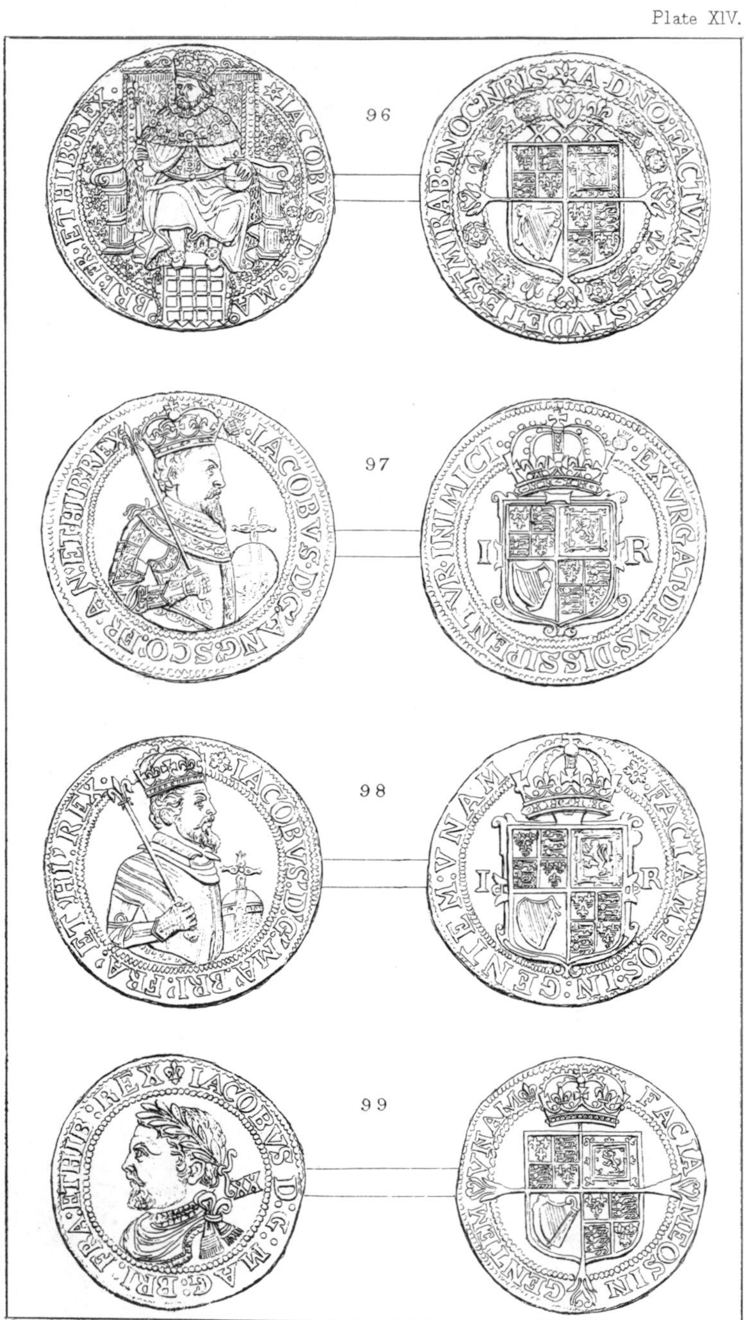

J. T. Lees.

Plate XV.

F. J. Lees. Delt.

JAMES I.

Plate XVI.

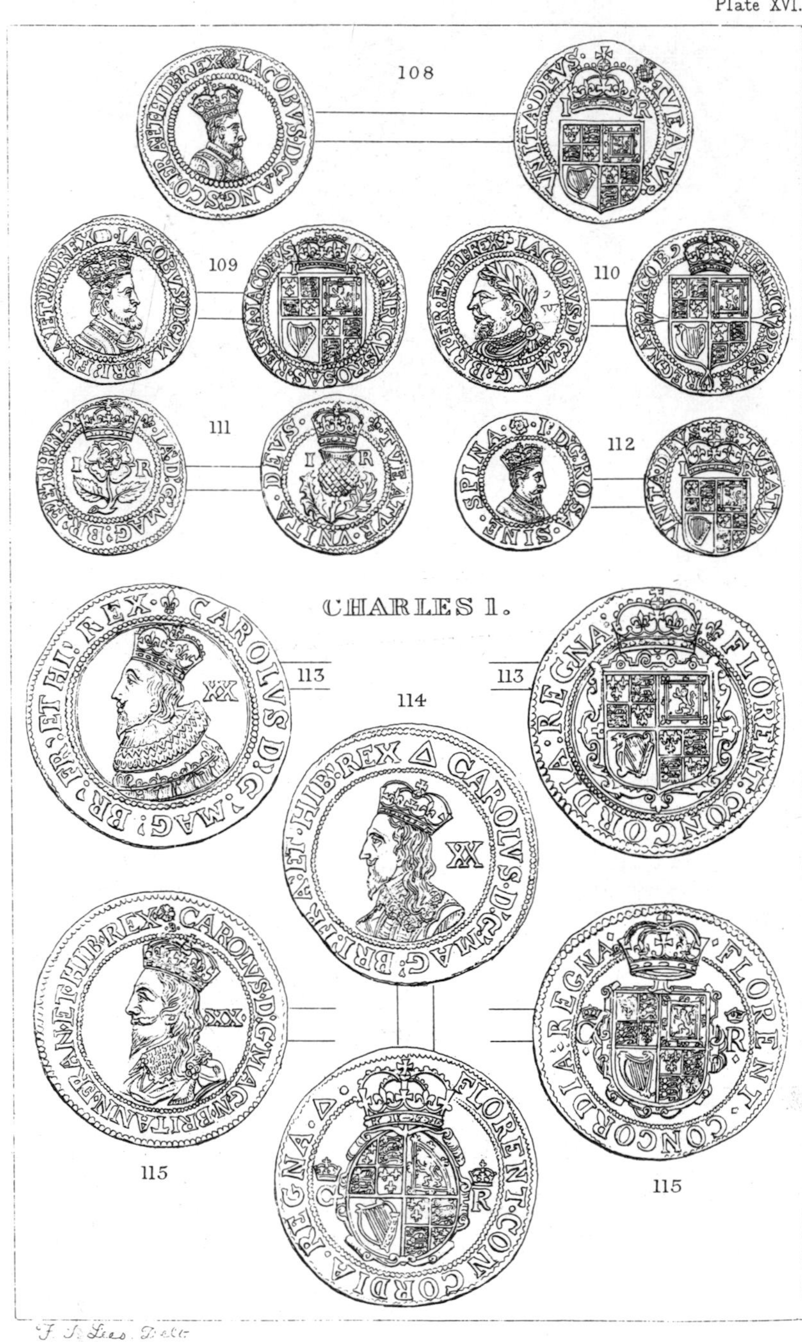

F. J. Lees. Delt.

CHARLES I.

Plate XVII.

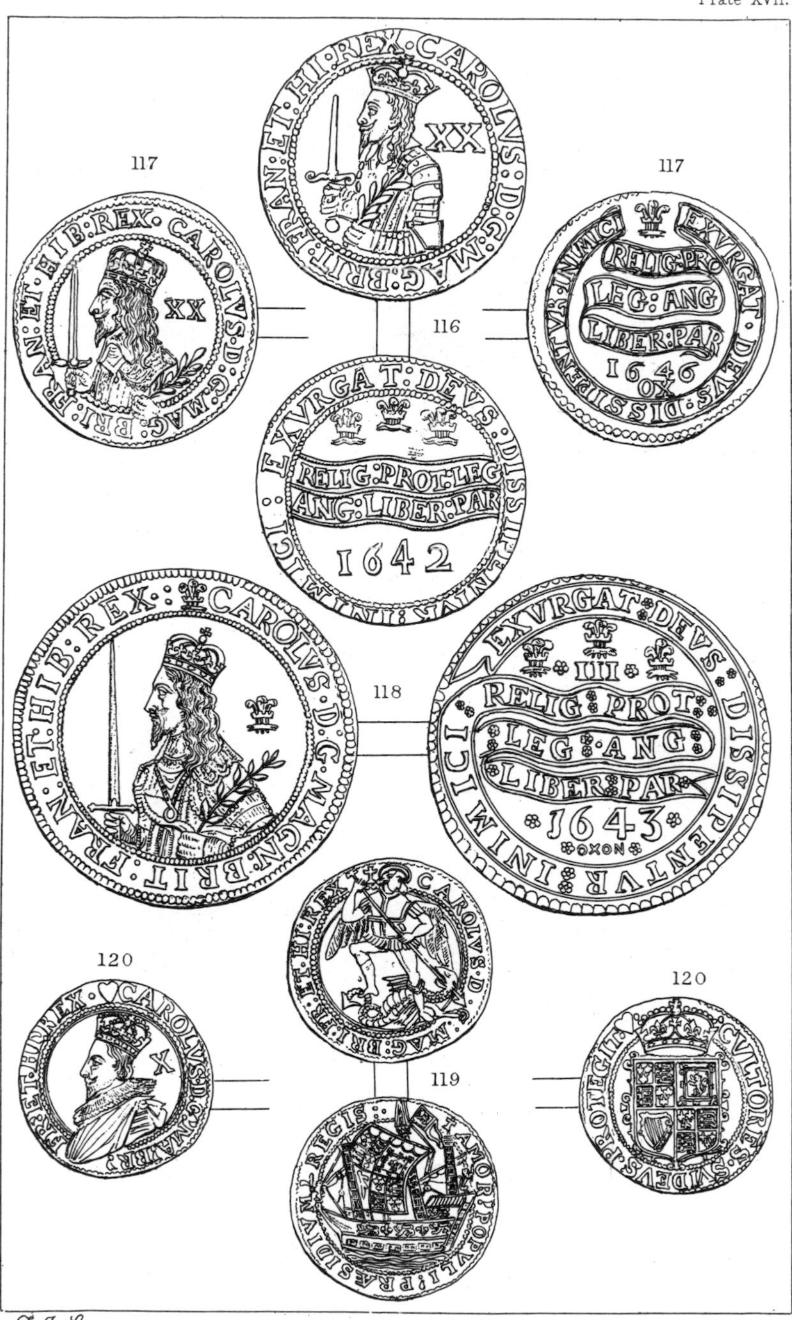

F. J. Lees.

CHARLES I.

Plate XVIII.

CHARLES II.

Plate XIX.

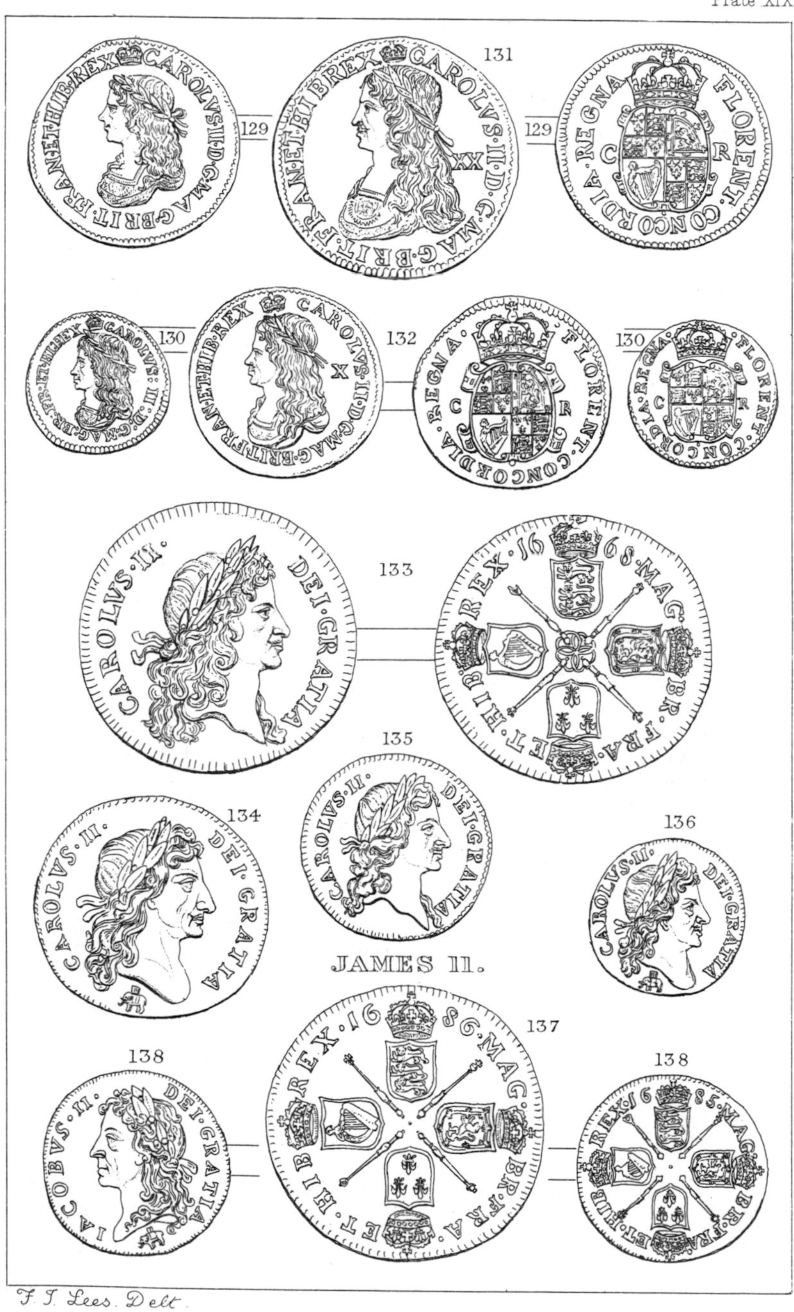

F. J. Lees. Delt.

WILLIAM and MARY.

Plate. XX.

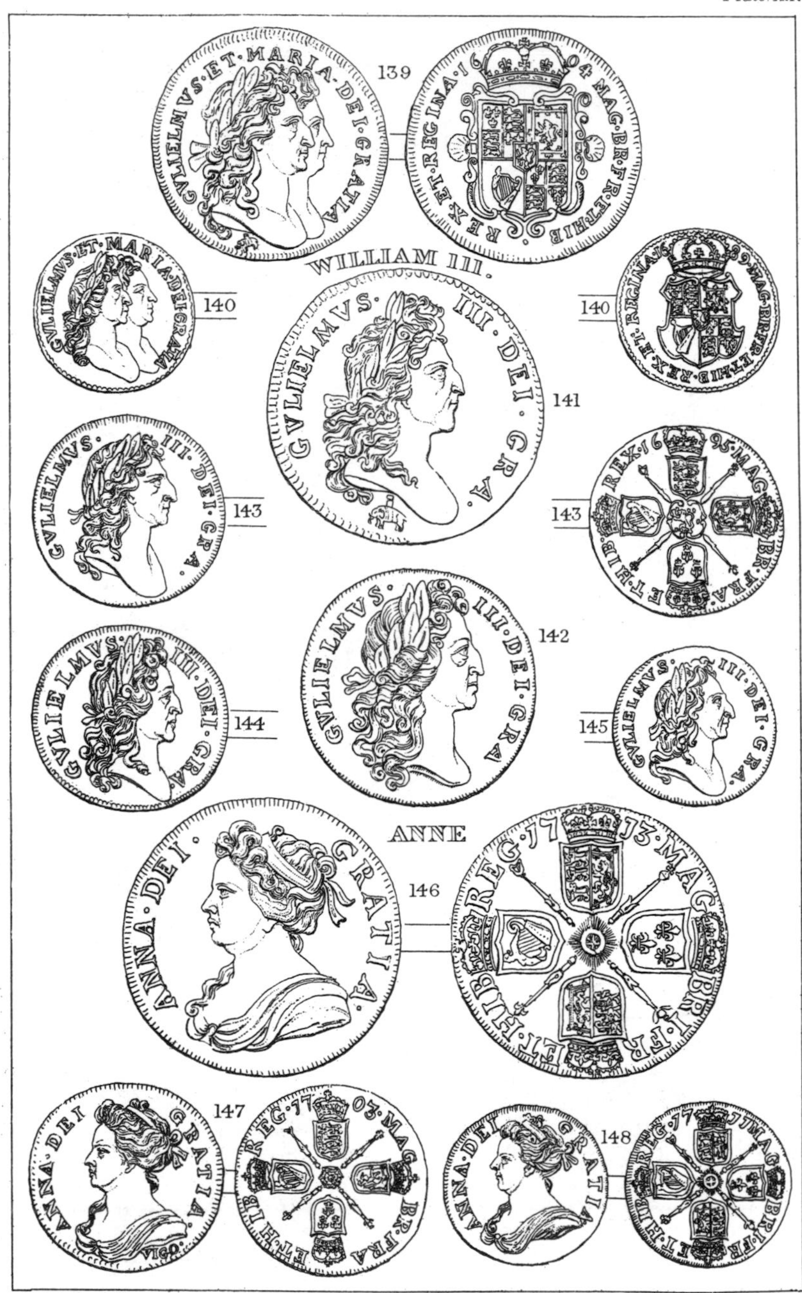

J.J. Lees D·elt

GEORGE I.

Plate XXI.

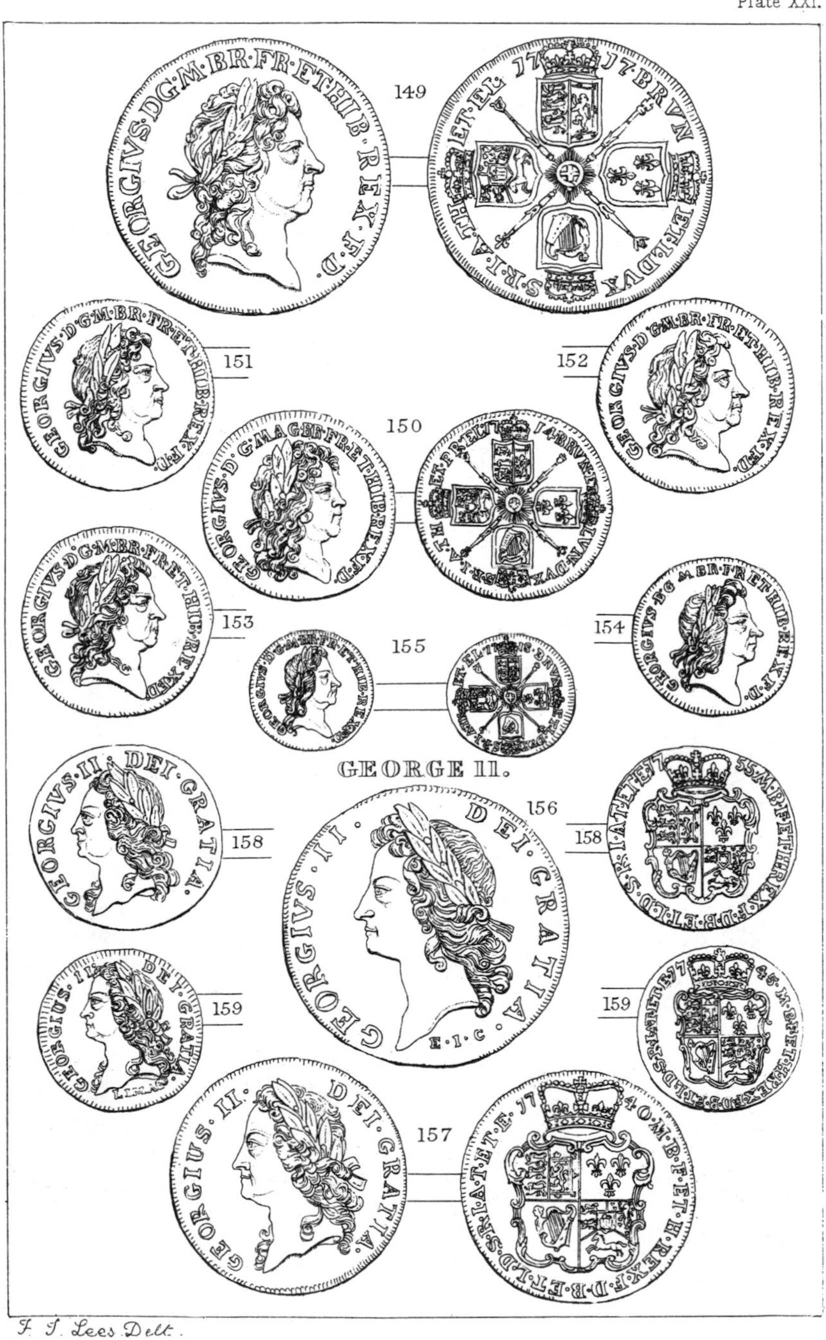

F. J. Lees Delt.

GEORGE III.

Plate XXII.

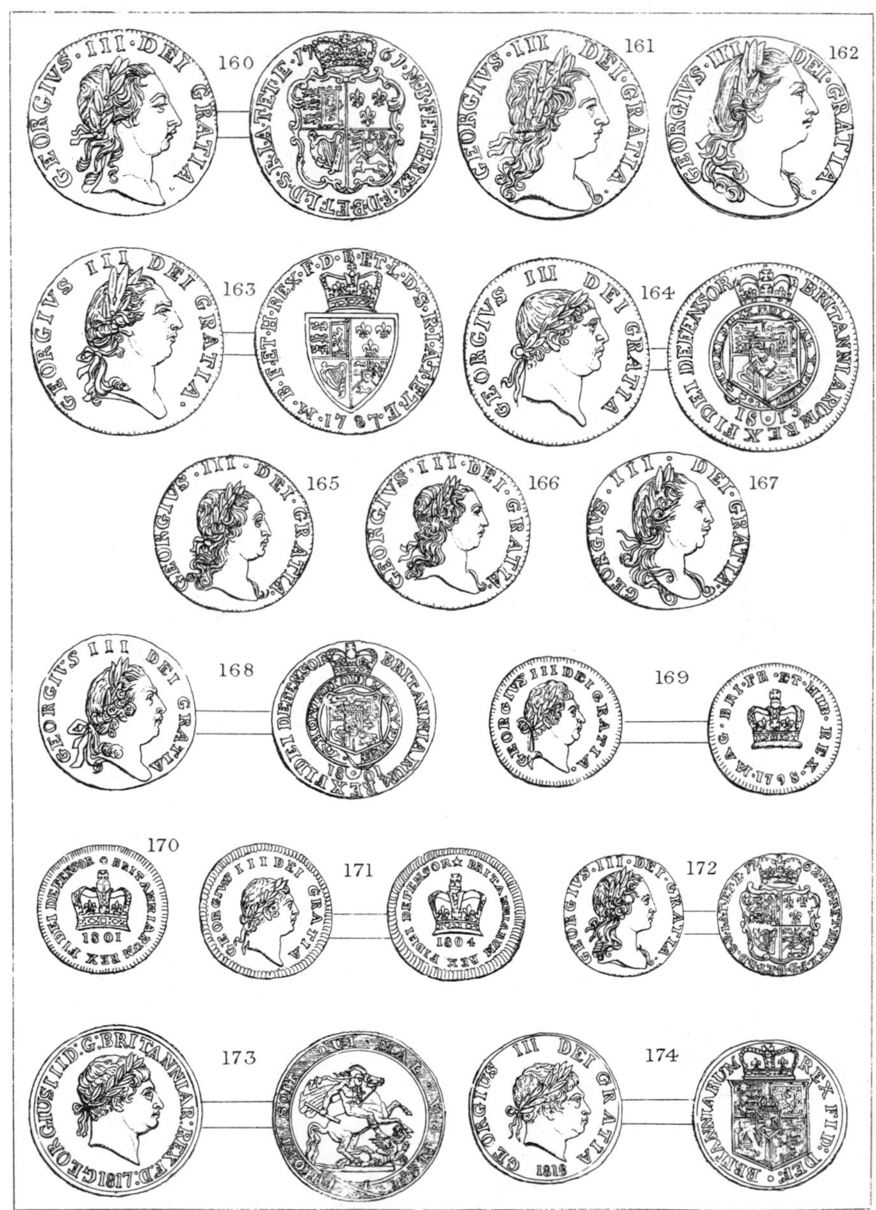

F. J. Lees. Delt

GEORGE IV.

F. T. Lees Delt.

SUPPLEMENT — LEGAL TENDER GOLD COINS OF THE IMPERIAL COINAGE

FIVE POUND PIECES

Quintuple sovereigns or five pound pieces dated 1887 or later are legal tender. Seven major varieties have been struck thus:

ROYAL MINT

Victoria			Mintages
Young Head	Una and the Lion (official pattern, six varieties exist)	1839	*c.* 180
Jubilee Head	(proof) uninitialled	1887	797
	(proof) initialled	1887	
	currency piece	1887	53,844
Old Veiled Head	proof	1893	773
	currency piece	1893	20,504
Edward VII			
	proof	1902	8,066
	matt proof	1902	
	currency piece	1902	34,911
George V			
	proof	1911	2,812
Edward VIII			
	pattern	1936	One or more exist
George VI			
	proof	1937	5,501
	matt proof	1937	Extremely rare
Elizabeth II			
	pattern	1953	None issued but at least 4 known

AUSTRALIA

	Sydney Mint	S Mintmark	
Victoria			
Jubilee Head	pattern	1887	None issued but 2 or 3 known
Edward VII			
	matt pattern	1902	None issued but 3 known

TWO POUND PIECES

No double sovereigns were struck with Victoria (Young Head).

ROYAL MINT

		Mintages
Victoria		
Jubilee Head	1887	initialled and uninitialled proofs (797) and as currency pieces (91,354)
Old Veiled Head	1893	As proof (773) and as currency pieces (52,212)
Edward VII		
	1902	Proof, and as matt proof (8,066) and as currency pieces (45,807)
George V		
	1911	Proof (2,812)
Edward VIII		
	1936	Pattern. One or more exist
George VI		
	1937	5,501 proofs, and an extremely rare matt proof
Elizabeth II		
	1953	None issued but at least 4 known

AUSTRALIA

	Sydney Mint	S Mintmark	
Victoria			
Jubilee Head	pattern	1887	None issued but 2 or 3 known
Edward VII			
	matt pattern	1902	None issued but 3 known

The development of the present-day sovereign.

1. The George III guinea of 1773. **2.** The last of the guineas, known as the military guinea, of 1813. **3.** A Victorian Young Head sovereign of 1851.

4. A Victorian Jubilee Head dated 1888, the reverse bearing Pistrucci's St. George and the Dragon which survives from 1817 and appears both on the George V sovereign (**5**) dated 1925 (but re-issued in 1949, 1950 and 1951) and the current Elizabeth II sovereign (**6**) of which that dated 1959 is the rarest.

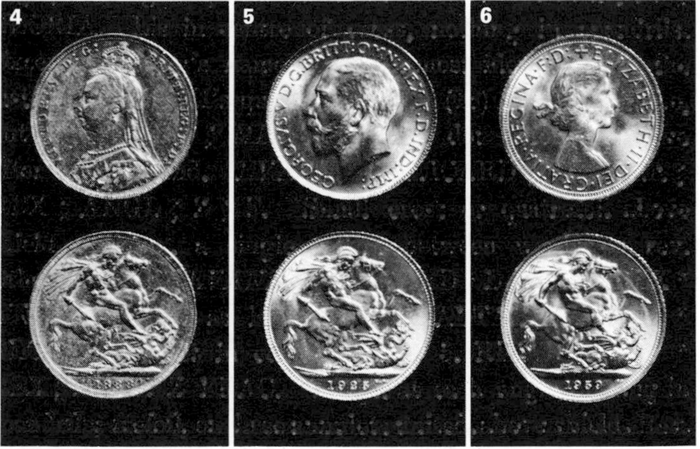

LEGAL TENDER

SOVEREIGNS OF THE IMPERIAL COINAGE 1838–1969

The total number of major varieties of the Imperial sovereign, excluding the 21 struck in the reign of George III, George IV and William IV in the period 1817–1837, and hence no longer tender, is as follows:

ROYAL MINT (*No mintmark*)

Victoria (Young Head Shield Reverse) without die numbers	1838–1864	31	None dated 1840. Two reverses in 1843, 1853, 1854; 1855 also with incuse initials; 1859 "Brittle" issue and non-brittle issue
Victoria (Young Head Shield Reverse) with die numbers	1863–1874	11	None issued dated 1867
Victoria (Young Head St. George Reverse)	1871–1885	15	None issued dated 1875, 1877, 1881, 1882; 1871 small and large initials, 1872 raised initials, 1878 with die numbers, 1880 uninitialled
Victoria (Jubilee Head)	1887–1892	7	1887 also in proof
Victoria (Old Veiled Head)	1893–1901	9	None dated 1897; 1893 also in proof
Edward VII	1902–1910	11	1902 in mirror and in matt proof
George V	1911–1917 and 1925	9	1911 also in proof
Edward VIII	1936	1	Proof only (unconfirmed)
George VI	1937	2	Proof and matt proof only
Elizabeth II	1953 and 1957–1969	12	1953 Proof only, none dated 1960 or 1961

SYDNEY MINT, AUSTRALIA

(*S Mintmark below dragon on the reverse*)

Victoria (Young Head, Shield Reverse)	1871–1887	15	None known dated 1874, 1876
Victoria (Young Head, St. George Reverse)	1871–1887	15	None known dated 1877, 1878
Victoria (Jubilee Head)	1887–1893	8	1877 rare proof
Victoria (Old Veiled Head)	1893–1901	9	
Edward VII	1902–1910	10	1902 rare proof
George V	1911–1926	16	
		73	

MELBOURNE MINT, AUSTRALIA

(*M Mintmark below dragon on the reverse*)

Victoria (Young Head, Shield Reverse)	1872–1887	16
Victoria (Young Head, Shield Reverse) St. George Reverse)	1872–1887	16
Victoria (Jubilee Head)	1887–1893	7
Victoria (Old Veiled Head)	1893–1901	9
Edward VII	1902–1910	9
George V (Large Head)	1911–1928	18
(Small Head)	1929–1931	3
		78

PERTH MINT, AUSTRALIA

(*P Mintmark below dragon on the reverse*)

Victoria (Old Veiled Head)	1899–1901	3	
Edward VII	1902–1910	9	
George V (Large Head)	1911–1928	18	
George V (Small Head)	1929–1931	3	
		33	

OTTAWA MINT, CANADA

(*C Mintmark below dragon on the reverse*)

Edward VII	1908–1910	3	
George V	1911–1919	7	None struck dated 1912 or 1915
		10	

BOMBAY MINT, INDIA

(*I Mintmark below dragon on the reverse*)

George V	1918	1	
		1	

PRETORIA MINT, SOUTH AFRICA

(*SA Mintmark below dragon on the reverse*)

George V (Large Head)	1923–1928	6	1923 as proof only
George V (Small Head)	1929–1932	4	
		10	

Totals:				
United Kingdom				108
Australia:	Sydney	73		
	Melbourne	78		
	Perth		33	185
Canada				10
India				1
South Africa				10
				313

HALF-SOVEREIGNS
ROYAL MINT

Victoria (Young Head without die numbers)	1838–1863 and 1883–1886	37	None struck for 1840, 1862, 1881 or 1882; 1853, 1856 and 1857 with small dates; 1850 and 1854 raised initials; 1854 incuse initials; 1839 plain edge proof; 1853 and 1885 in proof
Victoria (Young Head with die numbers)	1863–1880	17	None struck for 1868
Victoria (Jubilee Head)	1887–1893	8	Proof of 1887
Victoria (Old Veiled Head)	1893–1901	10	Proof of 1893
Edward VII	1902–1910	11	Proof mirror and matt proof of 1902. Those for 1902 and 1903 are uninitialled
George V	1911–1915	6	Proof of 1911
Edward VIII	1936	1	Unconfirmed proof
George VI	1937	2	Proof and matt proof only
Elizabeth II	1953	1	Proof only
		93	

SYDNEY MINT, AUSTRALIA (*S Mintmark*)

Victoria (Young Head, Shield Reverse)	1871–1887	13	None struck for 1873, 1877, 1884 and 1885
Victoria (Jubilee Head, St. George Reverse)	1887–1893	6	None struck for 1888 or 1890. 1887 also in proof
Victoria (Old Veiled Head)	1893–1900	5	None struck for 1894, 1895, 1896
Edward VII	1902–1910	6	None struck for 1904, 1905, 1907 or 1909. 1902 also in proof.
George V	1911–1916	5	None struck for 1913
		35	

MELBOURNE MINT, AUSTRALIA
(*M Mintmark*)

Victoria (Young Head, Shield Reverse)	1873–1887	8	None struck for 1874, 1875, 1876, 1878, 1879, 1880 or 1883
Victoria (Jubilee Head, St. George Reverse)	1887 and 1893	2	
Victoria (Old Veiled Head)	1896–1900	3	None struck for 1897 or 1898.
Edward VII	1906–1909	3	None struck for 1907.
George V	1915	1	
		17	

PERTH MINT, AUSTRALIA (*P Mintmark*)

Victoria (Old Veiled Head)	1900	1	
Edward VII	1904–1909	3	None struck for 1905, 1906 or 1907
George V	1911–1920	4	None struck for 1912, 1913, 1914, 1916, 1917, 1918
		8	

SOUTH AFRICA, PRETORIA MINT
(*SA Mintmark*)

George V	1925–1926	2	

Totals:			
	United Kingdom		93
	Australia: Sydney	35	
	Melbourne	17	
	Perth	8	60
	South Africa		2
			155

MINTAGE FIGURES

LEGAL TENDER SOVEREIGNS

The following table indicates the total mintages. These figures are not more than a guide to rarity since in some years large numbers were melted before issue, e.g. Royal Mint strikings of 1916 and 1917 while in the case of the Royal Mint sovereigns of 1925 these ceased to be rare after being re-struck and re-issued in 1949, 1951 and 1952.

No. Struck	*Year and mintmark*	*Remarks*
c. 2	1936	unconfirmed proof
c. 12	1953	proof only
636	1908 C	RR
719	1923 SA	proof only
773	1893	proof
797	1887	proof
3,184	1924 SA	RR
3,574	1819	RRRR
3,715	1913 C	RRR
3,764	1911	proof
5,501	1937	proof
6,111	1916 C	RRR
14,891	1914 C	R
15,123	1902	proof (mostly matt)
16,273	1909 C	R
20,013	1879	RR
28,012	1910 C	R
57,779	1931 M	R
58,845	1917 C	R
77,547	1930 M	R
107,516	1918 C	R
124,054	1841	R
135,889	1919 C	R
211,000	1926 M	R
240,000	1921 M	RRRR
256,946	1911 C	
278,000	1924 M	RR
310,000	1927 M	RRRR
360,000	1920 S	RRR
371,400	1882 M	
386,182	1828	RRR
394,000	1924 S	RR
413,000	1928 M	RRR
416,000	1923 S	RRRR
427,000	1883 M	
436,719	1929 M	RRR
503,695	1839	
510,870	1923 M	RRR
514,000	1919 M	RRR
520,713	1874	
530,000	1920 M	RRR
578,000	1922 S	RR
608,000	1922 M	RRR
616,770	1823	
690,992	1899 P	R

No. Struck	*Year and mintmark*	*Remarks*
717,723	1885	
723,441	1835	
803,234	1858	
839,000	1921 S	RRR
931,994	1820	
934,000	1917 M	
940,000	1887 M	
1,000,000	1887 S (Young Head)	
1,014,714	1917	RRRR
1,020,000	1887 S (Jubilee Head)	
1,031,050	1926 S	RR
1,066,680	1932 SA	
1,091,275	1878	
1,108,000	1883 S (both reverses)	
1,111,280	1887	
1,172,984	1837	
1,173,568	1931 P	
1,225,269	1833	
1,242,000	1916 S	
1,259,000	1878 S (both reverses)	
1,272,000	1916 M	
1,295,372	1918 I	
1,298,000	1882 S	
1,313,000	1926 P	RR
1,333,000	1928 P	R
1,346,000	1915 S	R
1,346,000	1893 S (Old Head)	
1,360,000	1881 S	
1,366,000	1879 S	
1,373,000	1874 M (Shield reverse)	
1,385,228	1959	
1,402,000	1850	
1,450,000	1865	
1,459,000	1880 S	
1,464,000	1924 P	
1,478,000	1873 S	
1,486,000	1885 S	
1,487,000	1877 M	
1,498,000	1893 S (Jubilee Head)	
1,540,000	1859	
1,554,000	1916	
1,578,000	1901	
1,590,000	1877 S	
1,595,000	1884	
1,606,000	1929 P	
1,613,000	1876 S	
1,623,000	1883 M	
1,637,000	1915 M	

Mintage figures, Legal Tender Sovereigns

No. Struck	Year and mintmark	Remarks
1,649,000	1893 M (Jubilee Head)	
1,650,000	1868	
1,666,000	1917 S	
1,667,000	1886 S	
1,710,000	1836	
1,755,000	1849	
1,769,000	1884	
1,774,000	1914 S	
1,815,000	1872 S (Shield reverse)	
1,835,000	1919 S	
1,837,000	1925 P	R
1,886,000	1900 P	
1,889,000	1875 M	
1,899,000	1874 S	
1,914,000	1893 M (Old Head)	
1,915,000	1930 P	
1,916,000	1887 M	
2,011,000	1914 M	
2,017,000	1908 S	
2,057,000	1909 S	
2,072,000	1957	
2,093,000	1882 M (St. George)	
2,122,000	1875 S (both)	
2,124,000	1923 P	
2,135,000	1910 S	
2,187,000	1888 S	
2,189,000	1873	
2,171,000	1878 M	
2,189,000	1870	
2,227,000	1912 S	
2,246,000	1848	
2,249,000	1913 S	
2,266,000	1827	
2,285,000	1895	
2,298,000	1922 P	
2,314,000	1921 P	
2,322,000	1913 M	
2,324,000	1881 M	
2,347,000	1818	
2,386,000	1873 (both)	
2,387,000	1830	
2,421,000	1920 P	
2,444,000	1829	
2,468,000	1912 M	
2,473,000	1890 M	
2,519,000	1911 S	
2,532,000	1897 S	
2,539,000	1907 S	
2,544,000	1896 S	R
2,548,000	1898 S	
2,555,000	1860	
2,596,000	1891 S	
2,718,000	1838	
2,732,000	1889 M	
2,740,000	1879 M	
2,749,000	1891 M	
2,758,000	1895 S	
2,777,000	1888	
2,788,000	1905 S	
2,792,000	1906 S	
2,806,000	1903 S	
2,808,000	1890 S	
2,813,000	1902 S	
2,814,000	1871 S	
2,830,000	1888 M	
2,850,000	1911 M	
2,889,000	1901 P	
2,901,000	1886 M	
2,942,000	1884 M	
2,966,000	1885 M	
2,986,000	1904 S	
2,995,000	1919 P	
3,000,000	1962	
3,000,445	1844	
3,012,000	1901 S	
3,028,000	1909 M	
3,052,800	1880 M (both)	
3,053,000	1910 M	
3,067,000	1894 S	
3,078,500	1908 M	
3,235,000	1817	
3,259,000	1899 S	
3,262,000	1889 S	
3,310,000	1925 M	
3,318,866	1876	
3,331,000	1907 M	
3,488,000	1892 M	
3,520,000	1903 M	
3,520,431	1925 (later 886,000 =4,406,431)	
3,586,000	1900 S	
3,589,611	1854	
3,632,000	1905 M	
3,650,080	1880	
3,656,000	1906 M	
3,716,000	1918 S	
3,737,000	1832	
3,742,000	1904 M	
3,767,000	1824	
3,782,611	1894	
3,800,845	1845	
3,802,947	1846	
3,812,884	1918 P	
3,986,000	1901 M	
4,013,624	1851	
4,047,288	1866	
4,096,771	1916 P	
4,110,286	1917 P	
4,165,000	1895 M	
4,166,000	1894 M	
4,200,343	1825 (both)	
4,265,000	1902 M	
4,278,144	1912 P	
4,289,112	1902 P	
4,305,000	1900 M	
4,361,347	1894	

Mintage figures, Legal Tender Sovereigns

No. Struck	*Year and mintmark*	*Remarks*
4,373,165	1911 P	
4,373,596	1915 P	
4,456,000	1896 M	
4,495,748	1857	
4,506,756	1904 P	
4,524,241	1909 P	
4,635,287	1913 P	
4,667,126	1847	
4,674,783	1903 P	
4,690,625	1910 P	
4,737,796	1902	
4,806,160	1856	
4,815,996	1914 P	
4,829,817	1906 P	
4,875,617	1908 P	
4,876,193	1905 P	
4,907,000	1918 M	
4,972,289	1907 P	
5,129,500	1897 M	
5,356,787	1822	
5,508,000	1898 M	
5,578,000	1899 M	
5,632,000	1925 S	
5,724,046	1826	
5,910,403	1905	
5,921,669	1863	
5,981,968	1843	
6,086,264	1925 SA	
6,329,476	1891	
6,441,322	1869	
6,529,887	1890	
6,898,260	1893	
7,104,720	1892	
7,257,455	1889	
7,400,000	1963	
7,515,478	1899	
7,624,736	1861	
7,836,413	1862	
8,053,435	1852	
8,448,482	1855	
8,511,792	1831 SA	
8,656,352	1864	
8,700,000	1958	
8,767,250	1871 (both)	
8,888,627	1903	
9,405,114	1821	
10,041,369	1904	
10,027,756	1930 SA	
10,466,981	1906	
10,597,993	1853	
10,846,741	1900	
11,107,611	1926 SA	
11,501,117	1914	
11,729,006	1908	
12,024,107	1929 SA	
12,157,009	1909	
13,486,708	1872 (both)	
16,379,704	1927 SA	
18,235,057	1928 SA	
18,458,663	1907	
20,295,280	1915	
22,379,624	1910	
24,539,672	1913	
30,044,105	1911	
30,317,921	1912	

Note:

c. = *circa.*
R = *rare.*
RR = *very rare.*
RRR = *extremely rare.*
RRRR = *of the highest rarity.*

C = *Ottawa mint, Canada.*
I = *Bombay mint. India.*
M = *Melbourne mint, Australia.*
P = *Perth mint, Australia.*
S = *Sydney mint, Australia.*
SA = *Pretoria mint, South Africa.*

— No designation indicates absence of mintmark and hence struck at the Royal Mint, London.

MINTAGE FIGURES

HALF-SOVEREIGNS

No. Struck	*Year and mintmark*	*Remarks*
? 2	1936	
(known) 3	1918 P	RRRR
c. 12	1953	proof
? 719	1923 SA	proof
773	1893	proof
797	1887	proof
1,230	1839	proof
3,764	1911	proof
5,501	1937	proof
11,000	1885 M	RR
15,123	1902	proof
24,668	1908 P	R
35,201	1879	
38,000	1886 M	
42,000	1881 M	
44,022	1909 P	R
48,000	1884 M	
52,000	1882 S	
60,030	1904 P	R
62,000	1881 S	
64,000	1887 M	R
80,000	1877 M	
82,000	1886 S	
82,042	1906 M	
84,000	1902 S	
94,000	1879 S	
97,221	1899 M	
106,000	1882 M	
110,024	1893 M	
134,000	1887 S	
154,000	1891 S	
165,000	1873 M	
179,595	1850	
218,946	1896 M	
220,000	1883 S	
250,000	1893 S	
260,000	1900 S	
273,341	1838	
356,000	1872 S	
410,595	1848	
508,835	1841	
516,240	1875	
728,223	1857	
773,573	1851	
806,540	1926 SA	
845,112	1849	
855,578	1858	
871,770	1887	
887,526	1845	
946,615	1925 SA	
982,636	1847	
992,795	1867	
1,009,049	1880	
1,063,928	1846	
1,079,286	1891	
1,125,144	1854	
1,127,007	1844	
1,130,867	1861	
1,131,500	1860	
1,133,756	1884	
1,159,544	1870	
1,251,762	1843	
1,371,574	1863	
1,377,671	1852	
1,717,440	1904	
1,758,490	1864	
1,834,750	1865	
1,861,764	1869	
1,884,432	1874	
1,927,050	1873	
2,037,664	1901	
2,042,747	1915	
2,058,776	1866	
2,062,970	1871	
2,081,941	1878	
2,197,482	1877	
2,203,813	1859	
2,223,352	1842	
2,226,023	1890	
2,391,362	1855	
2,391,909	1856	
2,522,057	1903	
2,708,786	1853	
2,785,187	1876	
2,869,183	1895	
2,870,457	1883	
2,878,527	1898	
2,946,605	1896	
3,023,993	1905	
3,248,627	1872	
3,361,881	1899	
3,568,156	1897	
3,794,591	1894	
3,996,992	1908	
4,010,715	1909	
4,233,421	1907	
4,244,457	1902	
4,245,437	1906	
4,307,372	1900	
4,426,625	1893	
4,468,871	1885	
5,023,881	1910	
6,094,290	1913	
6,104,106	1911	
6,224,316	1912	
7,251,124	1914	
13,680,486	1892	

VICTORIAN DIE NUMBERS

No complete list of die numbers used on Victorian Royal Mint sovereigns and half-sovereigns in the period 1863–1880 has ever been published nor indeed do Royal Mint records exist.

The following list shows all those noted in catalogues and sales in the twenty-four-year period 1945 to 1969.

SOVEREIGNS

1863 None, 1, 4, 6, 7*, 8, 10, 11, 12, 13 and 22.

1864 None, 7, 9, 14, 16, 18, 26, 29, 30, 34, 35, 38, 45, 48, 48*, 50, 56, 74, 75, 76, 78, 82, 84, 89, 90, 92, 93, 96, 99, 100, 101, 102, 105.

1865 1, 6, 10, 14, 15, 18, 20, 21, 26, 33.

1866 1, 2, 5, 7, 8, 11, 13, 15, 17, 18, 20, 21, 25, 27, 28, 41, 47, 48, 52, 54, 63, 66, 69, 70, 73, 75.

1868 3, 4, 6, 7, 12, 17, 31, 33.

1869 4, 5, 6, 8, 10, 11, 14, 16*, 27, 28, 29, 30, 33, 34, 37, 39, 40, 41, 44, 45, 46, 50, 57, 58, 60, 61, 64.

1870 34, 80, 82, 84, 87, 88, 93, 96, 119, 123.

1871 1, 4, 5, 9, 10, 13, 15, 17, 21, 25, 26, 28, 29, 30, 31, 33, 35, 36, 41, 58, 60, 61, 66, 72, 73, 75, 78, 97, 101, 105, 108, 110.

1872 None, 5, 6, 7, 12, 12*, 13, 14, 17*, 18, 21, 23, 24, 26, 27, 28, 33, 37, 39, 50, 60, 61, 66, 74, 75, 76, 87, 89, 90*, 95, 98, 99, 100, 104, 105, 108, 112.

1873 2, 4, 6, 9, 17, 20, 103, 163.

1874 15, 28, 34, 98.

**indicates the W.W. is incuse*

VICTORIAN DIE NUMBERS

HALF-SOVEREIGNS

1863 None, 3, 7, 9.

1864 8, 9, 14, 15, 16, 24, 27, 31, 33, 36.

1865 5, 13, 19, 22, 26, 37, 38, 39.

1866 1, 2, 7, 13, 21, 24, 31, 32, 33, 34, 55.

1867 5, 7, 9, 12, 13, 14, 15, 19, 21, 37.

1869 1, 6, 8, 12, 13, 16, 18, 20, 25.

1870 5, 36, 38, 40, 41, 42, 43, 44.

1871 7, 9, 10, 34, 61, 63, 64, 81.

1872 94, 100, 138, 141, 142, 143, 198, 203, 212, 214, 245, 335, 338, 341, 320, 346, 380.

1873 3, 65, 94, 147, 158, 171, 245, 275, 299, 300, 308, 335.

1874 8, 12, 26, 33, 45, 47, 74, 212.

1875 5, 23, 47, 72, 280.

1876 20, 27, 37, 43, 44, 45, 49, 51, 58, 65, 72, 73, 79, 83, 85, 88, 89, 98.

1877 11, 16, 25, 31, 37, 39, 46, 49, 51, 53, 54, 56, 66, 73, 85, 97, 108, 109, 110, 120, 124, 134, 137, 139, 143, 150, 151, 155.

1878 4, 11, 15, 17, 24, 25, 28, 32, 37, 40, 46, 53, 59, 65, 71, 72, 76, 78, 81, 98, 101, 105, 108, 113, 162.

1879 57, 119.

1880 None, 78, 103, 104, 111, 114, 115, 119, 125.

The numbers do not appear to be random but in clusters. The highest number recorded is 380 in the case of a 1872 half-sovereign. The lowest number unrecorded in this survey is Die No. 48.

It is believed that no single die number was used for more than 100,000 strikings.

COUNTERFEIT GOLD COINS

At least three half-sovereigns and thirty-four sovereign types are known to exist in counterfeit form.

These counterfeits are not invariably deficient in gold content and often possess the full 22 carat fineness (viz. 916.66 parts in 1,000 pure gold). The motive behind their manufacture is to collect the premium which the imprimatur of Imperial gold coins have weight for weight over bar gold in a way which escapes the instant detection of a weight check. Some counterfeits such as the 1914 half-sovereign are above standard weight while others such as the 1872 sovereigns are even of 920 fineness. Others however are seriously impure such as the crude 1923 George V sovereign (without a mintmark) which has a fineness of less than 770 parts in 1,000 and is of an otherwise non-existent date.

The following varieties have been reportedly forged:

FIVE POUND PIECE	1887
SOVEREIGNS	1878
	1879 (extremely rare date as a genuine coin)
	1889
	1892
	1894 M
	1896 M
	1906 P (two varieties of forgery)
	1909
	1910
	1911 (six varieties of forgery)
	1911 SA (non-existent date)
	1912
	1913
	1915
	1915 P
	1916 (very rare if genuine)
	1917 (very rare if genuine, two varieties)
	1917 P
	1918 I
	1918 P
	1920 (non-existent date)
	1923 (non-existent date)
	1925 SA
	1926 SA
	1927 (non-existent date, only one reported)
HALF-SOVEREIGNS	1913
	1914
	1917 (non-existent date)

Counterfeit Gold Coins

Counterfeits are for the most part easily detected by one or more of the following imperfections:

(1) Weight departure from half-sovereign and sovereign standard (3.994 and 7.988 grammes).

(2) Departure from standard fineness (916.66 parts in 1,000).

(3) Scarred or rough surface or pimples.

(4) Low relief.

(5) Irregular or shapeless beading.

(6) Missing or wrong punctuation of legend.

(7) Missing or mutilated engraver's initials, also B.F. for B.P.

(8) Oversized date figures or narrow spacing.

(9) Striations on the field.

(10) Streaming of St. George's crest on reverse irregular.

No. Struck	*Year and mintmark*	*Remarks*	*No. Struck*	*Year and mintmark*	*Remarks*

been the subject of an application under A), the full name and address of the prospective buyer (where established) and the following additional information :—

(i) for sale by auction—
the name and address of the auctioneer concerned;

(ii) for sale to private collectors resident in the United Kingdom—
the Bank of England's reference(s) relating to the buyer's authority;

(iii) for sale to overseas buyers—

(*a*) an application on a Form X for the issue of a Certificate C (the formal means of applying for permission to export gold coins : if the coins are to be held in the United Kingdom full details of the circumstances must be given instead),

(*b*) confirmation that payment is to be received in an approved manner (information on this question may be obtained from any Authorised Dealer in Gold),

(*c*) where a buyer is resident in another Scheduled Territory, evidence that the approval of the Local Authorities concerned has been obtained for the purchase and import.

C. The opportunity is taken to remind coin collectors that in accordance with Section 3 of the Exchange Control Act, 1947, bailees of gold coin must notify the Bank of England of the details of any such gold coin held by them unless, in accordance with the Exchange Control (Bailees Exemption) Order, 1947*, the bailee is satisfied that the owner is not required to surrender the coin.

BANK OF ENGLAND,
27th April 1966.

* Copies of the Order (1947 No. 2037) may be purchased from H.M. Stationery Office or through any bookseller.

AIDE MEMOIRE FOR COIN COLLECTORS.

THE EXCHANGE CONTROL (GOLD COINS EXEMPTION) ORDER 1966.

The Exchange Control (Gold Coins Exemption) Order 1966* came into force on the 27th April 1966. This Order revoked the Exchange Control (Collectors' Pieces Exemption) Order, 1947.

THE PROVISIONS OF THE NEW ORDER.

Under the new Order the holding, buying (or borrowing) and selling (or lending) of gold coins minted in or before 1837 are exempt from the requirements of Sections 1, 2 and 3 of the Exchange Control Act, 1947*. Also, any resident of the United Kingdom† who, on the 26th April 1966, held not more than FOUR gold coins minted after 1837 does not need permission to retain them.

Otherwise, ANY RESIDENT OF THE UNITED KINGDOM REQUIRES PERMISSION to :—

(1) HOLD any gold coin minted after 1837, and

(2) BUY (or borrow) or SELL (or lend) ANY gold coin minted after 1837 unless he is selling to an Authorised Dealer in Gold‡ or a Trader in Coin (as defined in Statutory Instrument No. 2042 of 1949*) or to a coin dealer specifically authorised by the Bank of England.

Applications, as set out under A and B below, may be submitted **direct** to the Dealing and Accounts Office, Bank of England, London, E.C.2., **except** in the case of B (iii) where applications must be submitted through an Authorised Dealer in Gold.

A. Applications for permission to MAINTAIN a collection of gold coins minted after 1837 held in excess of four in number on the 26th April 1966.

Applications should be submitted on Forms G.C.1.§ (Consideration will be given when dealing with these applications to the question of acquiring additional pieces.)

B. Applications for permission to SELL holdings of gold coins minted after 1837 other than to an Authorised Dealer in Gold, Trader in Coin or to a coin dealer specifically authorised by the Bank of England.

Applications should be submitted, by means of letters in duplicate, giving details of the coins which it is desired to sell, the Bank of England's reference(s) (where the holding has already

---

* Copies of the Order (1966 No. 438), of the Exchange Control Act, 1947, and of Statutory Instrument No. 2042 of 1949 may be purchased from H.M. Stationery Office or through any bookseller.

† References in this Aide Memoire to the United Kingdom should be read to include the Isle of Man and the Channel Islands.

‡ Most banks in the United Kingdom are also Authorised Dealers in Gold.

§ Obtainable from the Bank of England or any other Authorised Dealer in Gold.

STATUTORY INSTRUMENTS

1966 No. 438

EXCHANGE CONTROL

The Exchange Control (Gold Coins Exemption) Order 1966

Made - - - -	*19th April* 1966
Laid before Parliament	*26th April* 1966
Coming into Operation	*27th April* 1966

The Treasury, in exercise of the powers conferred upon them by sections 31 and 36(5) of the Exchange Control Act 1947(**a**), hereby make the following Order:—

1. The provisions contained in sections 1, 2 and 3 of the Exchange Control Act 1947 shall not apply in relation to any gold coin minted in or before 1837.

2. Any person resident in the United Kingdom shall be exempted from the provisions of section 2 of the Exchange Control Act 1947 to the extent that he may hold not more than four gold coins minted after 1837 and held by him on the coming into operation of this Order.

3. This Order shall extend to the Channel Islands, and any reference in this Order to the Exchange Control Act 1947 includes a reference to that Act as extended by the Exchange Control (Channel Islands) Order 1947(**b**).

4. The Interpretation Act 1889(**c**) shall apply for the interpretation of this Order as it applies for the interpretation of an Act of Parliament.

5. The Exchange Control (Collectors' Pieces Exemption) Order 1947(**d**) is hereby revoked.

6. This Order may be cited as the Exchange Control (Gold Coins Exemption) Order 1966, and shall come into operation on 27th April 1966.

19th April 1966.

William Whitlock,
Joseph Harper,
Two of the Lords Commissioners
of Her Majesty's Treasury

(**a**) 10 & 11 Geo. 6. c. 14. (**b**) S.R. & O. 1947/2034 (Rev. VI, p. 1001: 1947 I, p. 660).
(**c**) 52 & 53 Vict. c. 63. (**d**) S.R. & O. 1947/2040 (Rev. VI, p. 1023: 1947 I, p. 694).